Social Policy in a Developing World

T0329901

Social Policy in a Developing World

Edited by

Rebecca Surender

Lecturer in Social Policy, University of Oxford, UK

Robert Walker

Professor of Social Policy, University of Oxford, UK

Edward Elgar

Cheltenham, UK • Northampton, MA, USA

© Rebecca Surender and RobertWalker 2013

All rights reserved. No part of this publication may be reproduced, stored in a retrieval system or transmitted in any form or by any means, electronic, mechanical or photocopying, recording, or otherwise without the prior permission of the publisher.

Published by
Edward Elgar Publishing Limited
The Lypiatts
15 Lansdown Road
Cheltenham
Glos GL50 2JA
UK

Edward Elgar Publishing, Inc.
William Pratt House
9 Dewey Court
Northampton
Massachusetts 01060
USA

Paperback edition 2014
Paperback edition reprinted 2016

A catalogue record for this book
is available from the British Library

Library of Congress Control Number: 2012949717

This book is available electronically in the ElgarOnline.com Social and Political Science Subject Collection, E-ISBN 978 1 84980 993 1

ISBN   978 1 84980 990 0 (cased)
       978 1 78254 016 8 (paperback)

Typeset by Columns DesignXMLLtd, Reading
Printed and bound by CPI Group (UK) Ltd, Croydon, CR0 4YY

Contents

v

Figures and tables

FIGURES

TABLES

Contributors

Bob Deacon University of Sheffield, UK.

Jane Doherty School of Public Health, University of the Witwatersrand, South Africa.

Paul Dornan Department of International Development, University of Oxford, UK.

David Lewis Department of Social Policy, London School of Economics, UK.

Anna McCord Southern Africa Labour and Development Research Unit, University of Cape Town, South Africa.

Diane McIntyre Health Economics Unit, University of Cape Town, South Africa.

Charles Meth Department of Sociological Studies, University of Sheffield, UK.

Alex Nicholls Skoll Centre for Social Entrepreneurship, University of Oxford, UK.

Sony Pellissery National Law School, Bangalore, India.

Catherine Porter Department of Economics, University of Oxford, UK.

Rebecca Surender Department of Social Policy and Intervention, University of Oxford, UK.

Marian Urbina-Ferretjans Department of Social Policy and Intervention, University of Oxford, UK.

Antje Vetterlein Department of Business and Politics, Copenhagen Business School, Denmark.

Robert Walker Department of Social Policy and Intervention, University of Oxford, UK.

PART I

Contexts and conceptual frameworks

1. Introduction

Rebecca Surender

INTRODUCTION

While we now understand a great deal about the determinants, processes and distributional implications of social policies in developed countries, there is a continuing absence of knowledge about these matters in development contexts. The lack of basic descriptive information about the variety of mechanisms that poorer countries employ to address social needs and risks, together with a dearth of theoretical analysis explaining welfare policy or differences in cross-national arrangements, is widely bemoaned in the literature (Mares and Carnes 2009; Kennett 2004). There have been notable attempts since the turn of the century to address this deficit. The seminal work of Gough et al. (2004) explores the conditions under which social policy operates in developing countries and constructs a new conceptual framework for understanding different welfare regimes in the global South. The authors show how the management of social welfare and risk in developing countries is mediated under a very different set of institutional conditions from those in developed countries; formulated and implemented by a wider range of policy actors; and conveyed through a variety of different mechanisms and policy instruments. In short, the institutional welfare mix is much more complex and problematic. Others are also beginning to challenge the appropriateness of the analytic toolkit developed in the context of rich industrialized countries for understanding the development and dynamics of social protection in the global South (Hall and Midgley 2004; Mkandawire 2004; Haggard and Kaufman 2008; Yeates 2008; Mares and Carnes 2009). The accumulation of empirical data and research concerning the design and efficacy of various social protection instruments is also gathering momentum (Barrientos and Hulme 2008; Hanlon et al. 2010). Despite these notable contributions, the comparative welfare policy literature continues to be, if not consciously 'ethnocentric', then at least predominantly focused on the global North; and there remain several spaces and gaps in our knowledge about the variation, outcomes and

trajectories of welfare arrangements in other regions. It is to these spaces
and gaps that this volume is oriented.

The impetus for examining welfare and social policy in developing
country contexts has acquired additional momentum in recent years from
a number of factors. In the first instance, since the turn of the century we
have witnessed the steep and 'rapid rise of social protection up the policy
agendas of developing countries' (Devereux and Sabates-Wheeler 2007,
p. 1; Adésínà 2007, 2008). Previous scepticism about the affordability
and appropriateness of social expenditure and transfers in development
contexts has, it seems, given way to a discourse of 'pro poor', 'productivity enhancing' and 'transformative' social protection (DFID 2005,
2008; ILO 2001, 2008; World Bank 2009). Rather than being viewed as
an obstacle, the social dimension is now viewed as a major prerequisite
for successful development (Bird 2006). Understanding the reasons for
this seismic shift and its implications for practical policy choices and
preferences will improve our understanding not only of events in the
South but of comparative social policy analysis more generally. Second,
and arguably related to this, are the important transformations occurring
within some of the chief development institutions. There is now a wide
consensus that the various international development institutions (multilateral agencies, bilateral donors, regional organizations and regional
development banks) constitute an increasingly influential and global
dimension to the social policy agenda in developing countries (Deacon et
al. 1997; Deacon 2007; Vetterlein 2007). It is therefore important to
examine the changing nature of the ideas and activities of these institutions – and the implications of the new 'international institutional
architecture' for policy analysis. Third, the emergence of new global
actors in the form of powerful 'Southern donors' has additional practical
and substantive implications for global social welfare (Kwon 1997). It
raises important questions about whether a new South–South model of
social development is emerging, how it differs from traditional North–
South policy prescriptions, and, most crucially, whether it will achieve
more effective results in poverty reduction and economic and social
development (Malhotra 2010; Zimmerman and Smith 2011). Important
questions are also raised about how this new dynamic might potentially
influence Western development and international governance institutions
and, in turn, analysis of the politics and determinants of social policy in
developing countries.

Arguably, then, a 'changed global political order' is currently unfolding
in relation to social policy in a developing country context – one which
sees the emergence of new global actors and a weakening of the market
fundamentalist policy prescriptions of the Washington Consensus. This

collection seeks to examine the effects of these recent dynamics on the social policies of developing countries, in particular the increasing emphasis on social protection within policy discourses and the growing number of social protection policies and programmes being implemented. It seeks to describe and examine key areas of social policy both as substantive subjects and as examples to illustrate the issues and debates outlined above. Finally, it begins to explore the 'direction of travel' of these current social policy dynamics and their implications for social policy analysis. Do they represent a paradigm shift in policy ideas and a new emerging trajectory, or are they merely the re-embodiment of old debates and contestations?

SCOPE AND ORGANIZATION OF THE BOOK

The book is divided into four parts, each dealing with a subset of the issues and questions raised above.

Part I, 'Contexts and conceptual frameworks', provides a historical overview of the determinants and evolution of social protection systems in developing countries. From this historical approach we are able to identify several distinct yet interrelated themes which help to explain why the welfare mix in developing countries is more complex than that in the global North and why several of the assumptions and frameworks of mainstream policy analysis are inadequate.

Part II, 'Institutions and actors', addresses the concern that a much wider range of actors and organizations contributing to social policy needs to be examined in studies of developing countries than in a traditional welfare-state context.

To the state–market–family–Third-Sector matrix which underpins most Western policy models can be added a fifth sector, that of the supranational multilateral governance organizations. Despite ideological and institutional differences in perspective, the collective influence of international development institutions on the social policy of countries in the South is ubiquitous, including on the quantity of public expenditure, the choice of programmes and implementing mechanisms, and the very direction and nature of policy objectives (Wiman et al. 2006; Woods 2006; Deacon 2007; Ervik et al. 2009; Vetterlein 2010).

However, as Antje Vetterlein's chapter illustrates, this is a dynamic and fast-moving terrain, and developments since the mid-1990s open up several old debates as well as new ways of thinking about the drivers and determinants of social welfare in the South. The chapter seeks to understand and trace the shift in the approach of the World Bank and the

International Monetary Fund (IMF) to development. It compares the underlying values and theories of the Washington Consensus and the post-Washington Consensus, and evaluates these differences by comparing the new policy practice of poverty reduction strategy papers with the previous practice of structural adjustment lending.

In addition, NGOs feature as pivotal actors in contributing to social policy needs in developing countries. While Esping-Andersen (1990) in his typology of Western European states downplays the Third Sector as peripheral, in developing countries it is impossible to ignore the contribution this sector makes to public welfare (Lewis 2005; Mayhew 2005; Bebbington et al. 2007; Hearn 2007). Nevertheless, as David Lewis's chapter outlines, there is ambiguity about how these Third Sector organizations that are neither governmental nor part of the private for-profit business sector should be characterized, and questions remain about their effectiveness. The chapter explores the evolving nature and impact of NGOs in the context of the rise of new ideological agendas around neoliberalism from the 1980s, the emergent 'mixed economy of welfare', and the 'new public management' movement.

Equally, as Sony Pellissery's chapter shows, informal security regimes and the informal economy have to be an integral part of any global social policy analysis, both because a majority of the workforce in the global South gain their livelihood in the informal economy and because this workforce is constantly exposed to multiple vulnerabilities. In the context of increased pressures resulting from globalization, the chapter reviews the theoretical and explanatory positions shaping our understanding of the informal economy and summarizes various policy responses by the states in the global South in providing social protection for those in the informal economy.

Finally, the market assumes prominence in the form of private sector finance and provision of welfare for a minority of employees, as well as informal labour market mechanisms for the majority (Walt and Gilson 1994; Lund 2001; Frye 2006; De Haan 2007). While theories of market failure are often invoked to explain why richer countries have built comprehensive welfare states, the absence of large-scale public welfare systems in developing countries has led to a significant and growing emphasis on markets and the private sector for meeting welfare needs and mitigating social risks. The impact of markets in service, finance and provision is evident across all social policy sectors including health, education, housing, urban regeneration and pensions. It includes the privatization of health provision and pension schemes, the contracting out (or 'tertiarization') of services from the state to the private sector, and the expansion of internal markets.

Against this background, Jane Doherty's and Di McIntyre's chapter discusses the role and influence of the private sector in the welfare systems of developing countries through a detailed case-study examination of health care and health policy. The chapter highlights some of the issues and challenges that confront attempts to harness the strengths of the private sector in the service of social objectives, and reflects on the contextual differences between low- and middle-income countries on the one hand and high-income countries on the other, that affect the policy choices in this area.

Part III, 'Instruments and mechanisms', demonstrates how the institutional context outlined in Part II subsequently affects the range of formal and informal policy instruments and tools used to meet welfare needs. While some mechanisms such as public works programmes, emergency food aid and relief, and the regulation of remittances from migration are traditionally identified as 'developing-country specific', since the turn of the century social security mechanisms more typically associated with rich countries are equally finding their way on to the policy agenda of developing countries (Conway and Norton 2002; Wiman et al. 2006; Auerbach et al. 2007). These include contributory social insurance mechanisms and cash-transfer and social-assistance initiatives.

In this context, Robert Walker's chapter reviews current social security provisions in the global South and then elaborates on the structural constraints that must be negotiated if social security is to be further developed in low- and middle-income countries. The chapter draws attention to innovative ways of implementing social security in the context of development before finally engaging with recent claims that the promotion of social security may be a further example of cultural and economic imperialism.

As asserted earlier, social protection is increasingly accepted by the international donor community as being functional for broader development objectives (DFID 2005, 2008; ILO 2001; World Bank 2004). In the context of inadequate markets and public insurance systems, a broader role for non-contributory social assistance is deemed legitimate. Located within this wider trend is the rise of conditional cash transfers, that is, the idea of linking receipt of cash or income transfers to mandatory uptake of services or participation in income-generation activities. Though the preferred poverty alleviation instrument of governments and donors, the initiative is contentious and has generated widespread debate (Barrientos and De Jong 2006; Freeland 2007; Hanlon et al. 2010). It is against this background that Paul Dornan and Catherine Porter's chapter focuses on understanding the impact of conditionality within social protection instruments. Drawing on a wider debate and citing evidence from the authors'

longitudinal study of childhood poverty, the chapter considers some of
the different types of scheme often used to deliver social protection, with
a discussion of the conditionalities implied by each. The authors examine
both the positive effects for beneficiaries and possible unintended,
negative consequences for vulnerable household members.

Public works programmes typically provide a form of temporary social
assistance providing income or food in exchange for provision of labour
which is typically directed to the production of public goods. Though the
strategy takes various forms in different countries, it is arguably located
within a broader 'enterprise approach' based on an individualist ideology
which stresses the primacy of the market in social welfare and the centrality
of 'agency' over 'structure'. Income-generating programmes for instance
are similar, though they adopt a longer term strategy designed to encourage
and support participants to attain self sufficiency through engagement in
economic activity. Also, whereas income-generating programmes tend to
simulate normal market conditions, for example in the interest charged on
loans, 'wages' paid on public works programmes are often below market
rates. Such programmes are often underpinned by an ideological concern to
prevent the growth among recipients of a dependency on cash assistance
that is not earned. In this vein, social policy should encourage individual
responsibility and provide opportunity rather than 'hand-outs'.

Anna McCord and Charles Meth's chapter thus examines the role of
public works programmes and the 'enterprise' approach more generally
as instruments of welfare and social protection in developing countries. It
outlines the key components of public works programmes and challenges
to their implementation and examines the range of policy objectives. It
explores why such programmes (especially in the context of chronic and
structural labour market failures) have become popular policy options for
both policy makers and donors and the assumptions underlying their
selection over alternative interventions.

Similarly, governments of developing countries increasingly emphasize
creating opportunities for the poor to improve their own positions
through income-generating activities. Microcredit, income-generation
projects and social-entrepreneurship schemes are thus being given
increased prominence as mechanisms to address the critical challenges of
poverty and unemployment. It is argued that they encourage the poor to
utilize their most abundant asset – their labour – in order to generate an
income and sustain themselves independently. Secondary objectives
relating to supply-side improvements such as skills transfer, community
empowerment and capacity building are also frequently articulated.

Alex Nicholls's chapter explores the implications of social entrepreneurship in development contexts for the traditional objectives of

social policy and tests how far these implications challenge the boundaries of conventional policymaking and the responsibilities of policymakers. The chapter outlines the nature, scale and scope of global social entrepreneurship, and analyses the institutional drivers of the social entrepreneurship revolution to suggest some of the distinctive contributions that it can make in developing countries.

Part IV, 'Scenarios and trajectories', draws on the evidence presented throughout the volume to examine some key issues and politics of policymaking and implications for the normative and ideological debates surrounding the different goals of social policy. It assesses the implications of the different social policy dynamics for the conceptual frameworks of comparative social policy analysis and the extent to which these approaches can be considered 'new'. It evaluates the relevance of concepts that are well established and central in the study of social policy – equality, citizenship, social cohesion – in this new context and looks at future trajectories for social policy dynamics and welfare outcomes in these regions.

Bob Deacon's chapter is concerned with the ways in which increased world interconnectedness has affected the nature of social problems in the developing world and the nature of the social policies prescribed to address them. It reviews evidence of increased inequity within and between countries, and discusses the impact of globalization on global social structure, including the disembedding of the globalizing middle class, on the balance of power between capital and labour, on gender relations and on ethnic divisions. The extent to which the interests and ideas of the global South are reflected in the UN or in the G20 are examined briefly, and possible reforms to global social governance assessed. The ideas of de-globalization and world regionalism are introduced as a lead in to the chapter on South–South dialogues.

Following this, Rebecca Surender and Marian Urbina-Ferretjan's chapter explores the concept of South–South cooperation (SSC) and introduces its main characteristics, theories and actors, and the criteria used to classify them as such. The chapter examines the implications of SSC on social policy practices and analyses and discusses the extent to which these new developments represent a new model of social policy or paradigm shift (and a 'silent revolution'?) and the consequences for the analytical frameworks traditionally used within the subject.

DEFINITIONS AND TERMINOLOGY

Just as the welfare-regime approach has highlighted that there is no single homogeneous welfare state in OECD countries, so it is important to emphasize the distinctiveness and heterogeneity of developing countries' histories, institutions, values and policy arrangements.

Following the seminal work of Esping-Andersen (1990), we fully appreciate the limitations of using social expenditure as a gauge of welfare commitment. Nevertheless, most traditional measures and classification systems of 'development' still use narrow indicators of expenditure and GDP. But these narrow economic measures tell us little about the 'meaning of things' such as – for the purpose of this analysis – accessibility, coverage and performance of social protection arrangements or their distributional consequences. Although transparency indicators and the Human Development Index (HDI) of the United Nations Development Programme (UNDP) attempt to improve on this, even here we need to acknowledge that the macro and micro logics vary hugely depending on whether we are talking about East Asia, Sub-Saharan Africa or Latin America. Historical paths, existing institutional structures and governance are extremely heterogeneous and diverse; this fact militates against attempts to build typologies or theories.

Given the challenges involved in attempting to devise a generic tool to study the issues and countries addressed in this book, we adopt a 'sectoral system approach' to a specific social protection institution, actor or programme (UNRISD 2012). This approach is concerned with the institutions and policies constituting a specific social protection programme and the historical, political and structural factors affecting them. It avoids a methodological problem shared by many comparative studies on social policy, in particular the welfare regime approach, which pays insufficient attention to variations over time and across sectors and countries (Fine 2009). The perspective offered by the sectoral system approach reveals that the institutions and policies constituting specific social protection systems vary, as they are determined by specific historical legacies, socio-economic and political structures and cultures that differ in time and space. Issues of finance, human resource management, service provision and regulation, among others, are all discussed. Finally, while it is not the intention of this book to explicitly engage with or advance a framework of welfare typologies or classification, the comparative focus of the book wherever possible identifies patterns and common trends from which some analytic generalizations can be made. Though contributors use different language and terms to refer to the poorer countries of the world as a group (low income, developing, less developed, the global South and so on), the countries studied all fall within the World Bank classification of low-income/lower-middle-income economies (World Bank 2012) and have been selected in the light of criteria that include generalizability of the policy issue under consideration, geographical region, as well as indicators such as GNP, HDI status, and state and other institutional capacities and structures.

REFERENCES

Adésínà, J. (2007), 'Social policy and the quest for inclusive development research findings from Sub-Saharan Africa'. Programme Paper No. 33. Geneva: Research Institute for Social Development, Social Policy and Development, United Nations.

Adésínà, J. (2008), 'Transformative social policy in a postneoliberal African context: enhancing social citizenship'. Paper prepared for the RC19 Stockholm Annual Conference, 4–6 Sept.

Auerbach, P., M. Genoni and C. Pagés (2007), 'Social security coverage and the labor market in developing countries'. Discussion Paper No. 2979. Bonn: IZA, available at http://ftp.iza.org/dp2979.pdf.

Barrientos, A. and J. De Jong (2006), 'Reducing child poverty with cash transfers: a sure thing?', *Development Policy Review*, **24** (5), 537–52.

Barrientos, A. and D. Hulme (eds) (2008), *Social Protection for the Poor and Poorest*, Basingstoke: Palgrave Macmillan.

Bebbington, A., S. Hickey and D. Mitlin (eds) (2007), *Can NGOs Make A Difference?*, London: Zed Books.

Bird, K. (2006), *Pro-Poor Policy: How to Identify the Optimal Policy Mix and Tackle Challenges to Adoption*, London: Overseas Development Institute.

Conway, T. and A. Norton (2002), 'Nets, ropes, ladders and trampolines: the place of social protection within current debates on poverty reduction', *Development Policy Review*, **20** (5), 533–40.

Deacon, B. (2007), *Global Social Policy and Governance*, London: Sage.

Deacon, B., M. Hulse and P. Stubbs (1997), *Global Social Policy: International Organisations and the Future of Welfare*, London: Sage.

De Haan, A. (2007), *Reclaiming Social Policy*, Basingstoke: Palgrave Macmillan.

Devereux, S. and R. Sabates-Wheeler (eds) (2007), 'Debating social protection', *IDS Bulletin*, **38** (3), 1–7.

DFID (Department for International Development) (2005), 'Social transfers and chronic poverty: emerging evidence and the challenge ahead'. A DFID practice paper. London: DFID, available at http://www.globalaging.org/pension/world/2005/challenges.pdf (accessed 2010).

DFID (2008), *Leading the British Government's Fight Against World Poverty. Achieving the Millennium Development Goals in Africa: Working with China*, London: DFID.

Ervik, Rune, Nanna Kildal and Even Nilssen (2009), *The Role of International Organizations in Social Policy*, Cheltenham, UK and Northampton, MA, USA: Edward Elgar.

Esping-Andersen, G. (1990), *The Three Worlds of Welfare Capitalism*, Cambridge: Polity Press.

Fine, B. (2009), UNRISD Conference on 'Social and Political Dimensions of the Global Crisis', Geneva: UNRISD.

Freeland, N. (2007) 'Superfluous, pernicious, atrocious and abominable? The case against conditional cash transfers', *IDS Bulletin*, **38** (3), 75–8.

Frye, I. (2006), 'Extending social security to developing countries: particular emphasis on healthcare and informal economy workers'. Discussion Paper No. 1. Geneva: The Global Union Research Network, available at http://www.gurn.info/en/discussion-papers/healthcare05.pdf (accessed 2010).

Gough, I., G. Wood, A. Barrientos, P. Bevan, P. Davis and G. Room (2004), *Insecurity and Welfare Regimes in Asia, Africa and Latin America: Social Policy in Development Contexts*, Cambridge: Cambridge University Press.

Haggard, S. and R. Kaufmann (2008), *Development, Democracy and Welfare States*, Princeton, NJ: Princeton University Press.

Hall, A. and J. Midgley (2004), *Social Policy for Development*, London: Sage.

Hanlon, J., A. Barrientos and D. Hulme (2010), *Just Give Money to the Poor: The Development Revolution from the Global South*, Sterling, VA: Kumarian Press.

Hearn, J. (2007), 'African NGOs: the new compradors?', *Development and Change*, **38** (6), 1095–110.

ILO (International Labour Office) (2001), *Social Security: A New Consensus*, Geneva: ILO.

ILO (2008), 'Can low-income countries afford basic social security? Social Security Policy Briefings'. Paper 3. Geneva: ILO, available at http://www.ilo.org/public/english/protection/secsoc/downloads/policy/policy3e.pdf (accessed 2010).

Kennett, P. (2004), *A Handbook of Comparative Social Policy*, Cheltenham, UK and Northampton, MA, USA: Edward Elgar.

Kwon, H.-J. (1997), 'Beyond European welfare regimes: comparative perspectives on East Asian welfare systems', *Journal of Social Policy*, **26** (4), 467–84.

Lewis, David (2005), 'Actors, ideas and networks: trajectories of the non-governmental in development studies', in Uma Kothari (ed.), *A Radical History of Development Studies*, London: Zed Books, pp. 200–221.

Lund, F. (2001), 'A framework for the comparative analysis of social protection for workers in the informal economy', Durban: Mimeo.

Malhotra, K. (2010), 'South–South cooperation: potential benefits for the least developed countries', in *Poverty in Focus: South–South Cooperation: The Same Old Game or a New Paradigm?*, **20**, 7–9.

Mares, I. and M. Carnes (2009), 'Social policy in developing countries', *Annual Review of Political Science*, **12**, 93–113.

Mayhew, S. (2005), 'Hegemony, politics and ideology: the role of legislation in NGO–government relations in Asia', *Journal of Development Studies*, **41** (5), 727–58.

Mkandawire, T. (2004), *Social Policy in a Development Context*, Basingstoke: Palgrave Macmillan.

Seekings, J. (2000), 'The origins of social citizenship in pre-apartheid South Africa', *South African Journal of Philosophy*, **19** (4), 386–404.

UNRISD (United Nations Research Institute for Social Development) (2012), *The Universalisation of Social Security in Emerging Economies*, Geneva: UNRISD.

Vetterlein, A. (2007), 'Economic growth, poverty reduction and the role of social policies: the evolution of the World Bank's social development approach', *Global Governance*, **13** (4), 513–33.

Vetterlein, Antje (2010), 'Lacking ownership: the IMF and its engagement with social development as a global policy norm', in Susan Park and Antje Vetterlein (eds), *Owning Development: Creating Global Policy Norms in the IMF and the World Bank*, Cambridge: Cambridge University Press, pp. 93–112.

Walt, Gail and Lucy Gilson (1994), 'Reforming the health care sector in developing countries: the central role of policy analysis', *Health Policy and Planning*, **9** (4), 353–70.

Wiman, R., T. Voipio and M. Ylonen (eds) (2006), *Comprehensive Social Policies for Development in a Globalizing World*, Helsinki: The National Research and Development Centre for Welfare and Health, available at http://www.stakes.fi/social-policies-for-development (accessed 2011).

Woods, N. (2006), *The Globalizers: The IMF, the World Bank and their Borrowers*, New York: Cornell University Press.

World Bank (2004), *The Millennium Development Goals for Health. Rising to the Challenges*, Washington, DC: World Bank.

World Bank (2009), *World Development Report 2009: Reshaping Economic Geography*, Washington, DC: World Bank.

World Bank (2012), 'How we classify countries', available at http://data.worldbank.org/about/country-classifications (accessed 2012).

Yeates, N. (2008), *Understanding Global Social Policy*, Bristol: Policy Press.

Zimmermann, F. and K. Smith (2011), 'More actors, more money, more ideas for international development co-operation', *Journal of International Development*, **23**, 722–38.

2. The role of historical contexts in shaping social policy in the global South

Rebecca Surender

SOCIAL POLICY BUILDING BLOCKS: STATE CAPACITY AND LEGITIMACY

The emergence of new forms of social protection and welfare arrangements in developing countries has recently drawn attention to the extent to which the traditional frameworks and models of comparative welfare policy and advanced welfare capitalism are analytically applicable to the developing and transitional worlds of the South and the East. There are compelling grounds to argue that they are not. Gough et al. (2004) were among the first to direct our attention to the fact that the evolution of policies and activities oriented to welfare goals in the West has relied on several key factors that are largely absent in a development context: an autonomous, legitimized and capable state, a pervasive labour market and division of labour, robust financial markets and an established legal and judicial system – in short, a capitalist economic and a democratic political system. Key among these factors for the purpose of social policy analysis is the role of the state – both its capacity and its legitimacy. In a development context, it is recognized that the state has been historically weak in terms of institutional power (in particular, a mature and independent bureaucracy characterized by continuity, impartiality and expertise) and functional capability (the fiscal and human resource capacity of systems and staff) (Wood and Gough 2006). In the contexts of development and social policy, the state is neither a primary agent for programmatic development and implementation nor an enabling structure providing infrastructural or regulatory support (Gough 2005; Kohli 2006).

Equally, in terms of political legitimacy, states within the developing world typically suffer from several deficits, especially in terms of democratic processes such as the political mobilization of different constituencies and multiple political parties. Rather than acting as a corrective agent to labour market and other societal inequalities, the state frequently becomes captured by personal objectives and partisan interests and subsequently provides poor governance. As Collier (2007) and others have argued, in contrast to the idealized notion of a 'benign, liberal and pluralistic' state, the common view of the developing country state, held especially by those living under it in poverty, is of an institution which is far from impartial but serves the interests of dominant groups and sections. Those who have captured the state in turn use its apparatus as a 'crucial means of their own accumulation and reproduction' (Wood 2004, p. 50; Collier 2007), and lack of trust in official rules reinforces reliance on informal rights and mechanisms to secure welfare (Davis 2001). This becomes even more problematic in the context of ethnic divisions and conflicts where the politics of identity is based on local community membership rather than national or citizenship attachment (Collier and Hoefler 1998).

For all these reasons Yeates (2008) argues for a different set of theoretical constructs to replace the traditional functionalist and conflict theories of social policy and for a new global approach to replace the subject's methodological nationalism and emphasis on the nation state. In the context of weak capitalist modes of production and formal labour markets, theories of industrialization (Cutright 1965; Wilensky 1975, 2002) as key drivers of welfare state development lose their potency. Equally, theories of class mobilization (Korpi 1983; Swenson 2002; Yeates and Holden 2009), which hold that democratic class struggle is a core determinant of policy arrangements, shaping political settlements and social contracts, become redundant where class is not a privileged basis for mobilization and identity but coexists with multiple ethnic, religious, caste, clan and kinship cleavages (Collier and Hoefler 1998; Davis 2001; Wood 2004).

However, opposition to this critique of the developing country state is also evident in the literature. Some authors argue that, despite the challenges, state incapacity should not be exaggerated (though it frequently is by those opposed to the public sector for ideological reasons). Hall and Midgley (2004) remind us that the state remains the single most crucial social policy institution despite its failure in many contexts and despite the growing pressure on it from processes of globalization and localization. Central government expenditure has grown from an estimated average of 15 per cent of GDP in 1960 to between 13–35 per cent in most developing countries by 2002 (IMF various dates; World Bank 2006). Central government is still the primary agent responsible for basic social services, such as health and education, and increasingly provides social security and income support to large sectors of the population. Even more significantly, governments ultimately determine social policy priorities and interventions, albeit within the constraints of localization and globalization.

Walker and Wong (2005) argue that the traditional welfare policy models of advanced welfare capitalism have ignored the developing and transitional worlds of the South and the East, not because of material difference in their economic or political arrangements but because of the ethnocentric biases of the subject. They assert that, although democracy and capitalism have long been regarded as the two driving forces underlying welfare state development, historical evidence shows that state welfare services were first developed by authoritarian states such as those of Germany and Austria rather than by the most mature democratic capitalist societies. Furthermore, in terms of state fiscal capacity and expenditure, many modern Western welfare states do not guarantee a basic minimum income to their populations and offer only meagre benefits. Most important, the narrow focus on the functions and effects of the state sector tends to neglect the contributions of other non-statutory providers. Walker and Wong thus conclude that the unwillingness to incorporate non-OECD countries in existing welfare analysis stems not from material differences between the two hemispheres but rather from a chauvinistic refusal to develop more inclusive and pluralistic explanatory frameworks.

While recognizing the inherent political sensitivities of critiques of the state in development contexts, we nevertheless take as our point of departure the central premise that weak state capacity and legitimacy is central to understanding the varieties of welfare arrangements as well as the determinants and politics of social policy reforms in the developing world. In order to understand the limited reach and capacities of present-day central governments in poorer countries, we turn inevitably to the importance of historical contexts. As theories of historical institutionalism and path dependency have demonstrated (Skocpol and Amenta 1986; Hudson and Lowe 2004; Pierson 2007), in our understanding of social policy the past remains a central explanatory feature of current arrangements and of the way in which we understand and make sense of them. Nowhere is this more true than with the social protection systems of developing countries.

The following section provides a historical overview of the determinants and evolution of social protection systems in developing countries. With this historical approach we are able to identify several distinct yet interrelated themes that help to explain why the welfare mix in developing countries is more complex than that in the global North and why several of the assumptions and frameworks of mainstream policy analysis are inadequate.

First, the state in developing countries is very fragile and has therefore been constantly susceptible to exogenous ideas and influences during the entire post-colonial period.

Second, this weakness has opened up spaces for other actors to both shape and implement social welfare: Western governments, international donors and finance institutions, non-governmental organizations, the private sector and the informal sector. However, while many of these institutions and actors compensate for state deficit in the immediate term, paradoxically they further undermine the state in the longer term. Put simply, when external funders supply most of the welfare resources, there is no social contract which reflects processes of democratic struggle and internal political settlements between different social classes or cleavages. Traditional 'democratic feedback loops' that enforce accountability and representative governance are thus undermined (Midgley and Tang 2008).

Third, although ideas about the goals, roles, institutions and mechanisms of social policy have ebbed and flowed over time in Western and developing countries, the underlying tension between the economic and the social has remained a sharp and constant feature in developing contexts, and the position of social policy has always been precarious.

HISTORICAL ORIGIN AND EVOLUTION OF SOCIAL PROTECTION SYSTEMS IN DEVELOPING COUNTRIES

That most developing states were the creation of European (and later American) colonialism is well documented and requires no elaboration here (Ferro 1996; Clark 2006; Haggard and Kaufman 2008), other than perhaps to underscore the fact that colonial legacies have been instrumental in shaping (characteristically, undermining) state power in newly independent nations from the very beginning (Adésínà 2007; Midgley and Piachaud 2012). In most instances the formal arrangements of statehood had been externally introduced or imposed, typically joining together ethnically, culturally and linguistically diverse populations. Several 'Eurasian' states were 'multi-nations' and most African states were 'multi-tribal'. The imposition of arbitrary colonial borders frequently had disastrous consequences – trapping together often mutually antagonistic populations. In the immediate aftermath of colonisation this sometimes triggered civil wars and mass migration of populations, as in

Nigeria and India. In the longer term colonial borders made significant ethnic minorities vulnerable to long-term discrimination by dominant national groups who were able to capture the state (Sudan, Afghanistan). As Collier's work on the politics of identity reveals (Collier 2000), it is not possible to understand the present lack of trust in the state to deliver protection against risks in developing countries unless we begin with this historical analysis. In place of trust in formal state-level institutions (which are often distant, invisible and administered by dissimilar ethnic or religious groups), local populations turn to more visible and reliable networks of support and reciprocity – typically around physical, social or kinship-based communities (Davis 2001; Wood 2004).

Despite this foundation, it is striking that during the early post-colonial era (1950s–60s) when the process of independence got under way, many newly independent countries embarked on relatively expansive pro-grammes of social policy, building on the existing colonial infrastructure (Maclean 2002). Several (including most African) countries experienced improvements in social welfare – usually linked to public services run by the state. James Midgley and David Piachaud's recent work *Colonialism and Welfare* (2012) shows that although in the early stages colonial administrations were hardly concerned with social welfare, by the middle of the 20th century they had begun to expand public social services. Driven to some extent by the need to cater for European settler communities (mostly with public health facilities though some statutory social services also) and in part to quell growing civil unrest among 'native populations', colonial commissions began recommending that increased resources be made available for social welfare programmes – as seen in Britain's Colonial Development and Welfare Act of 1940. This trend was accelerated in the wake of the new post-war social contract when many European nations elected centrist and social democratic parties committed to redistributive social policies. Britain's embodiment of this new social contract, the Beveridge Report of 1942, was widely received not only in the UK but throughout the British Empire, and resulted in several commissions and inquiries in colonial states to examine the need for expanded government intervention in social and welfare services. The creation of India's social security system in the late 1940s (Hasan 1972) and the Gluckman Health Commission in South Africa (Van Niekerk 2009) are two examples. Similarly, the French government replicated its social security system in many of its African colonies (Midgley and Tang 2008).

Just as optimism and confidence in the 'possibility of politics' (Ringen 1987) were rising in Europe during post-war reconstruction, so too in the South many emerging independence leaders were 'statists', and the expansion of state welfare became an integral element in the quest for nation building and progress in newly independent countries. Many such leaders continued the expansion of public social services begun by the colonial authorities, ring-fencing government budgets for social pro-grammes, establishing separate ministries for implementing them and building schools, universities, hospitals and houses. Reflecting the opti-mism of the age, and financed by a booming world economy and demand for commodities and primary exports, this expanded social policy resulted in improved life chances and welfare for much of the population in the global South. In comparison with the situation 50 years earlier, access to education and health care widened and literacy rates, nutritional conditions and life expectancy all improved (Midgley 1995; Midgley and Piachaud 2012).

Of course, we should not allow our historical lens to become too rose-coloured. The political impact of colonialism varied across countries – leaving some countries with considerably more intact institutional architecture and functioning agencies (India and Korea, for example) than others (Nigeria and Tanzania). Many programmes were inappropri-ately modelled on Western forms (e.g. curative hospital-based health services) and largely 'residual' in nature. Perhaps most important, in contrast to their Western counterparts, which were embarking on expanded social services as a new expression of social solidarity and redistributive social justice, in developing countries the impetus for expanded social services was rooted in authoritarian political regimes in order to 'buy off' social unrest (Haggard and Kaufman 2008; Mares and Carnes 2009). Instead of the comprehensive social policy provision that came to the fore in European nations in the post-war period, underpinned by egalitarian principles and aspirations to social solidarity, a more incremental and minimalist safety-net approach emerged in the newly independent nations (MacPherson 1982).

SOCIAL POLICY INSTITUTIONS, IDEAS AND INSTRUMENTS IN THE LATER POST-COLONIAL ERA

Despite the early promise of some state-led social policy in the immedi-ate aftermath of independence, by the 1960s and during the 1970s the prevailing discourse surrounding social policy was very much one of 'growth first' and 'welfare after' (Mkandawire 2004; van Ginneken 2007). Just as Western confidence in bureaucratic and state-led solutions had exerted a strong influence on developing countries in the wake of independence, so again we see the influence of prevailing Western ideas about the role of social expenditure in this later post-colonial era.

At the very same time as Western welfare states were experiencing their 'golden age', mainstream Western theories asserted that in a development context economic growth, not social spending, was what was needed (Wade 1990, 2002). The benefits of growth and modernization through (centrally planned) urban industrialization and employment would result in poverty alleviation and development, and would invariably improve the welfare of the population. Public spending on social welfare was thus considered a wasteful diversion from the primary goal of economic growth. Accordingly, developing states confined their interventions to the 'disabled, infirm and to orphans', forcing the social needs of all others to be met through individual effort in the marketplace (Hall and Midgley 2004). A minimalist residual model of welfare provision (first introduced by some colonial administrations) was entrenched and social policies were expanded in a piecemeal and expedient manner – largely in response to political pressures and demands from the growing middle classes rather than to the needs of the majority of the poor (Midgley and Piachaud 2012).

Corresponding advice from donor agencies redoubled doubts about a 'welfare agenda' by insisting that Western-style welfare states could be established only at much higher levels of economic development than that achieved by most developing countries, and that social policy was to be pursued only after a certain development threshold had been reached (Kanbur 1999; Sen 2001; Fine et al. 2003). Furthermore, since labour markets in developing contexts were characterized by extreme dualism, such that large sections (the majority in some cases) of the population fell outside the formal wage economy, labour market-based welfare policies and contributory social insurance mechanisms were viewed as inappropriate and wider, universal social policies fiscally unaffordable. During the 1960s and 1970s interventions by the main development agencies reflected these views. They alternated between discrete project lending (focusing on building infrastructure, importing Western equipment and technology or installing electricity) and broader programmatic approaches intended to encourage more fundamental economic transformations in recipient countries. Loans were often used as instruments for delivering aid on the assumption that debt would be repaid with the profits from investments. The emphasis was placed on advancing production and promoting scientific knowledge rather than social welfare directly (Bräutigam 2009).

A Turn Towards Neoliberalism

By the mid-1980s, following the elections of the radical conservative Thatcher and Reagan administrations in the UK and the US respectively, the intellectual pendulum had swung even further in an anti-welfare direction with the ascendancy of neoliberal ideology in advanced economies and international donor institutions. In this era of the so-called Washington Consensus, neoliberal policies were based on the twin ideas of 'rolling back the state' and the opening up of the world economy to the free movement of goods, services and capital (Wade 1990). During this period, a strong critique of public sector institutions in both the global North and the global South resulted in prescriptions of 'trickle-down' free market economics but accompanied this time with the reduction in the size of the state, which was now viewed not as the solution to growth but as part of the problem (Fine et al. 2003; Weeks and Stein 2006; White 2006).

As in previous historical periods, we see a close alignment of the prevailing ideas and discourses in the West on the one hand and the activities and programmes being implemented in the South on the other. International development institutions, multilateral agencies and donors began during this time to add an extremely powerful global dimension to the social policy agendas of developing countries. Their collective influence on the policies of developing countries was pervasive, including on the quantity of public expenditure, the choice of programmes, and the direction and nature of policy goals (Vetterlein 2007). Amidst the turmoil of oil shocks, international economic downturn and large and mounting foreign debt, the economies of Latin America and Sub-Saharan Africa had little choice but to accept the external pressures and prescriptions of donor institutions (Thirlwarl 2006; Weeks and Stein 2006).

The World Bank and the International Monetary Fund (IMF), without doubt the most powerful international agencies of the time, led the development discourse, defined poverty and development, and influenced policy and policymakers in the global South (Woods and Narlikar 2001). Unlike other UN agencies, they exerted direct influence on developing countries by being able to recommend to them specific policies instead of merely shaping the policy dialogues (Armstrong et al. 2004; Deacon et al. 1997; Deacon 2007; Yeates 2008; Vetterlein 2010). Their loans represented the highest share of all official development aid and functioned to evaluate the creditworthiness of developing economies, thus effectively 'gate-keeping' their access to additional foreign capital. The Bank would lend money to aid-dependent countries on the basis that they accepted the conditions of structural adjustment. This entailed changes in their economic and social policies – in a liberal pro-market direction – and if they did not implement the changes, then the Bank could withhold funding (Pender 2001; Riddell 2007).

What did this mean for social policy in developing countries? The standard blueprint imposed strict fiscal discipline and restricted and redirected public expenditure in a process that gave little priority to human welfare. The conclusion of the Chief Economist of the Bank at the time – namely that the 'main task of the Washington Institutions ... was the storming of the citadel of statist development strategies' – perhaps illustrated that the project was an explicitly ideological one (Weeks and Stein 2006).The policy shift led to severe cutbacks in social investment, privatization of social programmes and the abandonment of social planning as an integral part of policymaking (Mkandawire 2005). Privatized health, pension and university education schemes and the expansion of internal markets were the preferred route to expanding access to services. There was a resurgence of residual safety nets for vulnerable groups since expansive welfare expenditure, it was argued, 'displaced informal social security mechanisms, crowded out the more efficient private sector, blunted the work ethic and fostered perverse incentives and dependency on unsustainable handouts' (Fine et al. 2003).

In order to bypass what were perceived to be weak, ineffective and corrupt central states, foreign aid was largely channelled via non-governmental organizations (NGOs), including international NGOs, whose numbers and influence grew hugely during this period (Hearn 2007). From occupying a relatively marginal position in the 1970s (typically as emergency relief agencies), NGOs became major social policy contributors and actors; and by the 1990s 12 per cent of all Western aid was being channelled through them. The withdrawal of the state from social services and the dramatic change in state–society relations forced those affected, particularly in Sub-Saharan Africa, to revert to the informal sector and rely once again on local mechanisms of reciprocity and risk pooling. The social policy vacuum created by structural adjustment thus resulted in the proliferation of alternative and traditional health services, self-help associations and rotational saving schemes, and, most crucially, extended family networks (Frye 2006).

Social Policy Beyond Neoliberalism

Since the late 1990s, however, discourse and philosophy concerning development and poverty reduction have shifted again in what appears to be quite a divergent direction (Devereux and Sabates-Wheeler 2007;

Dohlman and Soderback 2007). Explanations for this transformation are diverse, and range from rational policy learning in the face of failed strategies to theories of institutional change and the agency of individual actors (Wade 2002; Woods 2008).

Among the Washington institutions, a new initiative of Poverty Reduction Strategy Papers (PRSPs) replaced structural adjustment and led to a new vocabulary of 'pro-poor' and 'transformative' development policy (World Bank 2004, 2009). The aid relationship was recast as a partnership between donors and recipients (DFID 2005, 2008), where donors no longer imposed policies from on high on developing states but rather supported those policies that were (in theory) formed and 'owned' by recipients. Most relevant for the purposes of this analysis, there was a shift in the type of policies that was now being favoured by the Bank, away from the stark neoliberal agenda that focused primarily on monetary and fiscal policies as a means to promote economic growth and poverty reduction. The state was brought back into the frame, and there was a new focus on building the institutional capacity of developing states through governance reforms (Stiglitz 1998; Kanbur 1999).

The corresponding rise of social protection up the policy agenda of developing countries has been striking (Devereux and Sabates-Wheeler 2007; Barrientos and Hulme 2008; Hanlon et al. 2010; Mahon 2010). The new emphasis on enhancing human capital has translated into a focus on targeting social services and aid interventions to the needs of the most vulnerable and marginalized. There is a new consensus that extreme poverty and inequality need to be explicitly addressed if development targets are to be met and sustained, and that redistributive social protection interventions are at the centre in this endeavour (ILO 2008; World Bank 2004, 2009; OECD 2005). As illustrated throughout this volume, social pensions, conditional cash transfers, public works programmes and micro-financing strategies are all part of the new pro-poor social policy armoury. In fact the idea is more 'third way' (Craig and Porter 2006) than a full-scale turn to social democratic (command and control) welfare state models, since the recommended role of the state is to provide an 'enabling environment' for private (and other) social sector provision rather than taking a lead role in terms of finance or provision of services (Craig and Porter call this a 'third way for the third world'). Nevertheless, the new discourse acknowledges an explicit and enhanced role for the state and for redistributive social policy.

ASIAN TIGERS AND CHINESE DRAGON

However, just as social policy is (some would say, finally) gaining prominence on the agendas of developing states and international donors alike, a new set of actors is also emerging on the global policy scene and threatening to move the debate on to a different trajectory once more. A great deal has now been written about the developmental model forwarded by the 'Asian late industrializers', the so-called 'tiger economies' of South East Asia (Kwon 1997; Holliday 2000; Wilding 2000). Rejecting both classic Western welfare state models and the orthodox policies of the Washington Consensus, these economies arguably have forged an alternative and distinctive path. They spend less on welfare than Western economies, and rely mostly on non-state institutions – in particular the family and business. Also, in contrast to the social democratic ideal of universal, citizenship-based social welfare, they emphasize mutual self-help and independence from the state. Nevertheless, this developmental approach contravened the neoliberal mantra of the 1980s and advocated considerable government intervention. In particular, it involved an expansion of 'instrumental' social protection which would serve productivist goals, the most dramatic examples of which were the introduction of universal health care insurance by Taiwan and South Korea in the mid-1990s. Based on what had come to be known as the Japanese model, the developmental model pursued a social policy that served as the handmaiden of rapid industrialization. Though the state was a relatively low spender, it played a crucial role as facilitator and regulator, enforcing welfare programmes without providing direct finance. In particular, this involved regulating and incentivizing (and underwriting) the private sector so that it adopted more social responsibility in terms of corporate governance and occupational welfare.

The impact of the developmental model has attracted attention, for two main reasons. First, it has been phenomenally successful (especially prior to the late-1990s East Asian crisis) in achieving rapid economic and productivity growth within the domestic borders of this group of countries. Second, and progressively more important, the model has been exported to other developing countries through the activities of emerging donors, in particular China, in other poorer nations, especially in Africa (Alden 2008; Chin and Frolic 2007; Woods 2008).

China's increasing role as an 'emerging donor' in Africa, rooted in a classic developmental 'productivist' approach, seems to be driven less by explicit notions of citizenship and social rights and more by accumulation functions. Investment in education, training and health is justified in terms of broader economic development goals, and stands in contrast to the previous safety-net or 'welfarist' models of Western donors providing social protection from social contingencies and poverty.

There is now growing interest in the extent to which the approach pursued by China (and others) represents a paradigm change for social policy in developing countries and is influencing global debates on welfare and social policy in the context of international development. Initial research suggests that it is directly affecting programmes and policies in recipient countries and that policy learning and transfer has also begun to take place between new and traditional donors regarding the best instruments, institutions and ideas for social welfare (Urbina and Surender 2012; Woods 2006; Manning 2006). While any influence of the Chinese model on Western ideas and practice is still at a very early stage, this research shows that some changes in social policy thinking and practices seem to be under way among various traditional aid actors.

What is striking is the apparent attractiveness of the developmental model of emerging donor aid to recipients, particularly in Sub-Saharan Africa (Malhotra 2010; Urbina and Surender 2013). Part of the explanation undoubtedly lies in the lack of forced conditionality and the strong rhetoric of respect for the sovereign autonomy of aid recipients. But the enthusiastic embrace of this new developmental approach by recipient nations also reveals long-standing underlying tensions between the notions of 'welfare' and 'development' among donor beneficiaries. For many in the developing world, 'welfarism' is associated either with the colonial statism of the past or with notions of safety nets or charity – all undesirable. More attractive and immediately relevant is investment in infrastructure and other systems necessary for developing the supply side of developing economies. Eager to catch up with Western levels of economic growth and wealth, many in the developing world welcome a revival of the 'economic growth first and welfare after' approach now being advanced by the developmental model of new Southern donors. In this regard it is important to acknowledge a parallel between the views of traditional donor agencies outlined here and donor recipients themselves to the effect that 'welfare' consumes valuable resources and weakens attachment to the labour market, and to a large extent is an obstacle to economic growth.

REFLECTIONS AND SYNTHESIS

We began this chapter by arguing that a historical contextualization is necessary if we are to fully understand current social policy arrangements in developing countries. The overview of the evolution of social protection systems in developing countries presented here, though unavoidably cursory, allows us to discern a number of threads.

First, the experience and legacy of colonialism have meant that from the beginning the state in developing countries emerged as a weak institution in terms of both democratic processes (it was not underpinned by mobilization of different constituencies, multiple political parties, or a mature and independent bureaucracy) and functional capabilities (the fiscal and human resource capacity of state institutions and staff). The state was further undermined by the continuing influence of external forces and ideas (and, some world argue, resources), especially the 'direct attack' from the international development institutions during the era of the Washington Consensus and the expansion of the NGO sector. Both the early association of the state with the colonial project and the later rolling back of the state provided opportunities for other actors and sectors, and reinforced reliance on informal and local relationships and institutions. Thus, the management of social welfare and risk in developing countries is mediated by a very different set of institutional conditions, formulated and implemented by a much wider range of policy actors, and conveyed through a variety of different mechanisms and policy instruments.

Second, the relative fragility of the developing country state has made it susceptible to ideas and influences from outside. During the entire post-colonial period, we have evidence of diffusion if not direct transfer between the dominant ideas and discourses in the West and their applications in the South. The literature on policy diffusion teaches us that mechanisms of diffusion include learning, competitive and co-operative interdependence, and symbolic imitation (Braun and Gilardi 2006). Equally, the work of Dolowitz and Marsh (2000) describes policy transfer as the process of bringing ideas, programmes, institutions, policies or administrative arrangements from one place or time into another place or time. It can take the form of lesson drawing, coercive policy transfer, or policy harmonization across regions. The overview presented here displays evidence of all three process. Western policy ideas and discourses can be observed at all stages as a powerful determinant of national social policymaking in the global South, from the era of early post-colonialism and the Washington Consensus to the current Beijing Consensus via the Third Way in between.

Third, we also see that although ideas about the objectives and role of social policy have fluctuated over time, tension between the social and the economic, and the issue of the optimal relationship between the two, have remained constant. Debates about the optimal relationship between the economic and social spheres of policy are, of course, not new, and certainly not specific to developing countries (Mkandawire 2001). On one side is the argument that the social dimension is a crucial pre-condition and driver of economic development since it contributes to, among other things, human capital investment; and proponents point to the dysfunctionality of extreme poverty, inequality, and vulnerability to the achievement of development targets embodied in the Millennium Development Goals (MDGs) (Temple and Johnson 1998; Atkinson 1999; Sen 1999; Devereux and Sabates-Wheeler 2007). The other side of the spectrum sees social expenditure as an obstacle to economic growth because it reduces savings and investment and weakens labour-market attachment (Dornbusch and Edwards 1990). However, in the context of development we can see that before the mid-1990s the relationship could be mostly characterized by a social policy that had been largely subordi-nated to the overriding economic policy objective of economic growth. The tendency has consistently been towards a 'residual social policy' model which favours limited state intervention, a high degree of personal responsibility, the involvement of non-profit organizations in welfare and the maximum use of market mechanisms to meet social needs.

Fourth, it is significant therefore that since the mid-1990s the move-ment in social policy discourse has been radical and significant. Social policy in international forums and in developing countries themselves has become guided by the MDG framework, focusing on poverty alleviation and the promotion of basic human rights. Social welfare interventions have adopted a 'pro-poor' approach and implemented social protection measures involving both means-tested, targeted interventions to the poorest of the poor and a growing movement towards the 'universaliza-tion' of social protection (UNRISD 2012). Policy dialogue and pro-grammes of international donor organizations have supported public expenditure allocations for social protection with set measures and specific budgetary items. The establishment of dedicated public finance support for social protection at national and local levels is a radical and significant advance. It is somewhat paradoxical, then, that just as support for an expanded role for social policy has taken hold, a developmental, productivist approach has gained ground, bringing us full circle. It is important to examine the reasons for this.

Fifth, one interesting observation about these recent dynamics is that they reveal some congruence between the traditional 'supply' of ideas and programmes from the North and new 'demand' for them from the South. Barrientos (2012) and others question whether, increasingly for developing countries, the problem is not with the 'state' but rather with the 'welfare' element of the equation. There is certainly some evidence that, even though state capacity has grown and matured in developing countries, there has not been a corresponding embrace of 'welfarist' (state-led social transfer) solutions. Rather, Western-style welfare state models are frequently derided as redundant or even insidious (Midgley and Piachaud 2012). For many in the global South, 'welfare' has been associated with 'charitable voluntarism' (Gough et al. 2004), or a narrow concern with social services and safety nets, or – more extremely – as the cause of economic stagnation and dependency. Thus, new 'developmental' paradigms and 'empowerment' models, with their emphasis on autonomy, self-reliance and a comprehensive and integrated economic and human development approach, are rapidly being embraced in preference to Northern concepts of social policy.

This tension is paralleled to some extent in the debates and fault lines between development studies and social policy. Although the study of social protection and welfare arrangements in developing countries is becoming gradually more established within the development literature, much of it focuses on providing an effective response to poverty and vulnerability by evaluating what works in terms of sustainable development. For these analysts, a more intense focus on social policy is largely unnecessary, since social risk and vulnerability will be ultimately mitigated by development (and democracy). For social policy analysts, however, a wider understanding of the structural causes of vulnerability is needed if inclusion and empowerment are to be achieved.

A number of important and interesting questions about social policy in a developing world remain as we progress into the 21st century.

First, in the absence of a strong state and in the presence of a more complex institutional welfare mix, what are the current mechanisms in developing countries for managing social welfare and risk? Are they sufficient and adequate? What is the role of informal and local strategies for managing welfare and insecurity? What role for the market? Do NGOs continue to feature as pivotal actors in contributing to meeting social policy needs in developing countries, and is their presence a benign one? What are the mechanisms through which 'formal' state welfare provision is delivered, and how do they compare in intent or design with those in the North?

Second, given the current emphasis on the influential global dimension of the 'fifth sector' (the supranational multilateral donor organizations) for the social policy agenda of developing countries, what are the implications of the apparent recent changes in their ideas and activities for national policy formation and policy choices? Moreover, can we be certain of the direction of change in the wake of new South–South dynamics and pressures? Will the trajectory veer from the recent justification of social policy in 'advocacy and activist' terms towards a 'subordinate' social policy justified only in instrumental terms?

Third, what will be the repercussions of these new dynamics on the normative and ideological debates surrounding the different goals of social policy? Should social policy be directed towards minimal safety nets and managing social risk in the face of weak markets and states or towards more comprehensive and universal provision aimed at addressing structural inequality, social justice and development (Devereux and Sabates-Wheeler 2007)? Equally, what utility do principles such as citizenship, social rights, social justice and inclusion, long rehearsed in a Western context, have when applied to developing countries (Seekings 2000; Wood 2004; Sen 1999; Williams 2003; Marks 2005; Molyneux 2006; De Haan 2007; Freeland 2007; Adésínà 2008)?

Fourth and finally, what does all this mean for social policy theory? Given the hugely varying macro and micro logics of policy arrangements in developing countries, does the subject of comparative social policy need a different or expanded analytic toolkit to understand them? Does it make sense to search for a generic tool or framework for analysing these phenomena, or do we need to distinguish between policy sectors and different groups of countries and regional units? How relevant are the classical political economy approaches and explanatory variables for understanding the construction, evolution and transformation of welfare arrangements in the North (with the emphasis on class stratification, de-commodification, class/group mobilization, the role of ideas, actors, historical institutionalism, path dependency and policy transfer) for understanding developments in welfare arrangements in the South today?

REFERENCES

Adésínà, J. (2007), 'Social policy and the quest for inclusive development research findings from Sub-Saharan Africa'. Programme Paper No. 33. Geneva: Research Institute for Social Development, Social Policy and Development, United Nations.

Adésínà, J. (2008), 'Transformative social policy in a postneoliberal African context: enhancing social citizenship'. Paper prepared for the RC19 Stockholm Annual Conference, 4–6 Sept.

Alden, C. (2008), *China in Africa* (2nd edn), London: Zed Books.

Armstrong, D., L. Lloyd and J. Redmond (2004), *International Organisations in World Politics* (3rd edn), New York: Palgrave Macmillan.

Atkinson, A.B. (1999), 'Macroeconomics and the social dimension', in Division for Social Policy and Development (ed.), *Experts Discuss some Critical Social*

Development Issues, New York: United Nations department of Economic and Social Affairs.

Barrientos, A. (2012), Discussant comments at the conference 'Social Policy in a Developing World', Green Templeton College, University of Oxford, 8 June.

Barrientos, A. and D. Hulme (eds) (2008), *Social Protection for the Poor and Poorest*, Basingstoke: Palgrave Macmillan.

Braun, D. and F. Gilardi (2006), 'Taking "Galton's problem" seriously: towards a theory of policy diffusion', *Journal of Theoretical Politics*, **18** (3), 298–322.

Bräutigam, D. (2009), *The Dragon's Gift: The Real Story of China in Africa*, Oxford: Oxford University Press.

Chin, G. and B.M. Frolic (2007), 'Emerging donors in international development assistance: the China case'. Research report. Canada: Partnership and Business Development Division, IDRC.

Clark, D. (ed.) (2006), *The Elgar Companion to Development Studies*, Cheltenham, UK and Northampton, MA, USA: Edward Elgar.

Collier, P. (2000), 'Ethnicity, politics and economic performance', *Economics and Politics*, **12** (3), 225–45.

Collier, P. (2007), *The Bottom Billion: Why the Poorest Countries are Failing and What Can Be Done About It*, Oxford: Oxford University Press.

Collier, P. and A. Hoefler (1998), 'On economic causes of civil war', *Oxford Economic Papers*, **50** (4), 563–73.

Craig, D. and D. Porter (2006), *Development Beyond Neoliberalism?* London: Routledge.

Cutright, P. (1965), 'Political structure, economic development and national social security programs', *American Journal of Sociology*, **70** (5), 537–50.

Davis, P. (2001), 'Rethinking the welfare regime approach', *Global Social Policy*, **1** (1), 79–107.

De Haan, A. (2007), *Reclaiming Social Policy: Globalization, Social Exclusion and New Poverty Reduction Strategies*, Basingstoke: Palgrave Macmillan.

Deacon, B. (2007), *Global Social Policy and Governance*, London: Sage.

Deacon, B. (2010), 'Global social policy responses to the economic crisis', in K. Farnsworth and Z. Irving (eds), *Social Policy in Challenging Times: Economic Crisis and Welfare Systems*, Bristol: Policy Press, pp. 81–100.

Deacon, B., M. Hulse and P. Stubbs (1997), *Global Social Policy: International Organisations and the Future of Welfare*, London: Sage.

Devereux, S. and R. Sabates-Wheeler (eds) (2007), 'Debating social protection', *IDS Bulletin*, **38** (3), 1–7.

DFID (Department for International Development) (2005), *Fighting Poverty to Build a Safer World: A Strategy for Security and Development*, London: DFID.

DFID (2008), *Leading the British Government's Fight Against World Poverty. Achieving the Millennium Development Goals in Africa: Working with China*, London: DFID.

Dohlman, E. and M. Soderback (2007), 'Economic growth versus poverty reduction: a hollow debate?', *OECD Observer Magazine*, April.

Dolowitz, D.P. and David Marsh (2000), 'Learning from abroad: the role of policy transfer in contemporary policy-making', *Governance: An International Journal of Policy and Administration*, **13** (1), 5–24.

Dornbusch, R. and S. Edwards (1990), 'Macroeconomic populism', *Journal of Development Economics*, **32** (2), 247–77.

Ferro, M. (1996), *Colonisation: A Global History*, London: Routledge.

Fine, B., L. Costas and J. Pincus (2003), *Development Policy in the Twenty First Century: Beyond the Post Washington Consensus*, London: Routledge.

Freeland, N. (2007), 'Superfluous, pernicious, atrocious and abominable? The case against conditional cash transfers', *IDS Bulletin*, **38** (3), 75–8.

Frye, I. (2006), 'Extending social security to developing countries: particular emphasis on healthcare and informal economy workers'. Discussion Paper No. 1. Geneva: The Global Union Research Network, available at http://www.gurn.info/en/discussion-papers/healthcare05.pdf (accessed 2010).

Gough, I. (2005), 'European welfare states: explanations and lessons for developing countries'. Paper delivered to the World Bank conference New Frontiers of Social Policy, Arusha, 12–15 Dec.

Gough, I., G. Wood, A. Barrientos, P. Bevan, P. Davis and G. Room (2004), *Insecurity and Welfare Regimes in Asia, Africa and Latin America: Social Policy in Development Contexts*, Cambridge: Cambridge University Press.

Haggard, S. and R. Kaufmann (2008), *Development, Democracy and Welfare States*, Princeton, NJ: Princeton University Press.

Hall, A. and J. Midgley (2004), *Social Policy for Development*, London: Sage.

Hanlon, J., A. Barrientos and D. Hulme (2010), *Just Give Money to the Poor: The Development Revolution from the Global South*, Sterling, VA: Kumarian Press.

Hasan, N. (1972), *The Social Security System of India*, New Delhi: Chand.

Hearn, J. (2007), 'African NGOs: the new compradors?', *Development and Change*, **38** (6), 1095–110.

Holliday, I. (2000), 'Productivist welfare capitalism: social policy in East Asia', *Political Studies*, **48**, 703–23.

Hudson, J. and S. Lowe (2004), *Understanding the Policy Process*, Bristol: Policy Press.

ILO (International Labour Office) (2001), *Social Security: A New Consensus*, Geneva: ILO.

ILO (2008), 'Can low-income countries afford basic social security?'. Social Security Policy Briefings, Paper 3. Geneva: ILO, available at http://www.ilo.org/public/english/protection/secsoc/downloads/policy/policy3e.pdf (accessed 2011).

International Monetary Fund (1973–2005), *Government Finance Statistics Yearbook*, Washington, DC: International Monetary Fund.

Kanbur, R. (1999), 'The strange case of the Washington Consensus: a brief note on John Williamson's "What Should the Bank Think about the Washington Consensus?"', available at http://kanbur.dyson.cornell.edu/papers/Washington%20Consensus.pdf (accessed 2009).

Kohli, A. (ed.) (2006), *State Directed Development: Political Power and Industrialization in the Global Periphery*, Cambridge: Cambridge University Press.

Korpi, W. (1983), *The Democratic Class Struggle*, London: Routledge.

Kwon, H.-J. (1997), 'Beyond European welfare regimes: comparative perspectives on East Asian welfare systems', *Journal of Social Policy*, **26** (4), 467–84.

Maclean, L. (2002), 'Constructing social safety in Africa: an institutionalist analysis of colonial rule and the state of social policies in Ghana', *Studies in Comparative International Development*, **37** (3), 64–90.

MacPherson, S. (1982), *Social Policy in the Third World*, Brighton: Wheatsheaf.

Mahon, R. (2010), 'After neoliberalism? The OECD, the World Bank and the child', *Global Social Policy*, **10**, 172.

Malhotra, K. (2010), 'South–South cooperation: potential benefits for the least developed countries', in *Poverty in Focus: South–South Cooperation: The Same Old Game or a New Paradigm?*, **20**, 7–9.

Manning, R. (2006), 'Will emerging donors change the face of international cooperation?', Paris: OECD-DAC, available at http://www.oecd.org/dataoecd/35/38/36417541.pdf (accessed 2010).

Mares, I. and M. Carnes (2009), 'Social policy in developing countries', *Annual Review of Political Science*, **12**, 93–113.

Marks, S.P. (2005), 'Human rights in development: the significance of health', in Sofia Gruskin et al. (eds), *Perspectives on Health and Human Rights*, New York: Routledge, pp. 95–116.

Midgley, J. (1995), *Social Development: The Development Perspective in Social Welfare*, Thousand Oaks, CA: Sage.

Midgley, J. and D. Piachaud (eds) (2012), *Colonialism and Welfare: Social Policy and the British Imperial Legacy*, Cheltenham, UK and Northampton, MA, USA: Edward Elgar.

Midgley, J. and K.-L. Tang (2008), *Social Security, the Economy and Development*, Houndmills: Palgrave Macmillan.

Mkandawire, T. (2001), 'Social policy in a development context'. Social Policy and Development Programme Paper No. 7. Geneva: United Nations Research Institute for Social Development.

Mkandawire, T. (2004), *Social Policy in a Development Context*, Basingstoke: Palgrave Macmillan.

Molyneux, M. (2006), 'Mothers at the service of the New Poverty Agenda: Progresa/Oportunidades, Mexico's conditional transfer programme', *Social Policy & Administration*, **40** (4), 425–49.

OECD (Organisation for Economic Co-operation and Development) (2005), *Policy Coherence for Development: Promoting Institutional Good Practice*, Paris: OECD.

Pender, J. (2001), 'From structural adjustment to comprehensive development framework: conditionality transformed', *Third World Quarterly*, **22** (3), 397–411.

Pierson, C. (2007), *Beyond the Welfare State? The New Political Economy of Welfare* (3rd edn), Cambridge: Polity Press.

Riddell, R. (2007), *Does Foreign Aid Really Work?* Oxford: Oxford University Press.

Ringen, S. (1987), *The Possibility of Politics: A Study in the Political Economy of the Welfare State*, Oxford: Clarendon Press.

Seekings, J. (2000), 'The origins of social citizenship in pre-apartheid South Africa', *South African Journal of Philosophy*, **19** (4), 386–404.

Sen, A. (1999), *Development as Freedom*, Oxford: Oxford University Press.

Skocpol, T. and E. Amenta (1986), 'States and social policies', *Annual Review of Sociology*, **12**, 131–57.

Stiglitz, J. (1998), 'More instruments and broader goals: moving towards the post Washington consensus', UNU/WIDER Annual Lectures 2, Helsinki.

Swenson, P. (2002), *Capitalists Against Markets: The Making of Labour Markets and Welfare States in the United Sates and Sweden*, Oxford: Oxford University Press.

Temple, J. and P.A. Johnson (1998), 'Social capability and economic growth', *Quarterly Journal of Economics*, **113** (3), 965–90.

Thirlwal, A.P. (2006), 'Debt crisis', in D. Clark (ed.), *The Elgar Companion to Development Studies*, Cheltenham, UK and Northampton, MA, USA: Edward Elgar.

UNRISD (United Nations Research Institute for Social Development) (2012), *The Universalisation of Social Security in Emerging Economies*, Geneva: UNRISD.

Urbina-Ferretjans, M. and R. Surender (2012), 'China's developmental model in Africa: a new era for global social policy?' in Majela Kilkey, Gaby Ramia and Kevin Farnsworth (eds), *Social Policy Review 24. Analysis and Debate in Social Policy, 2012*, Bristol: Policy Press.

Urbina-Ferretjans, M. and R. Surender (2013), 'Social policy in the context of new global actors: how far is China's developmental model in Africa impacting traditional donors?' forthcoming in *Global Social Policy*.

van Ginneken, W. (2007), 'Extending social security coverage: concepts, global trends and policy issues', *International Social Security Review*, **60** (2–3), 39–57.

Van Niekerk, R. (2009), 'Social Policy, Social Citizenship and Contestation in South Africa since the 1940s', PhD thesis, Oxford University.

Vetterlein, A. (2007), 'Economic growth, poverty reduction and the role of social policies: the evolution of the World Bank's social development approach', *Global Governance*, **13** (4), 513–33.

Vetterlein, A. (2010), 'Lacking ownership: the IMF and its engagement with social development as a global policy norm', in Susan Park and Antje Vetterlein (eds), *Owning Development: Creating Global Policy Norms in the IMF and the World Bank*, Cambridge: Cambridge University Press, pp. 93–112.

Wade, R. (1990), *Governing the Market: Economic Theory and the Role of Government in East Asian Industrialisation*, Princeton, NJ: Princeton University Press.

Wade, R. (2002), 'US hegemony and the World Bank: the fight over people and ideas', *Review of Political International Economy*, **9** (2), 201–21.

Walker, A. and C.-K. Wong (2005), *East Asian Welfare Regimes in Transition*, Bristol: Policy Press.

Weeks, J. and H. Stein (2006), 'The Washington Consensus', in D. Clark (ed.), *The Elgar Companion to Development Studies*, Cheltenham, UK and Northampton, MA, USA: Edward Elgar, pp. 676–80.

White, H. (2006), 'Economic aid', in D. Clark (ed.), *The Elgar Companion to Development Studies*, Cheltenham, UK and Northampton, MA, USA: Edward Elgar.

Wilding, P. (2000), 'Review of Roger Goodman', Gordon White and Huck-ju Kwon (eds), *The East Asian Welfare Model: Welfare Orientalism and the State*', Public Administration and Policy, **9** (2), 71–82.

Wilensky, H. (1975), *The Welfare State and Equality: Structural and Ideological Roots of Public Expenditures*, Berkeley: University of California Press.

Wilensky, H. (2002), *Rich Democracies: Political Economy, Public Policy, and Performance*, Berkeley: University of California Press.

Williams, G. (2003), 'Studying development and explaining policies', *Oxford Development Studies*, **31** (1), 37–58.

Wood, G. (2004), 'Informal security regimes: the strength of relationships', in I. Gough et al., *Insecurity and Welfare Regimes in Asia, Africa and Latin America: Social Policy in Development Contexts*, Cambridge: Cambridge University Press, pp. 49–87.

Wood, G. and I. Gough (2006), 'A comparative welfare regime approach to global social policy', *World Development*, **34** (10), 1696–712.

Woods, N. (2008), *The Globalizers: The IMF, the World Bank and Their Borrowers*, New York: Cornell University Press.

Woods, N. and A. Narlikar (2001), 'Governance and the limits of accountability: the WTO, the IMF and the World Bank', *International Social Science Journal*, **53** (170), 569–83.

World Bank (2004), *The Millennium Development Goals for Health: Rising to the Challenges*, Washington, DC: World Bank.

World Bank (2006), *World Development Indicators, 2006*, Washington, DC: World Bank.

World Bank (2009), *World Development Report 2009: Reshaping Economic Geography*, Washington, DC: World Bank.

Yeates, N. (2008), *Understanding Global Social Policy*, Bristol: Policy Press.

Yeates, N. and C. Holden (eds) (2009), *The Global Social Policy Reader*, Bristol: Policy Press.

PART II

Institutions and actors

3. The role of the World Bank and the International Monetary Fund in poverty reduction: limits of policy change

Antje Vetterlein

INTRODUCTION

International development institutions now constitute an increasingly influential and global dimension of the social policy agenda in developing countries. The United Nations Development Programme (UNDP) is certainly the best-known amongst the international organizations that assist developing countries tackling social and political problems. Yet more economically oriented institutions such as the United Nations Conference on Trade and Development (UNCTAD) or the World Trade Organization (WTO) also shape social policies in developing countries by recommending economic policies regarding trade, for instance. Despite ideological and institutional differences, as well as different areas of competence, these organizations' collective influence on the social policies of countries in the South is ubiquitous, including on the amount of public expenditure, the choice of programmes and implementing mechanisms, and the very direction and nature of policy aspirations. Their main influence stems from the production of knowledge in the form of policy papers and analyses as well as policy advice, whereby they affect the global discourse on development. It is therefore imperative to know how specific development agencies view development and define it as a policy problem, since their perspectives shape the policies they frame and recommend to developing countries.

The World Bank and the International Monetary Fund (IMF) – two international financial institutions (IFIs) created by the Bretton Woods Conference of 1944 – are viewed as the most powerful international aid agencies of modern times. Their loans not only represent the greatest share of all official development aid, but they also serve to ensure the creditworthiness of developing countries and thus have a significant impact on international capital flows. Moreover, the World Bank and the IMF officially define poverty and development, and thus shape social policies in developing countries. In contrast to the UNDP, for example, they exert a direct influence on developing countries by recommending specific policies instead of merely shaping the policy discourse. In this context, the turn of the twenty-first century marked a critical juncture for both organizations, most noticeably reflected in their (re)dedication to poverty reduction through policy initiatives such as the Comprehensive Development Framework (CDF), the Highly Indebted Poor Countries Initiative (HIPC) and the Poverty Reduction Strategy Papers (PRSPs), all of which emphasize the importance of social policies.

The most significant characteristic of this changed notion of development is the reversal of the relationship between economic growth and poverty reduction, the two main objectives of development. In development theory and practice, their relationship has been contested. Approaches based on orthodox economic theory claim that economic growth is the optimal means to achieve poverty reduction. Alternative development approaches contend that poverty reduction itself, or sustainable (or social) development, is a precondition for economic growth. Depending on which theoretical position is adopted in the poverty–growth nexus, this has implications for whether economic or social policies will enjoy priority. A glance at the actual history of development theory and practice confirms these considerations, as aptly captured in the debate in the early 2000s between the Washington Consensus and the post-Washington Consensus. The recent emphasis on sustainable development and pro-poor growth signifies a greater emphasis in development discourse and practice on social policies. Yet, besides the ongoing criticism that the World Bank and the IMF impose a 'Western' view on developing countries and are used only for political reasons to benefit powerful states (among many such critics, see McMichael 2004 or Escobar 1995), even development critics who might accept a certain policy shift still argue that the social is instrumentalized and seriously considered only when it yields economic benefits. This speaks to an econocentric conception of development, or what I call the 'economization of the social'.

Against this backdrop, this chapter first seeks to understand and trace the shift in the World Bank and the IMF towards a more holistic approach to development. In so doing, it not only provides a summary of the underlying values and theories of the Washington Consensus and post-Washington Consensus, but also identifies five dimensions in which they are supposed to differ operationally. Second, it evaluates these differences by comparing the new policy practice of poverty reduction strategy papers (PRSPs) with the previous practice of structural adjustment lending (SAL). I argue that, despite the shift towards more social policies, Bank and Fund practice still falls into the trap of standardization and consequently economization because of bureaucracies' tendency to reduce complexity in order to be able to act. In other words, there are limits to policy change within these organizations.

The argument is developed in the following four steps. First, the chapter explains the logics behind the World Bank's and the IMF's social and economic policy prescriptions and critically assesses the main differences between the Washington Consensus and post-Washington Consensus. Second, it analyses the PRSP initiative as a policy tool in which the new holistic approach to development materialized. It thereby establishes the qualitative meaning of the social in current World Bank and IMF practice, by identifying five dimensions in which the new development operations differ from previous practice. Third, these proclaimed changes are assessed in operational practice by comparing the Policy Framework Papers (PFPs) with PRSPs (which replaced PFPs in 1999) with regard to their extent of standardization and economization. The final part of the chapter provides a critical assessment of the findings.

DEVELOPMENT POLICY AND DEVELOPMENT ECONOMICS: THE LOGICS BEHIND THE WORLD BANK'S AND THE IMF'S ECONOMIC AND SOCIAL POLICY ADVICE

The World Bank's and the IMF's understandings of development and, consequently, the significance of social policies as a tool to combat poverty have changed over time. The World Bank has been more involved with poverty and social policy. Yet the IMF has also implicitly dealt with social policy issues when making economic policy recommendations (Vetterlein 2010). While poverty reduction became a central focus for both organizations in the 1990s, they had long promoted it as an important objective of development. In the late 1960s the World Bank geared its policy efforts towards poverty alleviation as part of an overall Keynesian development strategy of massive investment in public infrastructure. The IMF, in turn, was briefly involved in designing a basic needs approach, incorporating social concerns into its economic models, in the late 1970s (Gerster 1982). In both organizations, the focus on poverty lapsed during the 1980s in favour of a development strategy that was based on classical economic theory. However, the 1990s witnessed a revival of the poverty alleviation agenda that culminated in the World Bank's Poverty Reduction Strategy Paper (PRSP) initiative, which the IMF joined in 1999.

This shift from a narrow-minded focus on economic growth that would automatically lead to poverty reduction towards a holistic understanding of development has also been known as the shift from the Washington Consensus to the post-Washington Consensus (Williamson 2003; Serra and Stiglitz 2008). But while development economists and practitioners now widely acknowledge that there is no single recipe in the form of a 'policy cocktail' that a country should follow in order to achieve high growth rates and decreasing levels of poverty (Rodrik and Rosenzweig 2009), international organizations, given their bureaucratic character, have an inherent tendency to develop simplified models that underestimate local knowledge and complex realities. Such simplified approximations – in the form of specific policy models, operational documents and standardized responses to policy problems – continue to form the basis for their policy recommendations and are used to justify their decisions (see the special issue of *New Political Economy* in 2012). The responsibility lies with a special policy elite, the staff of the World Bank and the IMF, who feed their expertise into the policy process (see for instance Chwieroth 2009; Park and Vetterlein 2010). Rodrik and Rosenzweig (2009) point out how development policies are informed by development economics since those organizations are staffed with economists whose everyday work is informed by their expertise.

This section, therefore, briefly revisits the underlying theoretical assumptions of the two opposing development strategies – the Washington Consensus and the post-Washington Consensus – in order to understand the logic behind the Bretton Woods institutions' social and economic policy advice. The development strategy adopted during the 1980s (the Washington Consensus) is based on the neoclassical economic model under which economic growth is the sole precondition for development. Economic growth, in turn, would be achieved if inflation was kept low and savings high or, alternatively, if the capital stock was enhanced and resource allocation was improved, which is achieved by self-regulating markets. This necessitated free and well-functioning competition as a precondition for a market economy that could be ensured by a government that set and guaranteed only the general conditions for economic development without further interventions. The underlying assumption held that economic growth automatically leads to further social 'progress' and development. Accordingly, the main aim of this development strategy was to increase per capita growth, which was treated as an end in itself. The main loci and primary actors this development strategy addressed were the market and market actors (i.e. the private sector) (for a summary of the content of this development strategy, see Table 3.1).

The two IFIs' policy prescriptions followed the reasoning of this perspective and, combined with the focus on macroeconomic stability since the 1980s, led to the adoption of policies such as privatization, liberalization and deregulation.[1] The foundation of this development strategy is technical knowledge and economic models that calculate, for instance, how much the inflation rate has to decrease in order for the national economy to grow at a certain rate. Hence, this development approach formulates very detailed goals, stating precise development objectives with quantifiable performance indicators. In this context, the role of the two IFIs embraces technical expertise, financial support as well as ensuring compliance with all the policy prescriptions via conditionality.

The post-Washington Consensus development strategy differs from the Washington Consensus in that it defines development in a holistic manner as a transformation process that affects the whole society. Development is not just economic but also entails paying attention to the imperatives of fostering sustainable, democratic and equitable growth. An increase in growth per capita is conceived as a means rather than an end in itself. Hence, economic growth is not considered as the sole precondition for attaining other development goals. Development is as much a cause as an effect of an increase in national growth (Stiglitz 1998a, b). This perspective broadens the objectives of a development approach. While an increase in growth per capita is still an integral part of successful development, it is not sufficient; it may not even be accomplished unless other objectives such as an increase in living standards, poverty reduction, environmental sustainability and democracy are pursued. Further, different actors are served by the suggested policies and means to achieve these aims, and the attention shifts towards different loci for the suggested policies. Instead of focusing only on the market, this perspective suggests fostering development in the private sector, the public sector, the community and family, as well as the individual (see Stiglitz 1998b).

The knowledge required for this development strategy transcends technical skills and economic models. If development is seen not just as a transformation of technology or progress in economic growth but as a

society-wide process of change, then there is a need to include performance indicators other than high return rates to projects and macroeconomic variables, which in turn requires a different kind of knowledge
drawn from disciplines such as anthropology, sociology or social psychology. It becomes important to know how (traditional) societies are
organized, what values underlie them and thus how this might influence
the economy. The social context of economic development becomes a
central focus (see Table 3.1). These changing theoretical assumptions
about development have had consequences for the policies of the World
Bank and the IMF.

The 1990s witnessed numerous new policy initiatives from the World
Bank including the Strategic Compact (1996), which was designed to
give greater attention to social issues; the Partnership Initiative (1997),
which sought to enhance country ownership of and participation in
programmes; the CDF, which was discussed by the World Bank in 1996
as a tool through which countries could manage knowledge and resources
to devise and execute effective strategies for economic development and
poverty alleviation; and the HIPC initiative (1996), which outlined for the
first time a framework for decreasing the external debt burdens of poor
countries to sustainable levels, and which was fused in 1999 with the
PRSP initiative. The adoption of these policies, together with new
cross-cutting procedural policies such as participation, ownership and
transparency, heralded significant changes in the World Bank's development strategy. They represented an acknowledgment that development
had to be seen in a holistic manner recognizing that social, institutional
as well as organizational aspects of a society are a precondition for
functioning markets.

This shift represented a fundamental break with the 1980s. Structural
adjustment conditionalities were supplemented with so-called 'green',
'people's' and 'governance' conditions (Dias 1994). The 1997 *World
Development Report* (World Bank 1997) supported this view by arguing
against state minimalism. Nonetheless, the report still emphasized the
market and economic growth as the main objectives of the institution's
policies; concerns about social, environmental and participatory aspects
were merely added as subsidiary elements to the overall economic
framework. This caused significant disagreement and conflict among
Bank staff. The first serious (and public) clash with this position was
Stiglitz's proposal for a new development approach in 1998, after which
he resigned as chief economist from the Bank. Ravi Kanbur's[2] resigna-
tion over the contents of the *World Development Report 2000/1* (World
Bank 2001) is another example of the outcome of voicing more radical
views on development policy departing from the Washington Consensus.[3]

Table 3.1   Two development strategies compared

	Washington Consensus	Post-Washington Consensus
Definition of development	Narrow approach Development as a technical problem, solvable by the laws of economics	Holistic approach Development as a transformation process of the whole society
Underlying assumptions	Economic growth as an end and modernization/progress is just an effect of it	Economic growth is a means and modernization is both a cause and effect of economic growth
Objectives/ values	Growth of GDP (increase in capital stock and efficient resource allocation)	In addition to growth in GDP, enhancement of living standards, poverty reduction, environmental sustainability, democratic development
Primary actors or loci for suggested policies	Market	Private and public sector, community, family, individual Government → ownership In particular NGOs and civil society → participation
Means/ policies	Fiscal discipline, reordering public expenditure priorities, tax reform, liberalizing interest rates, competitive exchange rate, trade liberalization, liberalization of inward foreign direct investment, privatization, deregulation, property rights	Macroeconomic stability, financial system, legal infrastructure, competition Government as a partner, enhancement of its capabilities (civil service) Participation, ownership, consensus Empowerment (education, health) Priority areas: education, infrastructure (communication and transport), health, knowledge, capacity-building (institutions and leadership)
Outlook of development strategy	Detailed planning documents Quantifiable performance indicators	Broad, less detailed, vision More ambitious and long term Comprehensive, coherent, consistent
Role of IFIs or aid assistance	Technical expertise and financial support Conditionality	Technical expertise and financial support Outside consultants (country is in the driver's seat) but no conditions
Type of knowledge	Technical knowledge, economic models So-called blueprint approach	As well as technical knowledge, consideration of the social context which implies non-economic knowledge such as political sciences, sociology, anthropology Country specificity

With the adoption of the PRSP initiative in 1999, the World Bank indeed tried to design an operational tool that could bring together many of the ideas that had been circulating in the organization to translate the new paradigm of a post-Washington Consensus into action.

The IMF also underwent major changes during the 1990s. The conditions attached to its loans changed to a set of secondary objectives such as poverty alleviation, environmental sustainability and good governance. Moreover, 'new' problems emerged on its agenda which brought it much closer to the World Bank. Over the course of the 1990s, the IMF developed three new instruments for crisis solution.[4] First, in 1990 it introduced economic growth policies, thrusting growth into central focus and diminishing the salience of balance-of-payments management. This enabled the IMF to give policy advice that moved beyond pure macroeconomic stability and embraced private sector development, tax policy and so on. Second, good governance guidelines were adopted in 1997 which embraced topics such as institution-building, designing and implementing anti-corruption policies, as well as promoting transparent and accountable administration and an efficient management of public resources. Third, the IMF established new facilities, such as the Contingent Credit Line, to enable it to lend larger amounts of money in the event of economic crisis, thereby restoring market confidence.

Yet the most crucial change in social policies and poverty reduction took place in 1999, when the IMF joined the World Bank's PRSP policy initiative and established a new facility – the so-called Poverty Reduction and Growth Facility (PRGF). A successor to the Enhanced Structural Adjustment Facility (ESAF), the PRGF has poverty reduction as its main goal. Although the IMF has remained largely responsible for macroeconomic policies within the PRSP process, this has nevertheless brought about operational changes that have, in turn, transformed the institution. Within the Fiscal Affairs Department, a new Poverty and Social Impact Analysis Unit has been established, which defines and measures poverty (reduction). Participation in the PRSP initiative has also resulted in the IMF increasingly collaborating with other development partners such as civil society organizations, elected institutions and key donors, thereby increasing pressure for greater accountability and transparency of the PRSP process. Moreover, for the first time in its history the IMF has recruited a few non-economic social scientists and also included social benchmarks among its conditionalities (for more detail, see Vetterlein 2010). Yet what precisely is the significance of this increased social focus in the Bank's and the Fund's development approach? A closer look at the objectives and background of the PRSP initiative will reveal the intended differences between the two development approaches. This policy analysis remains on the organizational level, which examines the policy conduct of the two IFIs instead of the implications of these policies on the ground in developing countries, an analysis of which would go beyond the framework of this chapter.

THE MEANING OF A HOLISTIC DEVELOPMENT APPROACH: UNRAVELLING THE PRSP

The PRSP process was initiated amid growing discontent at the limited impact on sustainable development of conditionality-based aid (Bwalya et al. 2004). The World Bank, usually more receptive to external critique (Park and Vetterlein 2010), underwent an 'identity crisis' (Pereira 1995) around the fiftieth anniversary of the two organizations, and frantically attempted to initiate policy reforms. For its part, the IMF started to react only at the prompting of two related events, namely, a damning external review of ESAF (Botchwey et al. 1998), and the simultaneous onset of the East Asian financial crisis, for whose detrimental social consequences the IMF was held principally responsible. These circumstances led to the endorsement of the PRSPs by both IFIs in September 1999 as a new framework for poverty reduction.

The PRSPs provide the basis for concessional assistance from the IFIs to low-income countries (LICs). The background to this new policy strategy was threefold. In the first instance, poverty reduction was made the ultimate goal of the strategy, and all other policies were subordinated to this overarching goal. Second, a prior consideration of the PRSP process was that it ought to be led by the governments of participating countries, also referred to as 'country ownership'. The Country Assistance Strategy (CAS, the World Bank's operational document dealing with countries) and the PRGF (the IMF's operational tool) have to be consistent with and based on the priorities set out in the PRSP. The PRSP replaced the Policy Framework Paper (PFP) as the basis for Bank CAS and Fund programmes. Third, the process ought to be open and participatory; it must be undertaken with broad participation from other social actors such as private firms, labour unions and non-governmental organizations.

The PRSP initiative signified a clear departure from the Washington Consensus. Whatever the new thinking on development is called, the PRSP process as a materialization of it seriously attempted to change operations in Bank and Fund practice. I argue that there are five key differences that distinguish both development strategies not only in discourse and policies but also on the operational level:

1.   the linkages between economic growth and poverty reduction;
2.   the underlying time horizon;
3.   the type of knowledge used to practise development;
4.   the focus on participation and ownership; and
5.   the centralization of aid activities.

Economic Growth or Poverty Reduction?

Undoubtedly, the most potent difference between the Washington Consensus and the new thinking on development lies in the understanding of the relationship between economic growth and poverty reduction. This is not to say that people no longer believe in a positive link between growth and poverty reduction; rather, the view that 'growth is everything' seems to have faded away (interviews conducted with Bank and Fund staff in 2004 and 2008). In other words, the underlying definition of the problem has changed. Development is perceived much more broadly than just in economic terms. Nevertheless, economic growth has not disappeared, but the related assumptions and explanations have changed and the growth objective is now combined with a strong emphasis on poverty reduction and therefore on social policies. While in the 1980s policies had to be made subject to the rules and discipline of the market, the policy package recommended now does not focus only on economic liberalization. Yet critics would still argue that this newly proclaimed understanding of development has not fully materialized on the ground.

A Different Understanding of Time

The PRSP explicitly adopts a long-term perspective on poverty reduction as one of its main features. What exactly does that mean? The underlying time horizon of the policies typical of the Washington Consensus is medium term. This is implicit in the economic theory based on the assumption of equilibria that underlies the Washington Consensus, since policy reforms relating to distribution and growth will yield results in five to ten years. This time perspective is also reflected in the way empirical analysis has been carried out in the World Bank and the IMF in the 1980s, which Gore (2000) calls the time of 'ahistorical performance assessment'. According to Gore, before the Washington Consensus development was understood as a long-term sequence of economic and social changes, a social transformation process with different stages. During the 1980s attention shifted to performance assessment, particularly economic performance, accompanied by a growing ahistoricism in development policy. As a consequence, IFIs were more concerned with monitoring the policy results and trying to improve performance as measured by specific indicators, such as the GDP growth rate, increases in poverty, the unemployment rate, and percentages of school enrolment or life expectancy, rather than considering development as a comprehensive process that goes beyond social and economic indicators. The perspective of long-term development strategies was lost. With the adoption of a holistic approach to development, we can observe a swing back to a long-term perspective on the one hand and also, on the other hand, to a short-term perspective. The former is captured by the term '*sustainable* development' whereas the latter is expressed in concerns about the immediate impact of policies on the poor.

A Different Type of Knowledge

In light of the objectives of the PRSP initiative, the knowledge used and required in the development process must change. Rather than only economic knowledge with its technical understanding of development and its focus on the cost-effectiveness of policies, much more contextual and social knowledge is now applied in both IFIs. This observation has two dimensions. On the one hand, a shift has taken place from the mere aggregation of economic data towards a more people-centred approach that focuses on qualitative rather than only quantitative information. On the other hand, development seen as a complex social transformation process implies that it is country-specific and path-dependent and thus requires contextual knowledge rather than blueprint approaches.

The best reflection of the shift towards a more 'people-centered' (see Cernea 1985) approach to development is the acknowledgment that poverty is a multi-dimensional problem (see World Bank 2001). Under the Washington Consensus, poverty analysis carried out by economists mainly consisted of measuring poverty in terms of income, that is, the poverty line of one dollar per person per day as well as correlations between the GDP level in a country and its poverty numbers. This method was increasingly criticized. Absolute numbers of people in poverty can fall while at the same time conditions in developing countries deteriorate. Furthermore, regional disparities as well as inequality in general need to be taken into account. Critics called for a broader understanding of poverty drawn in particular from the experiences of the poor themselves. The 'Voices of the Poor' project, which served as the basis for the *World Development Report 2000/1*, attempted to address this issue and was supposed to be taken into account in the PRSP process. Another example is the approach to conducting participatory poverty assessments (Kende-Robb 1999), which argues for the inclusion of the poor in poverty assessments. This type of qualitative knowledge provides information about the importance of the context in which development is taking place. In addition, while in the early 1980s state intervention was nowhere on the agenda in the recommended policy package, and thus development was not perceived as a national issue as such, this changed in the early 1990s when government activities were legitimized through the acknowledgment of market failure. Now, from a holistic development perspective, development is seen as a country-specific matter, contrary to so-called blueprint approaches. The PRSP is supposed to function in that way, as a policy plan tailored to one particular country. It describes all the special circumstances and tries to address them individually. Development policies are directed towards specific national and country-specific needs and objectives.

Participation and Ownership

This new type of knowledge further implies a shift from a patronizing system of negotiations between the respective IFI and developing countries to a so-called participatory process in which not only is the government of a country supposed to 'sit in the driver's seat', as a famous World Bank maxim goes, but civil society, the poor themselves and all other relevant development stakeholders are included. Both developments are captured by two buzzwords: country ownership and participation. In response to the criticism that the World Bank and the IMF have imposed their development notions on their clients, country ownership, in contrast, emphasizes the need for a government to decide what is best for its country and people. It is argued that country ownership will enhance the success of the development strategy by increasing the commitment and political will to carry out reforms.[5]

Participation is a closely related idea. If the new consensus is based on the acceptance that poverty is an overarching problem that concerns everyone, rather than a technical problem that can be solved through market mechanisms, this also implies the eradication of the divide between the IFIs, the government, and the people concerned (often represented by NGOs and other civil society groups). This new notion thus acknowledges new actors in the development arena, most notably NGOs. That way, it also changes policymaking practices from procedural rules in terms of negotiations and specific assessments to roundtable discussions with the participation of all the stakeholders as well as moving them on from mere consultancy to active funding and incorporation of NGOs. The PRSP process is supposed to address this issue by a comprehensive participatory process through which the strategy is developed. Even IMF staff now have to negotiate loans with development stakeholders other than the finance minister of a country.[6] Yet some critics of the World Bank and the IMF consider such activities as strategic moves by the two organizations to co-opt NGOs and other critical voices in order to pacify them or to enhance their own reputation. Ownership, on the other hand, is seen as a means to shift the responsibility for success to the countries themselves.

Centralization of Aid: Partnership and Donor Harmonization

A final point is the centralization of aid efforts in different countries. The PRSP initiative is an attempt to centralize development aid in one single strategy that combines all the aid activities under way in a given country. This has two consequences. First, it decreases the possibilities for countries to play one donor off against others or to receive financial aid for the same project from different sources, and thus, limits the scope for corruption. Second, it further prevents situations where different aid agencies give opposing policy recommendations to a country. Critical voices would, however, emphasize that all that information coming together in Washington DC might enhance the power that the Bank and the Fund can exert in the international development regime.

In sum, the PRSP initiative signifies change and an attempt to operationalize the holistic development approach referred to as the post-Washington Consensus.[7] These five dimensions address the main criticism the Bank and the Fund faced regarding their policy recommendations and practice during the 1980s and early 1990s.[8] It is therefore difficult to wholeheartedly criticize the two organizations. Yet this policy change seems to be limited. Despite the reforms, the Bank and the Fund continually fall short when it comes to the qualitative meaning of the 'social'. This critique is twofold. On the one hand, the Bank and the Fund are blamed for their continuing econocentric culture (Cernea 1996) despite focusing more on poverty issues and thus on social policies. I call this the 'economization of the social' whereby social policies are entertained only if they yield an economic benefit. On the other hand, and despite addressing this issue by looking into new types of knowledge focusing on people and finding country-specific solutions, Bank and Fund operations have been criticized for dealing only with issues that can be quantified, often offering standardized policy solutions based on technocratic economic modelling (the so-called blueprint approach). According to Scott (1998), the latter critique does not come as a surprise since bureaucracies, in order to function, produce a simplified reading of societies. The next and final section ties in to this point and argues that standardization in Bank and Fund practice is closely linked with economization. This will be further explained by comparing the content of two sets of operational documents, namely the PFPs and the PRSPs which replaced them in 1999.[9]

THE LIMITS OF POLICY CHANGE: ECONOMIZATION, QUANTIFICATION AND BLUEPRINTS

To revisit the five dimensions of difference identified above, poverty reduction became the driving theme in the PRSPs. The strategy begins with a comprehensive assessment of the main poverty issues in a given country and outlines priority areas and policy objectives to tackle them. Targets are in line with the aim of poverty reduction as well as the Millennium Development Goals (MDGs), and indicators are set to monitor whether or not the targets are met. The time frame is longer than the previous one under SAL. Further, PRSPs include a section on the participatory process to ensure that all stakeholders have had the chance to participate in the strategy and were able to voice their opinion. The PFP, in contrast, did not focus on either poverty or participation but was a short document identifying the main problems of a country, focusing on its macroeconomic framework, and establishing medium-term goals that should be monitored for policy success. Furthermore, it was a tripartite paper, written by the IMF and the Bank in consultation with the country.

Yet if we take a closer look at the last PFPs of four countries[10] and compare them with their first PRSPs, the differences are not so significant regarding the actual content and priority areas of the strategies (see also Oxfam 2004).[11] On the one hand, the PFPs not only focused on macroeconomic stability and structural policies but also paid attention to country specificities. Each of the four papers identified specific problems in its respective country and made specific recommendations on how to proceed. PFPs mainly referred to macroeconomic goals such as GDP growth, inflation rates and foreign exchange reserves; schooling and mortality rates were mentioned as the only indicators of social issues. Yet the PRSPs are prioritizing the same issues as did the PFPs. However, they provide a broader context by embedding the strategy in an overall analysis of poverty. Furthermore, targets are in line with the long-term MDGs; they are more precise and give detailed objectives in a macroeconomic framework but also trends in social expenditure, priority sectors and public finance in general. However, the targets and indicators are quantified and still prioritize economic areas or social policies that have a direct economic benefit, such as health and education. To summarize, first, the PRSP is evidence that poverty reduction has become the priority objective in Bank and Fund practice in LICs, yet economic growth is still as important as before. Second, already in the PFPs social problems in LICs were acknowledged and country specificities were taken into account. While targets are more refined and long-term in the PRSPs, the focus is still on policies where outcomes can actually be measured and quantified.

These two dimensions of the critique, economization on the one hand and quantification and standardization on the other, therefore still seem to hold. I argue that they are related to each other. Crouch (2007) points out that economic models fit nicely with modern bureaucracies and policy-making. In that sense the normative question of which development objective to pursue is interlinked with the operational and organizational conditions of a huge bureaucracy. Decisions in large bureaucracies such as the World Bank or the IMF are made on a rational basis, referring to rules, regulations, procedures, contracts and expertise. Even if it is acknowledged that poverty is a multidimensional problem and should be measured qualitatively, actionable knowledge is subject to targets, measurable indicators and thus quantification. Economic knowledge and models are in line with such imperatives. While the Bank and partly the Fund, too, have acknowledged that qualitative knowledge on poverty in terms of how it is perceived is important, it is nowhere to be found in the PRSPs. Instead poverty is measured, recorded and monitored in a quantitative way. A report from the Bank's Operations Evaluation Department (OED) concludes that the integration of social issues into Bank practice has been rather slow because its implementation depends on many factors and is hindered in particular by the fragmentation of responsibilities as a consequence of the cross-sectoral nature of many social development issues. This 'complexity' (see OED 2004, p. 27) of the topic runs counter to the Bank's culture and internal procedures. Scott (1998) would argue that this is not primarily related to the culture of an organization but that bureaucracies in general tend to struggle with complexity. So-called anti-poverty advocates (or 'change agents'; see Bebbington et al. 2006) have understood this problem and therefore employ one of their strategies of framing poverty in economic terms (interviews April 2004; see also Davis 2004; Vetterlein 2012). While they realise the inherent 'Faustian bargain' (Bebbington et al. 2006, p. 280) this strategy implies, the way in which knowledge about poverty that exists in the organization is translated into bankable policy solutions shows how operational and organizational conditions affect which understandings of the policy problem gain traction and become legitimate definitions beyond the organization. In other words, even if the Bank and the Fund would like to follow a holistic development approach that appreciates local knowledge based on participation and ownership, the very practices of an organization give way to actionable knowledge that can be easily adopted. In the case of the Bank and the Fund, economic knowledge fulfils the requirements of actionable knowledge and therefore wins over social and more complex knowledge about poverty. It is more manageable for both organizations to measure poverty in terms of income, life expectancy, school enrolment and so forth than to employ social knowledge such as the 'Voices of the Poor' project has produced.

But what exactly does that mean for the recommendations of the Bank and the Fund to developing countries and then, in turn, for the realities on the ground? While their policy agendas have changed[12] and they also spend more resources on social issues (Vetterlein 2012), the continuing focus on measurable targets and policies that have an immediate economic benefit might initially change little when it comes to the realities of developing countries. Thus, the main emphasis often remains on policies such as health and education, nutrition and population that have formed the core of the Bank's practice at least since the 1970s. Yet the change in procedures for framing these poverty strategies has the potential to eventually change practice by empowering people in developing countries. The cross-cutting themes that the more holistic social development agenda promotes, such as ownership, partnership and participation, are important in starting a process of building up capacities in developing countries to develop their own position *vis-à-vis* both IFIs. The participation stipulated by the PRSP process requires the active involvement of politicians, representatives of other (civil society) organizations as well as the people/beneficiaries of certain projects, which provides a chance for these people to make themselves heard but also to unite and strengthen their position and forces. Whether it would significantly decrease the power of organizations such as the Bank and the Fund is arguable.

On a more conceptual level, I would argue that in order to break with the strong practice of economization, quantification and standardization one might have to start at the normative level by disposing of the causal relationship established between economic growth and poverty reduction. For sure, economic growth and poverty reduction are related, but treating them as two separate objectives might allow following economic *and* social policies at the same time without treating this as a zero-sum game. This in turn might provide room for manoeuvre to accept that redistributional/social policies are inherently political, that is, based on values held in societies about what is just and what is not, and do not follow a standard grid. To narrow them down to their economic value will leave us in the quantification and consequently economization trap.

CONCLUSION

That the Bretton Woods institutions' conceptions of development have changed over time is patently evident. The erstwhile parochial focus on economic growth as the sole precondition for development has been supplanted by a more holistic understanding of development that places social policies at the centre of development and poverty reduction. This is in recognition of the fact that development is not merely about generating high economic growth rates but is also about fostering sustainable and equitable development. The new notion of development has been born out of a growing recognition of the complexity of the determinants of poverty and the reality that addressing its causes requires country-specific solutions. It is distinguishable from the Washington Consensus in terms of assumptions about the market structure and the linkages between economic growth and poverty reduction; the underlying time horizon; the type of knowledge used to practise development; the focus on participation and ownership; and the centralization of aid activities. Distilled in the PRSP process, this new policy thinking has defined, at least conceptually, the World Bank's and IMF's development approaches in recent years.

This change in development discourse within the Bretton Woods institutions has had implications at the policy level; and the usual criticism voiced against both organizations is therefore difficult to sustain. It no longer makes sense to deride them as instruments of powerful industrialized countries that exert geopolitical interests globally (McMichael 2004; Escobar 1995), that worsen the situation in developing countries through the specific policies adopted (Cornia et al. 1987), or that address poverty by merely engaging in a strategy of window-dressing (Fine 2001; Jayasuriya 1999). This is not to say, however, that critical discussions, for instance about the dominant role of the US Treasury in the Bank and the Fund (Wade 2002), the uneven allocation of voting power in both organizations (Woods 2006), or the ways in which these IFIs retain control while pushing responsibility on to developing countries are no longer relevant – far from it. Yet the intention of this chapter has been to show that even well-intended Bank and Fund policies might not escape the criticism of being standardized and econocentric responses to social problems. As large bureaucracies they have a tendency to ignore crucial local knowledge and produce policy responses that are administratively convenient. Since economic knowledge fulfils these criteria, there might always be a tendency to economization.

The chapter has analysed this problematique by tracing discourse, policies and operations in the field of poverty reduction and social policies within the World Bank and the IMF. The analysis shows that the underlying values and theories on which policymaking is based have changed over time and so have the Bank's and the Fund's policy recommendations. Since both IFIs are powerful organizations that shape world politics, not least by providing knowledge and expertise, it is crucial to understand these underlying values and theories. To this end, this chapter has first identified the main differences between the Washington Consensus and the post-Washington Consensus (see Table 3.1) and then undertaken a more fine-grained policy analysis of one of the policy tools that captures the newly adopted holistic development approach, namely the PRSPs. In a final step, a comparison between operational documents before and after the reforms reveals limits to the policy change in the Bank and the Fund. Both organizations seem to have a tendency towards a standardized and econocentric policy response to development. I have argued that the operational conditions of huge bureaucracies are such that economization, quantification and blueprint approaches prevail. I suggest that distinguishing between the normative and the organizational dimensions of the problem and acknowledging that economic growth and poverty reduction are not causally linked might help to improve the Bank's and Fund's approach to poverty and social issues.

NOTES

1. For a history of the Washington Consensus and the ten original policy recommendations, see Williamson (2008).
2. Ravi Kanbur worked as Economic Adviser, Senior Economic Adviser, Resident Representative in Ghana, Chief Economist of the African Region of the World Bank, and Principal Adviser to the Chief Economist of the World Bank. He also served as Staff Director of the *World Development Report 2000/1*. See Kanbur (2001).
3. For more details on both cases, see Wade (2001).
4. For more details regarding these new policies, see Riesenhuber (2001: 48).
5. Critics have noted that while this seems to be a good idea at first glance, it is always the taxi driver's client in the back seat who tells the driver where to go.
6. In particular among interviewees in the Fund (conducted in 2004 and 2008), this new technique was considered as a possible way to trigger learning processes on both sides of the table.
7. This chapter is about the Bank's and the Fund's response to criticism and evaluates the differences between SAL practice and the PRSP initiative. It does not seek to examine the triggers of policy change. For such a discussion, see for example Park

and Vetterlein (2010), who found three main triggers for change in the World Bank and the IMF: policy failure, external shocks and massive condemnation. Other scholars of IO studies suggest additional triggers such as change agents (Chwieroth 2009) and organizational culture (Weaver 2010) and also policy pressure by powerful member states in both organizations (Momani 2010).

8. See for instance the external review of ESAF (Botchwey et al. 1998).
9. Based on the PFP, lending under the Structural Adjustment Facility (SAF) and Enhanced Structural Adjustment Facility (ESAF) took place whereas the PRSP is the new operational document for the Poverty Reduction and Growth Facility (PRGF), which replaced (E)SAF lending to low-income countries (LICs).
10. Burkina Faso, Cambodia, Mauritania and Tajikistan.
11. The OED as well as the IMF's Independent Evaluation Office have also reviewed the PRSP approach, jointly as well as separately, and come to critical conclusions (OED 2004; IEO 2004; World Bank and IMF 2005). For a more critical view in particular of the concepts of ownership and participation in the PRSP, see Kamruzzaman (2009).
12. In order to incorporate a holistic development approach, the World Bank, for instance, has developed its social policy approach from traditional social policies (that is, social welfare and social protection) to social development with its own Bank-wide strategy paper (Vetterlein 2007).

REFERENCES

Bebbington, A., Michael Woolcock, Scott Guggenheim and Elizabeth Olson (eds) (2006), *The Search for Empowerment: Social Capital as Idea and Practice at the World Bank*, Bloomfield, CT: Kumarian Press.

Botchwey, Kwesi, Paul Collier, Jan Willem Gunning and Koichi Hamada (1998), *Report of the Group of Independent Persons Appointed to Conduct an Evaluation of Certain Aspects of the Enhanced Structural Adjustment Facility*, Part II, Washington, DC: IMF.

Bwalya, Edgar, Lise Rakner, Lars Svåsand, Arne Tostensen and Maxton Tsoka (2004), *Poverty Reduction Strategy and Processes in Malawi and Zambia*, CMI Reports, R 2004: 8, Bergen: Chr. Michelsen Institute.

Cernea, Michael M. (ed.) (1985), *Putting People First: Sociological Variables in Development*, New York: Oxford University Press.

Cernea, Michael M. (1996), 'Social Organization and Development Anthropology', 1995 Malinowski Award Lecture. Environmentally Sustainable Development Studies and Monographs Series 6, Washington, DC: World Bank.

Chwieroth, J.M. (2009), *Capital Ideas: The IMF and the Rise of Financial Liberalization*, Princeton, NJ: Princeton University Press.

Cornia, Giovanni Andrea, Richard Jolly and Frances Stewart (1987), *Adjustment with a Human Face*, 2 vols, Oxford: Oxford University Press.

Crouch, Colin (2007), 'Neoinstitutionalism: still no intellectual hegemony?', *Regulation and Governance*, **1**(3), 261–70.

Davis, Gloria (2004), *A History of the Social Development Network in The World Bank, 1973–2002*, SDV Paper 56, Washington, DC: World Bank.

Dias, Clarence J. (1994), 'Governance, democracy and conditionality: NGO positions and roles', in Andrew Clayton (ed.), *Governance, Democracy and Conditionality: What Role for NGOs?*, Oxford: INTRAC.

Escobar, Arturo (1995) [1952], *Encountering Development: The Making and Unmaking of the Third World*, Princeton, NJ: Princeton University Press.

Fine, Ben (2001), 'Neither the Washington nor the post-Washington Consensus: an introduction', in Ben Fine, Costas Lapavitsas and Jonathan Pincus (eds), *Development Policy in the Twenty-First Century*, London, New York: Routledge, pp. 1–27.

Gerster, Richard (1982), 'The IMF and basic needs conditionality', *Journal of World Trade Law*, **16** (6), 497–517.

Gore, Charles (2000), 'The rise and fall of the Washington Consensus as a paradigm for developing countries', *World Development*, **28**(5), 789–804.

IEO (Independent Evaluation Office) (2004), *Evaluation of the IMF's Role in Poverty Reduction Strategy Papers and the Poverty Reduction and Growth Facility*, Washington, DC: IMF.

Jayasuriya, Kanishka (1999), 'The new touchy-feely Washington', *AQ: Journal of Contemporary Analysis*, **71**(6), 5–7.

Kamruzzaman, Palash (2009), 'Poverty Reduction Strategy Papers and the rhetoric of participation', *Development in Practice*, **19**(1), 61–71.

Kanbur, Ravi (2001), 'Economic policy distribution and poverty: the nature of disagreements', *World Development*, **29**(6), 1083–94.

Kende-Robb, Caroline (1999), *Can the Poor Influence Policy? Participatory Poverty Assessments in the Developing World*, Washington, DC: World Bank.

McMichael, Philip (2004), *Development and Social Change: A Global Perspective*, London: Pine Forge Press. (This book provides essential historical background.)

Momani, Bessma (2010), 'Internal or external norm champions: the IMF and debt relief', in Susan Park and Antje Vetterlein (eds), *Owning Development: Creating Global Policy Norms in the IMF and the World Bank*, Cambridge: Cambridge University Press, pp. 29–47.

OED (Operations Evaluation Department) (2004), *An OED Review of Social Development in Bank Activities*, Washington, DC: World Bank.

Oxfam (2004), 'From "Donorship" to Ownership? Moving Towards PRSP Round Two', Oxfam Briefing Paper 51, Oxford: Oxfam International.

Park, Susan and Antje Vetterlein (2010), *Owning Development: Creating Global Policy Norms in the IMF and the World Bank*, Cambridge: Cambridge University Press.

Pereira, L. (1995), 'Development economics and the World Bank's identity crisis', *Review of International Political Economy*, **2**(2), 211–47.

Riesenhuber, Eva (2001), *The International Monetary Fund under Constraint: Legitimacy of its Crisis Management*, The Hague, London: Kluwer Law International.

Rodrik, Dani and Mark R. Rosenzweig (2009), 'Introduction: linking development policy with development research', in Dani Rodrik and Mark R. Rosenzweig (eds), *Handbook of Development Economics*, Amsterdam: North-Holland.

Scott, James C. (1998), *Seeing Like a State: How Certain Schemes to Improve the Human Condition Have Failed*, New Haven, CT: Yale University Press.

Serra, Narcis and Joseph E. Stiglitz (2008), *The Washington Consensus Reconsidered: Towards a New Global Governance*, Oxford: Oxford University Press.

Stiglitz, Joseph E. (1998a), 'More Instruments and Broader Goals: Moving Toward the Post-Washington Consensus', 1998 WIDER Annual Lecture, Helsinki, 7 January, available at http://www.globalpolicy.org/socecon/bwi-wto/stig.htm (accessed 11 February 2002).

Stiglitz, Joseph E. (1998b), 'Towards a New Paradigm for Development: Strategies, Policies, and Processes', 1998 Prebisch Lecture at UNCTAD, Geneva, available at http://www.worldbank.org/html/extdr/extme/jssp101998.htm (accessed 11 February 2002).

Vetterlein, Antje (2007), 'Economic growth, poverty reduction and the role of social policies: the evolution of the World Bank's social development approach', *Global Governance, Global Governance*, **13**(4), 513–33.

Vetterlein, Antje (2010), 'Lacking ownership: the IMF and its engagement with social development as a global policy norm', in Susan Park and Antje Vetterlein (eds), *Owning Development: Creating Global Policy Norms in the IMF and the World Bank*, Cambridge: Cambridge University Press, pp. 93–112.

Vetterlein, Antje (2012), 'Seeing like the World Bank on poverty', *New Political Economy*, **17**(1), 35–58, available at http://www.tandfonline.com/doi/abs/10.1080/13563467.2011.569023.

Wade, Robert (2001), 'Showdown at the World Bank', *New Left Review*, **7**(Jan./Feb.), 124–37.

Wade, Robert (2002), 'US Hegemony and the World Bank: the fight over people and ideas', *Review of International Political Economy*, **9**(2), 215–43.

Weaver, Catherine (2010), 'The strategic social construction of the World Bank's Gender and Development Agenda', in Susan Park and Antje Vetterlein (eds), *Owning Development: Creating Global Policy Norms in the IMF and the World Bank*, Cambridge: Cambridge University Press, pp. 70–90.

Williamson, John (2003), 'The Washington Consensus and beyond', *Economic and Political Weekly*, **38**(15), 1475–81.

Williamson, John (2008), 'A short history of the Washington Consensus', in N. Serra and J. Stiglitz (eds), *The Washington Consensus Reconsidered: Towards a New Global Governance*, Oxford: Oxford University Press, pp. 14–30.

Woods, Ngaire (2006), *The Globalizers: the IMF, the World Bank and their Borrowers*, Ithaca, NY: Cornell University Press.

World Bank (1996), *The World Bank Participation Sourcebook*, Environmental Department Papers 019, Washington, DC: World Bank.

World Bank (1997), *World Development Report: The State in a Changing World*, New York: Oxford University Press.

World Bank (2001), *World Development Report 2000/1: Attacking Poverty*, New York: Oxford University Press.

World Bank and IMF (International Monetary Fund) (2005), *2005 Review of the PRS Approach: Balancing Accountabilities and Scaling Up Results*, Washington, DC: World Bank and IMF.

4. Building the welfare mix or sidelining the state? Non-governmental organizations in developing countries as social policy actors

David Lewis

INTRODUCTION

When almost half a century ago Arthur Livingstone (1969, pp. 60–61) noted that the 'voluntary worker' was a key figure in community-level work in developing countries in his review of social policy and development, he was perhaps a little ahead of his time:

> Not for many years to come will many developing countries possess even the rudimentary professional services to make comprehensive welfare programmes effective. In the meantime, assistance to the present skeleton staff of specialists must be provided by either voluntary or partly qualified assistants.

Today, both local and international non-governmental organizations (NGOs) have come to be regarded as key players in international development and poverty reduction work across the world. They play roles in what has sometimes been termed 'big D' development in terms of projects and programmes, as well as in 'little d' development as diverse actors within wider processes of capitalist change and transformation (Bebbington et al. 2008). An estimated 10 per cent of total overseas development assistance is channelled through NGOs, and international NGOs based in developing countries raise an estimated USD 20 billion–25 billion annually in the form of additional development assistance to low-income countries (OECD 2009). Some NGOs remain voluntaristic and small-scale in forms that Livingstone might still recognize, while others have grown to become highly professionalized, even corporate, entities. Still, questions remain as to the effectiveness of these organizations, and whether NGOs complement or substitute for governments.

Although a major topic within development studies since the 1980s, the subject of NGOs in developing countries has only recently begun to interest social policy researchers. In social policy a state-centred approach has dominated, in which non-governmental actors were frequently underplayed. For example, Esping-Andersen's (1990) influential threefold typology of industrialized country 'welfare regimes', which has formed the basis of much subsequent thinking about comparative social policy, had remarkably little to say about non-state actors. Given the centrality to mainstream social policy of the idea of a welfare state based on citizenship rights, created in order to replace patchy private and charitable service provision, the ambiguous view of this so-called 'third sector' of organizations that is neither governmental nor part of the private for-profit business sector is in many ways understandable (see Evers 2010). But it is increasingly out of date, and somewhat at odds with reality. If we adopt Deacon's (2008) conceptual framework that suggests four interrelated approaches to understanding social policy (sector policy, redistribution and rights, social issues, and welfare regime theory), we will be able to see in this chapter that NGOs may play important roles in each.

The rise of new ideological agendas around neoliberalism from the 1980s onwards brought non-state actors more sharply into focus as social policy actors, as the state was restructured. A new language of the 'mixed economy of welfare' emerged, with its explicit recognition of third-sector roles in welfare provision, along with the 'new public management' movement that emphasized the growing role of markets and partnerships in attempts to reform and reshape the services that remained within the state sector (Dean 2006). The crisis of the welfare state under neoliberalism, and the idea of a welfare mix that included both public and private elements, therefore helped to focus new attention on non-governmental actors. They were seen as agents of the new policy agendas of privatization and contracting, but also in some cases as sites of resistance to these new agendas. This chapter aims to provide an overview of these issues and to explore briefly key issues using selective examples.

ENGAGING WITH NGOS: TRANSCENDING A DOUBLE KNOWLEDGE GAP IN SOCIAL POLICY?

Despite early work on 'social planning' approaches in developing countries by writers such as Livingstone (1969) and Hardiman and Midgley

(1982), the study of social policy has remained predominantly focused on rich industrialized country contexts and has tended to downplay non-state actors. This gap in our knowledge is beginning to be filled with the rise of a 'social policy and development' agenda that is based on evolving conversations between researchers in social policy and those within development studies. Gough and Wood's book *Insecurity and Welfare Regimes in Asia, Africa and Latin America: Social Policy in Development Contexts* (Gough 2004) was a landmark text in this cross-disciplinary dialogue. It also served to address a second gap – that of the third sector. The book was one of the first to bring non-state actors more fully and more systematically into the analysis of social policy and development alongside government, market and household. Gough (2004, p. 30) explicitly recognized the key role of the non-governmental sector in developing country social policy:

> A wider range of institutions and actors are involved in modifying livelihoods structures and their outcomes. At the domestic level, 'communities', informal groups and more formal NGOs, figure as informal actors and add a fourth institutional actor to the state–market–family trinity.

The growth of a new field of global social policy has also moved forward the study of NGOs. For example, Yeates (2001, p. 8) shows how an increase in processes of globalization has intensified transnational politics such that non-state actors increasingly play roles in both national and international political arenas. One consequence is that

> social policies and politics are no longer confined to the domestic sphere, or to the governmental sphere – if they ever were – and greater account must be taken of the transnational realm in charting the development of social policy.

The increased profile of the non-governmental sector and the welfare mix idea, linked as it is to the rise of neoliberal policy agendas and the privatization of the state, remains deeply controversial for many social policy researchers. Few would disagree with the vision of transformative social policy that is put forward by the United Nations Research Institute for Social Development in its 2010 report *Combating Poverty and Inequality* that

> Despite the important role played by such non-state and private actors in reducing vulnerability and destitution, as well as in advocating social rights, they cannot act as substitutes for public action by the state. (UNRISD 2010, p. 139)

Yet whether one takes a positive or a negative view of the increased role of this third sector, the gap in our knowledge has been problematic, for two main reasons. First, it has crowded out 'society-centred approaches' that engage with the roles of citizen groups in shaping the institutions and processes of social policy. Second, the state-centric view has placed the field of social policy at odds with current policy realities around the world – whether in relation to the 'big society' agenda under way in the UK, or to the 'good governance' agenda that continues to inform international development policies among donors such as the World Bank or the UK Department for International Development (DFID) (Ishkanian and Szreter 2012). At home and abroad, non-state actors such as NGOs and other 'civil society' organizations are increasingly playing, for better or for worse, a set of important roles as service delivery agents, as vehicles for self-help and as policy advocates. Indeed, in many areas of the developing world, people depend upon them for key services.

DEFINING NGOS: A WAY THROUGH THE MUDDLE?

The origin of the term 'NGO' can be traced back to the establishment of the United Nations (UN) in 1945, when the acronym was coined to denote the UN observer status that was awarded to selected international non-state actors. In the period since then, 'NGO' has become a notoriously imprecise abbreviation that is used in both broad and narrow senses. At its broadest, it refers to a diverse range of actors, from small-scale community-based organizations to large-scale professionalized agencies. NGOs are engaged across most fields of human endeavour, from arts and leisure to human rights and environment.

NGOs are normally understood as a subset of a wider 'third sector', made up of a diverse universe of non-state and non-profit organizations. The term 'non-governmental organization' is often used interchangeably with similar terms such as 'voluntary', 'non-profit', 'civil society' and 'community-based' organization, each of which has its own cultural and ideological origins. At its narrowest, NGO is commonly used to refer to the subgroup of third-sector organizations active in the development fields, funded primarily – but not exclusively – from within the international aid system.

Much effort has been expended in attempts to define and explain NGOs as responses to the failure of states and markets. Definitions of what constitutes an NGO have been either legal (focusing on the type of formal registration and status of organizations in a specific context), economic (focused on where an organization's resources come from) or functional (based on the types of activities undertaken). The work of Salamon and Anheier (1992) attempted clarification by developing a more holistic approach to the study of what they called the 'nonprofit sector'. Finding the mix of approaches unsatisfactory and inconsistent, they instead constructed a 'structural/operational' definition drawn from a more rounded analysis of an organization's observable features. Five key characteristics were identified as central prerequisites of any non-profit organization: it needs to be formal, that is, the organization is institution-alized with regular meetings, office bearers and some organizational permanence; private, in that it is institutionally separate from government although it may get some resources from government; non-profit distrib-uting, and if a financial surplus is generated it does not accrue to owners or directors (often termed the 'non-distribution constraint'); self-governing and therefore able to manage its own affairs; and finally voluntary, and even if it does not use volunteers as such, there is some degree of voluntary participation in the management of the organization, such as having a voluntary board of directors.

For the purposes of social policy analysis, NGOs can be understood as part of the subset of third-sector or non-profit organizations that are engaged in development or humanitarian action at local, national and international levels. Vakil (1997, p. 2060) defines NGOs as 'self-governing, private, not-for-profit organizations that are geared to improv-ing the quality of life for disadvantaged people'. This is one of the simplest and best definitions. It refines Salamon and Anheier's 'structural/operational' criteria for the specific context of development policy and practice. Using this framework, we can therefore maintain an inclusive focus that takes into account the broad diversity of NGOs, while still retaining the capacity to contrast development NGOs with other types of third-sector groups such as trade unions, organizations concerned with arts or sport, and professional associations. While there is a wide range of non-state development actors and a lack of agreement about defining NGOs in relation to wider civil society organizations, this chapter focuses on the broad general category of 'NGOs'. Examples are provided of three main types of NGO – international NGOs, national developing country organizations, and local level grass-roots membership or self-help organizations.

NGOS AND DEVELOPMENT – A SHORT HISTORY

Development studies began taking an interest in NGOs during the late 1980s, when the profile of NGOs began to increase. There were at least three sets of reasons for this new prominence. First there was the perceived failure of top-down forms of government-to-government, project-based aid, which was by the 1980s seen as having led to disappointing results in the struggle to reduce poverty. NGOs were seen to offer an alternative way of working. Second was the rise of people-centred, community development approaches that were primarily associated with the work of the NGO sector. These approaches challenged the top-down orthodoxy with a set of new ideas about participation, empowerment, rights and social justice. Third was the emerging ideological climate of neoliberalism, which emphasized downsizing what were seen as inefficient and over-large developing-country states, and the creation of more space for privatized market-based actors and policies (Lewis 2005). This tendency gathered additional momentum after the end of the Cold War, crystallizing into what Edwards and Hulme (1995) termed development's 'new policy agenda', which also became seen as part of what was known in aid circles as the principles of 'good governance'. This agenda emphasized the role of NGOs on the one hand as efficient private service providers, and on the other as innovative citizen advocates with the potential to campaign for social transformation and better governance.

NGOs have a far longer history, predating their rise to prominence in the 1980s. Three main historical trajectories in their evolution can be noted: (a) national historical processes in developing countries in which political, religious, economic and charitable impulses have helped to generate local forms of third-sector organization, sometimes in conjunction with international aid flows; (b) the work of missionaries and other forms of humanitarian action from the colonial period onwards and the subsequent growth of a modern international NGO sector; and (c) the rise of a Western donor neoliberal development policy framework that has favoured state withdrawal and helped to generate an ideology of 'non-governmentalism', as part of universalist ideas about 'good governance'.

First, national level processes in developing countries have helped to shape the emergence of NGOs. NGO approaches, structures and values vary, and this diversity is in part rooted within specific histories and contexts. For example, in Latin America histories of peasant movements seeking land rights, and political radicals seeking to build more open democratic societies, have both contributed to the evolution of NGOs. Some were influenced by 'liberation theology', which influenced the Church's work with the poor. In Brazil, Paulo Freire's radical ideas about 'education for critical consciousness' and organized community action were influential, and inspired many other NGOs around the Third World. Alongside these radical influences there have been professionalized organizations with close relationships with donors and governments (Pearce 1997).

In Asia, distinctive influences on the growth of NGOs have included Christian missionaries and reformist urban middle classes; and in India traditions have drawn on Mahatma Gandhi's ideas of voluntary action and village-level self-reliance. Local self-help traditions such as rotating credit groups, in which households pool resources into a central fund and then take turns in borrowing and repaying, have influenced the emergence of micro-finance and credit services, associated with organizations such as Bangladesh's internationally renowned Grameen Bank. Also in Bangladesh, BRAC has evolved into one of the largest NGOs in the world, operating in a wide range of sectors including education, health, agriculture and legal services. It has grown and developed steadily since being established in 1972, breaking its earlier dependence on donor funds to generate its own revenue, and internationalizing to become the first Southern NGO to operate on a global level (Smillie 2009). Local associational third-sector activity has underpinned African societies, including the home-town associations common in Nigeria, or the well-documented 'harambee' self-help movement of Kenya. In countries of Eastern Europe and the former Soviet Union, increasing NGO numbers were the result both of local activists rediscovering ideas of civil society, as Buxton (2011) shows in the context of Central Asia, and of the democracy promotion and civil society development efforts of Western donors.

A second strand of the evolution of NGO work in developing countries can be linked to the histories of colonialism, such as the missionary work tradition. As Barrow and Jennings (2001, p. 10) explain, in the UK the provision of welfare services for non-European populations was part of the agenda for the 19th-century evangelical Protestant movement, leading to

> the rise of missionary organisations dedicated to assisting ideologically and economically impoverished peoples, as well as bearing the torch for Western civilisation … [they] began to accompany their conversion work with social work – providing health care, educational opportunities and relief in times of distress to communities ravaged (as they saw it) by disease, rampant poverty, the depravations of the slave trade and 'heathen customs'.

In Uganda, Christian missionaries arrived during the late 19th century and were providing health and education services before the state, with this tradition now representing 'the most enduring element of the NGO sector in the country' and continuing through the country's independence in 1962 up to the present day (Cannon Lorgen 2002, p. 293). In the UK, organizations such as the Church Missionary Society and the Universities Mission to Central Africa were part of the early movement to provide charitable relief to people overseas. The latter provided relief in the form of food aid for 1371 people in a single week during the 1899 northern Tanganyika famine (Barrow and Jennings 2001).

A more secular Western strand of NGO work also emerged, embodied for example in the Red Cross organization established by Henri Dunant in 1864 in order to uphold the principles of the Geneva Convention on the rules of war. Such organizations became part of a growing tradition of international organizations that worked outside the state in pursuit of wider humanitarian objectives. For example, the 1910 World Congress of International Associations brought 132 international associations together to engage with issues that included narcotics control, transport, intellectual property rights, public health, agriculture and conservation. NGOs became prominent during the League of Nations after the First World War, active on issues such as labour rights (Charnovitz 1997). Save the Children Fund was established by Eglantyne Jebb in 1919, following the First World War. Oxfam, then known as the Oxford Committee Against the Famine, was created in 1942 with the aim of sending famine relief during the Greek civil war. In 1946 CARE started sending food from the US to Europe following the Second World War. Indeed, Western NGOs have existed at least since the 18th century, when there were national level issue-based organizations that campaigned for peace and advocated against the slave trade.

Third, as we have seen, NGOs assumed a far greater role in international development from the 1980s onwards. There was a period of discovery and celebration of NGOs among international donors as they became seen as a possible 'magic bullet' that would bring new solutions to long-standing development challenges that had up to that point been characterized by inefficient government-to-government aid programmes and frequently ineffective and unsustainable development projects. More important still, and as we have seen, NGOs as private non-state actors fitted neatly into the ensuing effort to liberalize developing economies and roll back the state as part of World Bank and International Monetary Fund (IMF) structural adjustment policies, and NGOs quickly came to be seen as cheaper alternatives to public sector services. After the Cold War, Western international donors such as the World Bank and the British Overseas Development Administration (later known as DFID) began to advance the 'good governance' policy. Though it was never a single coherent set of ideas, this was broadly based on the belief that positive development outcomes could emerge only from a properly balanced relationship between government, market and third sector. Within this paradigm, development NGOs came to be conceptualized as being part of an emerging 'civil society', a synonym for this third sector.

The 'discovery' of NGOs by the development policy community as the neoliberal international development agenda gained traction in the 1980s attracted new attention to NGOs, and far larger quantities of aid resources than had existed before. The idea of NGOs as an all-purpose 'magic bullet' for development problems was quickly discredited, for reasons that are discussed below. But the new centrality of NGOs to development was regarded by many people as positive, in that it helped bring new and often 'alternative' ideas into mainstream thinking and practice (Mitlin et al. 2007). These included new ideas about participation, empowerment, gender, and rights-based development approaches. It also ushered in an optimistic, transformative set of ideas for a more inclusive and innovative approach to development and poverty reduction. For example, Michael Cernea (1988, p. 8), one of the main advocates of NGOs at the time, suggested that NGOs as organizations embodied 'a philosophy that recognizes the centrality of people in development policies', and that along with their good local relationships NGOs possessed important 'comparative advantages' over government. As well as increasing their funding to international and local NGOs, and encouraging partnerships between governments and NGOs in the delivery of key services, donors began to direct efforts towards building the capacity of developing country or 'Southern' NGOs, and to encouraging these organizations to 'scale up' their often small-scale and local activities. Such efforts often had mixed results.

Both advocates and detractors of NGOs tend to assume that NGOs have standardized characteristics. Yet a crucial though often overlooked point is that NGOs tend to take very different forms in different settings based on context, culture and institutions. For example, while the third sector is a recognized part of most Western liberal democracies, there are wide variations in the level of government funding for it. In developing countries the domestic third sector is further complicated by other factors, such as funding from outside development agencies. Carroll's (1992, p. 38) tenet that 'all NGOs operate within a contextual matrix derived from specific locational and historic circumstances that change over time' is one that remains apposite. For example, while it is usual to make a distinction between international NGOs (INGOs) and developing country or 'Southern' NGOs, and to assume the dominance of INGOs over their local counterparts in many developing countries, this too varies across contexts. In countries such as India, Bangladesh and the Philippines, where there are well-developed and locally resourced domestic

NGO sectors, the influence of INGOs is lower than in some contexts in Sub-Saharan Africa, where local NGOs may be less well established and heavily dependent on INGO 'partners' and other donors for resources (Lewis and Kanji 2009).

NGOS AS SOCIAL POLICY ACTORS: UNDERSTANDING THEIR ROLES

Like development, social policy can be framed within both broad and narrow definitions. At its narrowest, social policy can refer to social sectors such as health and education and welfare services such as income support and pensions. At its broadest, social policy is concerned with the ways in which a society facilitates or constrains the capacity of its citizens to flourish. NGOs contribute at both levels, with some engaged in meeting direct needs and others seeking to make a wider contribution to the functioning of institutions, the pursuit of human rights, and struggles for social or environmental justice. NGOs are a broad category and it follows that NGOs can play a wide range of roles within social policy, from the relief and emergency work of the international NGO community after the devastating Haiti earthquake in 2009, to the small local NGOs campaigning for local government transparency in India. Though diverse, these roles can be simplified and broadly classified into three categories or clusters: those of 'implementer', 'partner' and 'catalyst' (Lewis 2007). This section outlines, using selected illustrative examples, the wide range of roles that NGOs play within social policy and the 'welfare mix' in terms of these three essential types.

The implementer role involves the mobilization of resources towards providing people with goods and services. NGO service delivery work often originates from, or is rooted in, citizen's own efforts to address unmet needs under existing provision. For example, in the Western Kasai province of Western Congo a grass-roots NGO called Butoke is helping to build food security and social welfare by providing village associations with agricultural seeds and farm tools to strengthen people's efforts to help themselves. Service delivery work is performed by NGOs across a wide range of social policy fields such as health care, education, financial services, emergency relief and human rights. For example, in Zambia, Hodi is an NGO that provides community services for unaccompanied minors, women and children, along with basic education services, in two refugee camps that host around 40,000 refugees from the Congo (OECD 2009). The role of NGOs as service providers has become perhaps the most visible of NGO roles in many developing country settings. There are a range of broader institutional contexts in which NGOs may be providing services, including gap-filling, substituting for government providers, and complementing existing provision. Some NGOs provided services in a gap-filling role, often to populations in places where government services are unavailable or insufficient, in order to complement government. Others are specifically contracted by government to provide services in place of government, often in contexts where public services are being restructured and withdrawn. Since the 1990s NGOs have therefore substituted for government service provision in many developing countries. In some cases this may provide improved quality or choice for service users, but in many cases researchers report a decline in provision, especially for the poorest. Critics of the increasing role of NGOs in service provision have pointed to a range of problems, including erratic quality of provision, limited accountability to service users and a lack of coordination between organizations (Lewis and Kanji 2009). In Bangladesh, Wood (1997) identified the potential problem of creating 'states without citizens', in which government engaged subcontractors to provide basic services in a franchise model where the accountability link between citizens and government became unclear or broken.

The role of partner reflects the growing trend for NGOs to work jointly with government, donors and the private sector, performing tasks such as provision of particular inputs within multi-agency projects, or working with companies on socially responsible business initiatives. For example, the IBON Foundation in the Philippines is a capacity-development NGO concerned with knowledge building in the education sector. Church activists and professionals originally established the NGO in 1978 in order to disseminate politically sensitive socio-economic information during the country's long period of authoritarian rule. After democracy was restored in 1986, the NGO began building the IBON Partnership in Education for Development (IPED) in response to demands from the formal education sector for new ideas to revitalize the curriculum. There are now more than 200 partner schools subscribing to IBON's education materials service, and the NGO has become an accredited service provider with the Professional Regulatory Commission (OECD 2009). Under the partnership role we also find community-level 'capacity building' work which seeks to develop and strengthen local capabilities. Partnership is also used to describe the working relationships between international NGOs and the local organizations that they fund and work with in developing countries. Partnership became a policy buzzword central to the 'new public management' agenda, part of which aimed to create more productive relationships between the sectors. In relation to government and NGOs, new logics of 'synergy', 'partnership' and 'co-production' began to become a key part of social policy discourse and practice. Research began to suggest that such partnerships could be highly effective if they were set within effective institutional frameworks and the provision of adequate resources (White and Robinson 1998). While such relationships could work, many researchers also focused on the problems and tensions involved when government and NGOs come together, and highlighted the unequal power relations that lie behind some of the more cosy discourses of partnership. For example, a study by Batley (2006) found, in a comparative study of contracting in six countries, that non-state service provider relationships are often rather unsupportive and that government–NGO relationships remain 'surrounded by mistrust'. Indeed, the idea of partnership has become increasingly contested as more and more NGOs are 'contracted' by governments and donors provide services within privatizing policy agendas. International development donors have, through the 'good governance' policy agenda, encouraged the idea – common also in many areas of the 'developed' world – that the effectiveness and efficiency of service delivery in areas such as health care and education could be improved if collaboration and partnership were built between government and non-state providers. The result has been the emergence of a wide range of contracting relationships.

The catalyst role refers to the ability of NGOs to contribute to processes of change, either locally in small ways or within higher levels of policy processes. Advocacy NGOs try to shape international, national or local policy processes in support of particular values or on behalf of specific communities. For Najam (1999), there are key points or stages within the 'policy process' in which NGOs can shape or contribute to outcomes, including agenda setting, policy development and policy implementation. In addition, Najam argues that NGOs can play important roles as watchdogs, seeking to 'keep policy honest' (1999, p. 152). At the local or organizational levels, NGOs may be able to develop new insights and approaches or facilitate new thinking and innovation. Such efforts may be at the level of community-based action, such as new forms of micro-lending, gender budgeting or community business, or they may be directed at others actors in development such as government, business or donors. For example, the 'right to information' movement in India has worked to try to increase the accountability of officials to local people through improving public scrutiny. These efforts may include grass-roots organizing and group formation, gender and empowerment work, lobbying and advocacy, and attempts to secure wider influence through policy entrepreneurship. Citizen engagement, as Gaventa and McGee (2010) have shown, can make an important difference to governance and developmental outcomes.

Moving away from more linear models of policy that separate out policy and implementation, McGee's (2004) 'multi-range model' of the policy process adopts a more political perspective. This shows the ways NGOs may serve as political actor catalysts that influence policy at international and local levels. Here, policy is conceptualized as a dynamic process containing 'actors' who frame ideas and implement action, and 'policy spaces' in which different types of actor interact and which may be both 'closed' or 'invited', and where policy narratives in relation to poverty and development are constructed from diverse sources of knowledge, ranging from official data to people's stories and experiences. For example, in the context of Uganda, Karen Brock provides a valuable account of the ways in which the growing participation of non-governmental actors in formal policy 'spaces' can achieve positive policy influence in relation to poverty reduction agendas, such as in 'changing attitudes among government actors' (2004, p. 106) in relation to the Uganda Participatory Poverty Assessment Programme. At the same time, she shows how influence may also be exerted through informal participation in policy spaces, such as the work of the Ugandan Joint Council of Churches in relation to lobbying and alliance building in relation to the parliamentary process. Such work also shows the limits to such efforts, since Brock also suggests that pushing too hard can create oppressive responses from the state. Another catalyst role, that of innovation, may contribute to improved service delivery as well, as in the case of BRAC developing new teaching approaches that are now used in government primary schools in Bangladesh.

Within the wide range of such work, the three NGO roles outlined above easily become blurred within the messy everyday realities of NGO activity. For example, for some NGOs the implementation role becomes a prerequisite for seeking wider policy influence, since they need to secure income through contracting arrangements, the opportunity to demonstrate good practice to government in service delivery, and the fact that being seen to do something practical increases an organization's credibility among both its service users and government officials.

NGOS: CLAIMS AND COUNTERCLAIMS

As we have seen, when development NGOs were 'discovered' during the 1980s they were eagerly embraced in the world of international development. They were seen as providing a source of new alternatives to improve upon the limited achievements of three decades of conventional government-to-government approaches to aid that had characterized the post-war era of international aid. At the same time, an enhanced role for NGOs seemed to appeal to both sides of the development debate (Lewis and Kanji 2009). For radicals, NGOs reflected a new activist grass-roots approach to promoting social change in developing countries. For the new advocates of markets and privatization, NGOs were seen as important private actors with the potential to deliver public services more efficiently than government, and to a wider range of previously excluded sections of the population.

The claims that were made for an increased role for NGOs in development centred on two main sets of issues. First, for mainstream agencies such as the World Bank and other donors the new importance of NGOs was framed in terms of areas of 'comparative advantage' over other public or private policy actors in service delivery, based on NGOs' organizational strengths. NGOs were seen as flexible, value-driven organizations that contrasted with bureaucratic and self-interested government agencies. They were seen as having a strong capacity to represent and serve communities, a high level of cost-effectiveness based on strong social values and a voluntarist spirit, and an organizational culture that made possible a high degree of learning and experimentation, resulting in the innovation of practices and ideas. NGOs also filled in the gaps left by mainstream approaches, in particular working with poorer communities ignored by government and markets. For example, in many rural areas NGOs could be found providing services to rural households that had long been ignored or discriminated against by mainstream public-sector agricultural extension agents, and some NGOs set about developing new approaches and technologies that could serve the needs of these excluded sections of society (Lewis 1993). The Grameen Bank in Bangladesh argued that poor rural people were failed both by private loan services that were too costly and by government loan services that were captured by elites (Yunus, 2010).

Second, for those advocating alternative development approaches, the political role of NGOs as vehicles for enhancing citizen voice and action and the construction of 'social capital' was particularly emphasized. The formation of community-level groups was seen as contributing to greater empowerment and local voice. NGOs were seen to have important roles in local communities where they were organizing local communities in ways that followed the Grameen Bank's group-based collateral approach to building social solidarity, or more radical empowerment-based forms of organization reflecting on Freirean theory. NGOs also gained a profile

as advocates seeking to influence national-level policymaking, challenging existing policies or bringing new issues to the policy agenda based on
the demands of their members or supporters. At the same time, income
generation support, training and credit by NGOs was seen as strengthening local livelihoods in sustainable ways. The creation of self-help groups
was seen as contributing to economic security and social solidarity.

Yet the belief that NGOs represented a 'quick fix' for long-standing
development problems did not last. Criticisms centred on several key
issues. The first central problem was that, despite the rhetoric, many
NGOs tended to lack strong accountability relationships to the people
that they claim to serve, and instead acted as agents of those donors,
companies or governments that provided them with funding. In a detailed
study of 300 NGOs in Uganda, for example, it was recently found that
NGOs were less than transparent in the way that they reported their work
to funders and government (Burger and Owens 2010). In the context of
Pakistan, Bano (2012) argues that foreign aid has tended to undermine
local efforts at community-based collective action and altruism in the
wider third sector. A second set of criticisms revolves around the fact that
many otherwise effective NGOs may be too small to make much of a
difference beyond small islands of success. If they grow and formalize,
they often lose their original comparative advantage as their values and
organizational structures become confused. Also, Tendler (2004) is
critical of the tendency towards 'projectization' in which social policy is
increasingly seen as being implemented with micro-level initiatives rather
than at the level of broader social reform, and suggests that the rise of
NGOs has contributed to this problem. Third, a set of political criticisms
point to the compromised role of NGOs within unfolding patterns of
neoliberalism. Some argue that local NGO sectors and the foreign aid
that supports them lead the emerging middle classes away from more
developmental activities, and contribute to privatization processes. Such
critics point out that NGOs all too often are substitutes for government,
and serve to undermine already fragile states in many developing country
contexts.

Part of this critique is the view that NGOs serve as agents of
neoliberalism, supported by international development agencies, and
undermine rather than build on local community structures and relationships. Critics argue that the emerging support for self-help groups – often
seen as a form of bonding social capital – among international development agencies such as the World Bank and the United Nations Development Programme may use the language of localism, but remains firmly
aligned with the aims of neoliberal policies. For example, the microcredit
agenda, an activity strongly – though not exclusively – associated with

the role of NGOs, has recently come in for considerable criticism. Pattenden (2010) describes the growth of women's self-help groups in India, where there are now believed to be 31 million members of three million microcredit groups that have been formed by NGOs and government. He shows how these groups are part of the expansion of microcredit as a strategy for promoting economic growth in rural areas, where they are seen as

> advancing the goals of economic development and poverty reduction by thickening civil society, strengthening the poor's stocks of social capital, engendering development, and complementing decentralised good governance with empowering participatory processes. (p. 508)

These efforts, he argues, ultimately have a depoliticizing effect on the organizational efforts of poor people, because while they provide 'marginal' economic benefits they leave untouched the deep-rooted structural inequalities that require a more political, transformative approach to civil society and social transformation.

Eventually, these criticisms of NGOs began to coalesce into a wider disillusionment and finally evolved into a backlash against NGOs. New evidence began to suggest that the advantages of NGOs were sometimes overstated, and that NGOs often fell short of the level of performance that was expected. It was not only critics from the Left who remained critical of the ways that 'alternative' NGO agendas had become co-opted by mainstream development agencies, but many donors themselves found that NGO performance and accountability when evaluated systematically were disappointing. Ever eager to move on to the next development fashion, the wider development industry had scaled down its interest in NGOs by the late 1990s and moved on to new approaches that emphasized a return to working more directly with developing country governments, using newly tooled managerialist mechanisms such as 'budget support' and 'sector-wide approaches' (Lewis 2007).

The critical discourse around NGOs highlights the complexities of NGO roles in development and social policy, which, as we have seen, are strongly context-specific. It is rarely useful to try to generalize about NGO roles and capabilities since developing-country settings vary considerably. For example, in Bangladesh the NGO sector, despite international influences and resources, can be seen to have evolved in a manner that has been strongly locally conditioned, based on the political and charitable impulses of local activists and social entrepreneurs in the period since Bangladesh emerged as a new independent country in 1971 (Lewis 2011). Organizations such as BRAC and Grameen Bank have overcome the limits to scale that are normally encountered by development NGOs, and challenged many of the prevailing assumptions about NGOs. India, too, contains an NGO sector that is more the product of local than of international influences. By contrast, and perhaps more typically among the countries of Sub-Saharan Africa, the context of Mozambique highlights an NGO sector which remains dominated by international NGOs, and which has evolved in a manner that is still strongly externally determined through the operation of both international donors and international NGOs. At least until comparatively recently, the donor community has tended to bypass and weaken the government by deploying NGOs as service contractors (Hanlon 1991).

The latter problem is illustrated by the case of international NGOs and primary health care in Mozambique (Pfeffer 2003). After gaining independence from Portugal in 1975, Mozambique had developed a highly effective primary health care system that received acclaim from the World Health Organization. During the 1980s, the system was undermined both by the South Africa-backed civil war that destabilized the country, and by the external imposition of the IMF's structural adjustment programmes that cut state spending and deepened poverty and insecurity. Unlike the case of Bangladesh, where most NGO activity is indigenous, the NGO sector in Mozambique is dominated by a mix of different types of Western international NGOs. These organizations moved into the vacuum left after the collapse of the socialist bloc as a source of funding for the Mozambique government. The result has been a lack of coordination between NGOs, and between NGOs and government, and a problem of competing organizations that all too often leads to duplicated efforts and parallel services. Large numbers of expatriate personnel have tended to disrupt national planning processes and local services, and intensified local social inequalities. According to Pfeffer (2003, p. 726):

> Rather than redistributing resources to promote greater equity and help alleviate poverty, the flood of NGOs and their expatriate personnel has fragmented the health system and contributed to intensifying social inequality in local communities with important consequences for primary health care delivery.

More research is needed within social policy and development if the theoretical and practical implications of the rise of NGOs are to be fully understood for issues such as citizenship and accountability. The relative lack of a strong research base, and sound theoretical development, remains a problem for those studying NGOs and social policy. The result is also a weak and underdeveloped evidence base for understanding how NGOs might contribute more effectively to social policy in different contexts, settings and sectors.

DEVELOPMENT AND SOCIAL PROTECTION

'Social protection' – the broad idea of public action to address socially unacceptable levels of poverty, risk and vulnerability within a society – has emerged as the dominant 'paradigm for social policy in developing countries' (Barrientos and Hulme 2008, p. 3). The social protection discourse originated from the International Labour Office (ILO), and more recently gained support within a range of UN agencies and the World Bank. Although there are different strands of thinking around social protection, the idea has recently become influential among many donors and national governments in developing countries in support of efforts to link social policy interventions across government departments in ways that move beyond the traditional reliance on welfare ministries.

Discussions about social protection have in general been more inclusive of the non-governmental sector than more traditional social policy discourses. In some cases, social protection has simply involved the development NGOs as contracting partners. The context of Bangladesh can be seen as a good example of this. A range of cash transfer programmes organized by line ministries has tended to involve partnership arrangements with international, national or local NGOs. The Vulnerable Group Development programme is one example that has provided welfare-based food transfers to meet immediate needs alongside opportunities for people to reduce their vulnerability by accessing micro-finance services to strengthen assets and build livelihoods through group-based lending and 'self-help' (Lewis 2011). At the same time, more recently there have also been more innovative NGO-led initiatives. For example, BRAC's 'Challenging the Frontiers of Poverty Programme', which was established in 2002, has aimed to challenge and break with mainstream welfare-based approaches to social protection using an asset-transfer approach coupled with education services, health support and rights awareness training. It also seeks to go further towards an empowerment as opposed to a welfare approach by helping to build coalitions for change with non-poor groups in some areas of the country. This has led to the setting up of local-level 'poverty reduction committees' that have made some progress with improving the situation of the poorest by, for example, building new village sanitation facilities (Smillie 2009).

Interestingly, according to Barrientos and Hulme (2008), many of the international development NGOs have been slower than their national counterparts to engage with social protection. Many INGOs have remained locked into project-based approaches within limited time frames, and others continue to provide fragmented services that operate in parallel to government structures. Advocacy NGOs concerned with rights-based work, such as Help Age International or the Pensions Not Poverty Coalition, have embraced the idea of social protection more readily, and argue for extending social protection more widely within developing country contexts. International NGOs working in the field of humanitarian assistance have also been more responsive to the social protection agenda than many development NGOs, perhaps because they see the agenda as offering a long-term response to problems of emergency and conflict.

The social protection agenda promotes ideas about the welfare mix by re-anchoring social policy and development agendas more firmly to the state. As Barrientos and Hulme (2008, p. 12) observe,

> Social protection acknowledges, in both principle and practice, the advantages of mixed provision, but at the same time it assigns to public agencies a primary role in policy development, co-ordination and regulation. NGOs engaged in social protection will need to adjust to this parameter.

This perspective restores the centrality of government to social policy provision, and may also help us to move beyond the somewhat mechanistic ideas of government–NGO 'partnership' that have dominated since the 'new policy agenda' of the 1990s, by suggesting more dynamic forms of interaction between state and non-state actors.

CONCLUSION

In moving away from a predominantly state-centric, Western-based approach to social policy, the challenge now is to strive towards a balanced view that gives increased recognition to NGOs and other non-state actors within the different perspectives on social policy that have emerged. Such an approach recognizes the importance of NGOs to social policy in almost all societies, developed or developing, their diverse forms and roles, and the important debates that inform the choices available to policymakers around the social roles NGOs should play in any given context.

While NGOs remain important to social policy, some key paradoxes remain. With a few important exceptions, most NGOs are relatively small organizations that are capable of making only limited inroads into the major challenges posed by global poverty and inequality. Understanding the roles of NGOs must always therefore be linked to a wider institutional analysis that includes the state. In this context, two rather different views of NGOs tend to dominate. One sees NGOs essentially in a 'sticking plaster' role, able to respond in an often imperfect but necessary way to emergencies or disadvantage in the short term, but as a stopgap to more sustainable and longer-term public provision by government. Such a view takes us all the way back to Arthur Livingstone (1969). Another sees NGOs in a more idealized way, as effective actors with distinctive advantages over government agencies and market-based organizations, working alongside other institutions in the welfare mix. These different views of NGOs are to some extent reconciled in a third view, namely that a healthy and vibrant third sector, containing different types of NGOs operating at varying levels of effectiveness, is a valuable asset to any society.

We can situate non-state actors in Deacon's (2008) framework that sets out four main approaches to understanding social policy as sector policy, redistribution and rights, social issues, and welfare regime theory. Within sector policy, increased subcontracting to NGOs has in some cases provided for more flexible and effective service delivery, while in others it has raised problems of accountability and quality. In relation to redistribution and rights, NGOs have emerged as advocacy organizations seeking to shape the formulation and the implementation of social policies on behalf of citizens, but have also attracted criticism among those who question their legitimacy. In terms of social issues, NGOs in the development field have served to raise and promote issues of empowerment, gender, social development and participation within development processes. Finally, within welfare regime theory, NGOs have achieved increasing recognition as key actors within newly identified insecurity and informal security regimes.

More broadly, studying NGOs can also help us better understand state formation processes, the interface between local and international politics, and the ways that social development policy discourses operate. To do this, we will need to journey beyond the mainstream social policy literature into development studies research. Within a more integrated study of social policy and development that takes full account of non-state actors, we will also need to move forward research in ways that can challenge still-dominant instrumental views of NGOs in the literature as merely service providers and advocates, to focus also on the expressive dimensions of these non-state actors and the values that they represent. At the same time, in the realm of policy the key challenge is to find ways that allow NGOs to play constructive roles within the emerging welfare mix within development settings in ways that complement, rather than sideline, the state.

REFERENCES

Bano, Masooda (2012), *Breakdown in Pakistan: How Aid is Eroding Institutions for Collective Action*, Stanford, CA: Stanford University Press.

Barrientos, Armando and David Hulme (2008), 'Social protection for the poorest: an introduction', in A. Barrientos and D. Hulme (eds), *Social Protection for the Poorest: Concepts, Policies and Politics*, London: Macmillan, pp. 3–26.

Barrow, Ondine and Michael Jennings (eds) (2001), *The Charitable Impulse: NGOs and Development in East and North-East Africa*, Oxford: James Currey.

Batley, Richard (2006), 'Engaged or divorced? Cross-service findings on government relations with non-state service providers', *Public Administration and Development*, **26**, 241–51.

Bebbington, Anthony, Samuel Hickey and Diana C. Mitlin (eds) (2008), 'Introduction', in *Can NGOs Make a Difference? The Challenge of Development Alternatives*, London: Zed Books, pp. 3–37.

Brock, Karen (2004), 'Ugandan civil society in the policy process: challenging orthodox narratives', in K. Brock, R. McGee and J. Gaventa (eds), *Knowledge, Actors and Spaces in Poverty Reduction in Uganda and Nigeria*, Kampala: Fountain Publishers, pp. 94–112.

Burger, Ronelle and Trudy Owens (2010), 'Promoting transparency in the NGO sector: examining the availability and reliability of self-reported data', *World Development*, **38** (9), 1263–77.

Buxton, Charles (2011), *The Struggle for Civil Society in Central Asia: Crisis and Transformation*, Sterling, VA: Kumarian.

Cannon Lorgen, Christy (2002), 'The case of indigenous NGOs in Uganda's health sector', in Judith Heyer, Frances Stewart and Rosemary Thorp (eds), *Group Behaviour and Development: Is the Market Destroying Cooperation?*, Oxford: Oxford University Press, pp. 291–306.

Carroll, Thomas F. (1992), *Intermediary NGOs: The Supporting Link in Grassroots Development*, West Hartford, CT: Kumarian Press.

Cernea, Michael (1988), 'Non-governmental organisations and local development', Discussion Paper 40, Washington, DC: World Bank.

Charnovitz, S. (1997), 'Two centuries of participation: NGOs and international governance', *Michigan Journal of International Law*, **18** (2), 183–286.

Deacon, Bob (2008), *Global Social Policy and Governance*, London: Sage.

Dean, Hartley (2006), *Social Policy*, Cambridge: Polity Press.

Edwards, Michael and David Hulme (eds) (1995), *Beyond the Magic Bullet: NGO Performance and Accountability in the Post-Cold War World*, London: Earthscan.

Esping-Andersen, G. (1990), *The Three Worlds of Welfare Capitalism*, Cambridge: Polity Press.

Evers, Adalbert (2010), 'Welfare', in Jean-Louis Laville and Antonio Cattani (eds), *The Human Economy*, Cambridge: Polity Press, pp. 175–9.

Gaventa, John and Rosemary McGee (2010), *Citizen Action and National Policy Reform: Making Change Happen*, London: Zed Books.

Gough, Ian (2004), 'Welfare regimes in development contexts: a global and regional analysis', in Ian Gough and Geof Wood (eds), *Insecurity and Welfare Regimes in Asia, Africa and Latin America: Social Policy in Developing Countries*, Cambridge: Cambridge University Press, pp. 15–48.

Hanlon, Joseph (1991), *Mozambique: Who Calls the Shots?*, London: James Currey.

Hardiman, Margaret and James Midgley (1982), *The Social Dimensions of Development: Social Policy and Planning in the Third World*, Chichester: John Wiley.

Ishkanian, Armine and Simon Szreter (eds) (2012), *The Big Society Debate: A New Agenda for Social Policy?*, Cheltenham, UK and Northampton, MA, USA: Edward Elgar.

Lewis, David (1993), 'Bangladesh overview', in John Farrington and David Lewis (eds), *NGOs and the State in Asia: Rethinking Roles in Sustainable Agricultural Development*, London: Routledge.

Lewis, David (2005), 'Actors, ideas and networks: trajectories of the non-governmental in development studies', in Uma Kothari (ed.), *A Radical History of Development Studies*, London: Zed Books, pp. 200–221.

Lewis, David (2007), *The Management of Non-Governmental Development Organisations* (2nd edn), London: Routledge.

Lewis, David (2011), *Bangladesh: Politics, Economy and Civil Society*, Cambridge: Cambridge University Press.

Lewis, David and Nazneen Kanji (2009), *Non-Governmental Organisations and Development*, London: Routledge.

Livingstone, Arthur (1969), *Social Policy in Developing Countries*, London: Routledge and Kegan Paul.

McGee, Rosemary (2004), 'Unpacking policy: actors, knowledge and spaces', in K. Brock, R. McGee and J. Gaventa (eds), *Knowledge, Actors and Spaces in Poverty Reduction in Uganda and Nigeria*, Kampala: Fountain Publishers, pp. 1–26.

Mitlin, Diana, Sam Hickey and Anthony Bebbington (2007), 'Reclaiming development? NGOs and the challenge of alternatives', *World Development*, **35** (10), 1699–720.

Najam, Adil (1999), 'Citizen organizations as policy entrepreneurs', in D. Lewis (ed.), *International Perspectives on Voluntary Action: Reshaping the Third Sector*, London: Earthscan, pp. 142–81.

OECD (Organisation for Economic Co-operation and Development) (2009), *Better Aid – Civil Society and Aid Effectiveness: Findings, Recommendations and Good Practice*, Paris: OECD.

Pattenden, Jonathan (2010), 'A neoliberalisation of civil society? Self-help groups and the labouring class poor in rural South India', *Journal of Peasant Studies*, **37** (3), 485–512.

Pearce, J. (1997) 'Between co-option and irrelevance? Latin American NGOs in the 1990s', in D. Hulme and M. Edwards (eds), *Too Close for Comfort? NGOs, States and Donors*, London: Macmillan, pp. 257–74.

Pfeffer, James (2003), 'International NGOs and primary health care in Mozambique: the need for a new model of collaboration', *Social Science and Medicine*, **56**, 725–38.

Salamon, L. and H.K. Anheier (1992), 'In search of the non-profit sector: in search of definitions', *Voluntas*, **13** (2), 125–52.

Smillie, Ian (2009), *Freedom From Want: The Remarkable Success Story of BRAC, the Global Grassroots Organization That's Winning the Fight Against Poverty*, Stirling, VA: Kumarian Press.

Tendler, Judith (2004), 'Why social policy is condemned to a residual category of safety nets and what to do about it', in T. Mkandawire (ed.), *Social Policy in a Development Context*, Basingstoke: Palgrave Macmillan, pp. 119–42.

UNRISD (United Nations Research Institute for Social Development) (2010), *Combating Poverty and Inequality: Structural Change, Social Policy and Politics*, Geneva: UNRISD.

Vakil, A. (1997), 'Confronting the classification problem: toward a taxonomy of NGOs', *World Development*, **25** (12), 2057–71.

White, Gordon and Mark Robinson (1998), 'Towards synergy in social provision: civic organisations and the state', in M. Minogue, C. Polidano and D. Hulme (eds), *Beyond the New Public Management*, Cheltenham, UK and Lyme, USA: Edward Elgar, pp. 94–116.

Wood, Geof (1997), 'States without citizens: the problem of the franchise state', in D. Hulme and M. Edwards (eds), *Too Close for Comfort? NGOs, States and Donors*, London: Macmillan, pp. 79–92.

Yeates, Nicola (2001), *Globalization and Social Policy*, London: Sage.

Yunus, Muhammad (2010), *Building Social Business*, New York: Public Affairs.

5. The informal economy: dilemmas and policy responses

Sony Pellissery

INTRODUCTION

Since it escapes the state's regulatory framework, the informal economy challenges the wider notion of social contract, which is the cornerstone for the legitimacy of the state. At the same time, the informal economy is the sole source of livelihood for the vast majority of households in the global South. Is this paradox good news for the welfare state? Or does it indicate that the welfare state is a straightjacket when the European model is emulated in the global South? Answering these questions, the chapter argues that, while dealing with the complex issue of the informal economy, nation states in the global South are creating welfare institutions very different in substance and form from those of industrialized countries.

The chapter has two parts. The first part deals with the conceptual issues about the nature of the informal economy. It summarizes how four decades of academic research have shaped the discipline of the informal economy. Further, it attempts to uncover the structure and map of the informal economy, which is defined by a variety of systemic embeddedness between social and economic motivations, and variations across occupational categories. This part ends by providing evidence of how the globalization process intensifies the informal economy. The second part deals with policy responses by nation states in dealing with the challenge of informality. The early attempts at formalization, attempts to organize informal labourers, the model of the welfare fund and the task of broadening social protection are also discussed in this part.

PART I: CONSTITUENTS OF INFORMAL ECONOMY

Defining Informality

Since the International Labour Office's (ILO) study of urban labour markets in Africa (ILO 1972), there has been extensive research on the informal economy. The ILO defined economic informality as a 'way of doing things, characterized by: (i) ease of entry; (ii) reliance on indigenous resources; (iii) family ownership of resources; (iv) small scale of operations; (v) labour intensive and adapted technology; (vi) skill acquired outside the formal school system; and (vii) unregulated and competitive markets' (cited in Bromley 1978, p. 1033). Since this definition was drafted, academic research on informality has evolved through three symbiotic strands. These three related developments can shed light on what exactly informality is.

The first strand is a movement away from the thinking of informal labourers as marginal to heroic entrepreneurs.[1] The rapid urbanization in Third World economies was the direct consequence of limited opportunities in the agriculture sector in rural areas and the expanding opportunities in the cities. The population that moved to the cities occupied unwanted pieces of land as well as public spaces, slowly transforming them into slums. This population was defined by the experience of 'marginality' (Portes and Shauffler 1993) since the slums lacked the basic services of urban societies, and their inhabitants lacked official legal title to the properties on which they lived. This migrant population also did not take on mainstream formal jobs in urban areas but undertook peripheral jobs and provided support services to the formal economy. Thus, the nature of employment was survivalist. However, this view has been undermined by Hernando de Soto's (1989, 2001) claim that informal sector workers are not helpless and affected by insecurity. He argues that, in a context of legal systems[2] that do not adequately protect ownership and thereby allow people to accumulate and retain the capital necessary to increase productivity and ultimately wages, self-employment should be perceived as heroic entrepreneurship. Weak states which fail to uphold legal titles and contracts between citizens would be thus hotbeds of mushrooming informal sectors. Recognizing the heroism of informal-sector workers, one policy response has been to provide a simple legal environment that facilitates exchange and upholds citizens' legal titles (Rodrik 2002).

The second strand through which informality has been conceptualized is the discovery of the roots of informality in academic work undertaken before the birth of the term 'informality'. The modernization school (Lewis 1954) plays a key role in this respect. The economy was divided into 'traditional' and 'modern' sectors. This categorization envisaged that rural subsistence workers (the surplus labour), whose marginal productivity was zero, would be absorbed by technology-driven production processes. This thesis is also known as the 'dual economies' or the 'segmented market' approach (Bromley 1978). Under the aegis of the modernization school it was imagined that eventually the informal sector would evaporate and employment would occur exclusively in the formal economy. To understand why this has not happened, we need to understand alternative ways of thinking about the economy. Polanyi (1944) is relevant here. Polanyi's analysis of the historical development of capitalism in Europe conceptualized the process of restructuring the economy through market development in which a process of commodification of land, labour and money takes place.[3] This would be marked by a 'double movement': on the one hand laissez-faire and on the other hand attempts to insulate the social fabric from market forces. In societies where this commodification was incomplete, the moral economy continued to prevail (Scott 2005; Maddison 1998). This economy is characterized by reciprocity and mutual obligations rather than rights guaranteed by the state. This aspect of the embeddedness of markets and capitalism has challenged the modernization schools. It is recognized that firms and businesses require flexibility and innovation, which often thrive in contexts of mutual trust, for capital formation (Granovetter 1985; Uzzi 1997).[4] This second strand, which has revolutionized understanding of the informal economy, is primarily about the nature of the good that is transacted. Many goods that are produced by informal labour are non-tradable. For instance, the trust that is required to run a family business can operate only with informal labour as the knowledge required to run the business is tacit knowledge, not knowledge acquired by formal training. How could this be effectively exchanged with formal labour? Another contribution of this second strand is the nature of the regulation of market exchanges. When the informal economy is defined by the yardstick of regulation, which is being evaded, it is seen not as an aberration but as 'a necessary outgrowth of advanced capitalism' (Sassen 1994, p. 2291).

A third strand of academic work that has contributed to our understanding of the informal economy concerns the artificiality of the formal–informal distinction itself. The sectoral view of the economy retained the distinction and initially referred to the 'informal sector'. However, when it was realized that the informal sector was integrated with the rest of economy it was renamed the 'informal economy'. The works of Douglass North (1990, 1991), empirically observing institutions like tied labour, sharecropping, insurance and risk-pooling mechanisms, have revealed the close similarity between the underlying structures of the informal and the formal economies. This finding challenges the common misconception that informality means an absence of rules. Rather, what exists is a continuum running from the formal economy to the informal economy. Evidence of the lack of segmentation has come from informal labourers as well as firms. On the one hand, surveys have shown that many self-employed workers participate in the informal economy to supplement their incomes (Maloney 2004). On the other hand, surveys of informal firms or household businesses have shown that they work closely with the large-scale production processes of the formal sector. This third contribution to the literature about the informal economy has radicalized the understanding of 'law as a social process' (Berry 1993; Holston 2007), where the interpretations shaped by the vested interests leave law as an open arena of contestation.

The Structure of Informality

Different terms that are used to refer to the informal economy include 'shadow', 'underground', 'second', 'parallel', 'black' and 'cash'. All of them indicate the unaccountable nature of income in general and transactions in particular in the informal economy.[5] This is specifically so with reference to the state machinery, which can legitimately acquire information about the economic transactions occurring on its territory. It was argued that when a state is unable to obtain this information (let alone regulate the economy), the emergence and persistence of informality is a symptom of a weak state failing to regulate social forces[6] (Myrdal 1968). More recently Harriss-White (2003) has pointed out that informality is a creation of a state that is controlled by the politics of the market. This 'politics of the market' guides anti-competitive practices through the operations of social networks, funds political parties so as to defend illegality in the market, keeps the societal principles and rules in market transactions upfront while underplaying state regulations, and undertakes small charity activities to maintain the dependency of the workforce on it. Thus, the structure of the market shapes the nature of state.[7]

The demand-side explanation of the persistence of the informal economy is that so many people are too poor to be able to afford formal exchanges. Thus, the majority of consumers of street food are lower-class employees of factories, offices or construction sites. This does not mean that the supply side is driven by the household production alone. Very often branded multinational products (e.g. Coca Cola) are retailed through informal outlets.

The informal economy creates its own incentives and disincentives. Incentives include working for relatives, gaining training and unobserved payments such as food and lodging, and greater freedom to do what one enjoys. These incentives are to be compared with what one forgoes. These are precisely the incentives for formal work, namely a pension, work security, insurance against injury at the workplace, subsidies for housing and the education of children, and health insurance. Comparing these packages of incentives is essential to judging whether an informal worker is disadvantaged or remains vulnerable.

A widely accepted classification of workers in the informal economy largely consists of three categories: employers (owners and operators of informal enterprises), self-employed (own-account workers, heads of family businesses, unpaid family workers) and wage earners (home-based workers, casual workers without fixed employers, domestic workers, temporary and part-time workers, unregistered workers and employees of informal enterprises). Apart from this categorization, the workplace and the degree of dependence or independence reveal the vulnerability of the labourer (Carr and Chen 2002). A large-scale National Sample Survey in India in 2005 revealed that 57 per cent of enterprises were own-account workers.

This categorization has to be seen as very closely linked with two other issues. The International Labour Office distinguishes the informal economy from the formal economy as well as from the criminal economy and the care economy (ILO 2002b). The care economy is primarily served by women, and is considered to be more a household affair than an economic affair. Feminist movements have argued that participation in the care economy is an unpaid reproductive activity where women often forgo productive opportunities in the market. Though women's labour in the care economy is to be accounted for, it is important to distinguish it from informal labour that receives monetary benefits from outside the home.

The criminal economy is more complex. It is a matter of fact that violence and criminal activities are more rampant in informal settlements. Often, drug peddlers and arm dealers find shanty towns to be havens. The complexity lies not in identifying which activities are illegal but rather in diagnosing why illegal activities coexist with the informal economy. As noted earlier, the absence of formal rules governing exchanges requires force to be used to secure compliance. This has been reported in studies of the mafia in Italy (Gambetta 1993) and Russia (Varese 2001).[8]

Mapping the Informal Economy

The forgoing discussion reveals the difficulty involved in mapping the informal economy. It varies considerably among countries[9] and occupational categories. Further, the boundaries of the informal economy are in constant flux. Despite these ambiguities, some of the oft-used measures to understand the extent of the informal economy are size of the firm, scale of entrepreneurship, payment of taxes, coverage of social security benefits, legal protection in terms of registration of firms, and the contractual nature of employment. Since the early 1990s the ILO has been working with national statistical establishments to define the informal economy so as to enable many types of marginal workers to be identified in statistical systems. An important challenge for this mapping exercise has been the multiple jobs undertaken by the same informal labourer (who is sometimes engaged in formal-sector jobs as well). However, some indicative trends can be observed, though precise data will continue to be elusive.

Non-agricultural work constitutes 78 per cent of the informal economy in African countries, 57 per cent in Latin America and the Caribbean, and 45–85 per cent in Asia (Becker 2004). In all these regions the informal economy has grown since 1990, when economic liberalization occurred in different parts of the world. The exception is in South East Asia, where manufacturing expanded in the late 1980s and the informal economy shrank. In all the countries, more women than men work in the informal economy. In Africa, there were 20 per cent more informal-economy job opportunities outside agriculture for women than for men (ILO 2002b). Nearly 95 per cent of informal economy jobs are undertaken by self-employed persons, and half of these informal jobs are in street trade.

The governments of both India and China have encouraged the informal economy by promoting small and micro enterprises outside the formal economy. Nearly 50 per cent of urban workers in China have no formal contracts (Huitfeldt and Jutting 2009). In China these workers are primarily participants in the massive rural–urban migration or have been laid off in the formal urban economy. In India it is estimated that close to 90 per cent of labourers work in the informal economy and produce 60 per cent of GDP (Sinha 2005). In both countries underemployment is a huge problem. In India, the workforce is growing at a rate of 2.5 per cent annually but employment is growing at only 2.3 per cent. China's workforce is increasing by 13 million per year, and every year about seven million workers are laid off by state-owned enterprises. Since only about 11 million jobs are created every year, the unemployment rate is predicted to grow beyond 10 per cent (Chandrasekhar et al. 2006).

Schneider and Enste (2000) attempted to map the informal economy in terms of its contribution to GNP and the workforce in 110 countries.[10] The study revealed that the informal economy is thriving in many OECD countries, too, though not on the same scale as in the global South. In European countries the informal economy grew between 5.7 and 16.5 per cent during 1960–95 (Schneider and Enste 2000, table 3). Among west European OECD countries, Austria's shadow economy is 10.2 per cent of its GNP (and 16 per cent of its workers in the informal workforce), compared with 16.3 per cent of Germany's (23 per cent of its workers in informal workforce) and 28.6 per cent in Greece's (workforce data not available). Among non-European OECD countries, in the United States the informal economy makes up 8.8 per cent of GNP; in Australia the figure is 15.5 per cent. However, it is to be noted that informal workers in advanced economies are not as vulnerable as those in the global South. Informal workers are often called 'atypical' or 'non-standard' workers, who are often eligible for insurance and health benefits but without employment security.

Increasing Informality in the Wake of Globalization

Informality has attracted serious attention in modern times in the wake of new equations emerging between global networked capitalism and the democratic struggle to contain local or social forces. Many scholars have argued that the traditional role of the state has undergone tremendous changes in the context of globalization (e.g. Castells 1999). One important change is the state's reluctance to ensure labour protection, since this would be a direct intervention in capitalist production that would impair the intense competition of the globalized economy (Tilly 1995; Held et al. 1999). The competition induced through globalization has changed the relationship between capital and labour in a significant way. For instance, 'a shift from the import substituting policy regime to an export promoting one involves a corresponding shift in factors of production' (Chakravarty 1999, p. 163). If firms wish to remain in business, becoming more productive through adapting to new technology, rapidly changing the aspirations of customers, and making profits by engaging in the production chain system and altering production organizations have become mandatory. Thus, firms are looking for various ways to reduce costs, to increase efficiency and to remain profitable. The new game of profitability and competitiveness has made companies look at using labour as efficiently as possible – employing the right worker in the right job at the right time. Nation states are encouraging appropriate job strategies to meet this challenge:

In a world where trade in good and services as well as international investment flows developed much faster than domestic economies, where technologies are developed and diffused extremely rapidly, and where domestic markets are being liberalized, competition is constantly increasing. To stay in the race, firms – and their staff – must continuously innovate and increase their efficiency. This objective is essential and is the basis for the general recommendations [of the jobs strategy]. (OECD 1996, p. 5)

At the macro level these job strategies gave rise to a set of laws that closely followed the precepts of neo-liberalism. These 'liberal employment and labor laws', according to the McKinsey Global Institute (2003, p. 2) 'allow companies greater flexibility in reassigning tasks and eliminating jobs. This flexibility is essential to capture offshoring opportunities effectively'. What does this flexibility mean? At the macro level, the important determinants of labour flexibility include regulation on employers' hiring and firing of workers, higher unemployment and welfare benefits, tight working hours, trade union power to protect workers, and a legal environment creating psychological and financial costs in initiating lawsuits (Sundar 2005). Beyond this macro-level flexibility, firm-level flexibility is important to understanding how the job strategies of nation states affect workers through legal frameworks.

The demands on the labour market change in line with parallel changes in product markets, production systems, work organization, technology, and so on. Changes in the global organization of production, trade liberalization and the processes of economic restructuring are accompanied by the trend towards labour market flexibility (Eyck 2003). A firm could adopt either internal or external forms of flexibility in this regard. Internal flexibility strategies include overtime, shift work, part-time work, hiring and firing, multi-skilling, and in-house transfer. External flexibility strategies include employing temporary and contract workers, increasingly amount of labour on-call, laying off, engaging freelance workers and consultants, outsourcing and secondment (Pfeifer 2005, p. 406). This has been possible because of the global commodity chain that disperses the production process across the globe. Workers face two closely linked challenges: (a) the limited possibility to experience power through collectivization;[11] (b) the priority of the learning logic (by experimentation, risk taking and reflection) over the production logic (standardization and problem solving) for use value. This has been made possible by buyer-driven commodity chains being controlled by technology (Gereffi 1994), a development which allowed the informal economy to coexist with growth.

In the Asian 'tiger' economies (Thailand, Singapore, Malaysia, the Philippines and Korea), street vending increased after the financial crisis of 1998 (Bhowmik 2005). Kohpaiboob et al. (2009) has documented how various informalized production processes emerged after the Thai automotive industry experienced shocks in the global economic crisis of 2008. Verick (2010) has documented the impact of the global crisis on the informal sector in South Africa, showing that the informal labour market is not a natural absorber of workers laid off in the formal sector.

Interconnected global business has shown that nation states are finding it difficult to provide adequate protection for labourers when a crisis begins in one part of the world. Global crises are increasingly affecting local economies and casual and contract labourers especially severely. Many micro-level studies have been undertaken since the 2008–09 global financial recession. A study of its impact on gem-polishing workers and construction workers in the Indian state of Rajasthan showed a systematic reduction in health and education expenditures in the early part of the crisis and in food and clothing expenditure when the crisis became severe (Mohanakumar and Singh 2011). The knitwear industry of the Indian state of Tamil Nadu was similarly vulnerable (Vijayabaskar 2011). In both locations the workers mobilized to demand from the state increased social services in the form of food provision and other welfare measures.

There is a growing consensus not merely that the informal economy deserves policy attention on the part of nation states, but that global social policy needs to address it with the same urgency. Social policy is able to address the problem of risk that emerges from informality because of the direct link between informal labour and poverty.[12] Part II of this chapter examines different policy responses to the informal economy.

PART II: POLICY RESPONSES

Is it not a contradiction to assume that policy measures adopted by the state can improve the conditions of labourers in the informal economy, which by definition contains enterprises that do not come under state regulation? This dilemma represents the difficulty in designing comprehensive policies to ameliorate conditions in the informal economy. Another important debate that poses policy challenges is whether workers choose to work in the informal economy or whether they are forced into it. The policy response depends significantly on the answer to this question. In Part II of this chapter an attempt is made to document some of the policy responses by different nation states to the question of the informal economy.

The Clash Between the Modern State and the Moral Economy

To fully appreciate how social rights are operationalized in the context of the informal economy, it is important to understand the nature of exchanges in the moral economy. It is also important to recognize that exchanges came first; formalization and legal frameworks to govern exchanges (let alone modern states and their laws) came later. In other words, the informal economy is prior to the formal economy. The rules of exchanges within the moral economy secure for all members their social right to minimum subsistence (Scott 1979). The guiding principles of the organization of the moral economy include trust, reciprocity, face-to-face networks and mechanisms to ostracize those who fail to observe the community's norms of reciprocity.[13]

Unlike the evolution in the West of the welfare state and citizenship rights in the context of industrialization and residual elements of charity, in many East Asian and African countries a welfare system was woven into the fabric of society. Thus, Gandhi's philosophy of *Sarvodaya* (welfare for all) visualized individual well being of the last person in the society rather than the happiness of the majority. Similarly, the philosophy of *Ubuntu* in Africa emphasized interpersonal allegiances and relations. These Southern versions of welfare systems place very little importance on the state and its regulations.

However, the moral economy is confined within familial, religious, caste and geographical boundaries. This mechanism of a 'closure of opportunities using externally identifiable characteristics' (Weber 1978, p. 173) is one of the strategies used in traditional societies to curb competition. A similar phenomenon has been reported to be abundant in the informal sector (Varcin 2000). Such closure, based on ethnicity and localism, gives power to both enterprise owners and customers. Accumulation processes are increasingly ethnicized. The informal nature of the operation allows the money that would have been paid in tax to be saved,[14] and reinvested in further accumulation, which in turn deepens ethnic ties. This social structure of accumulation undercuts the legitimacy of the state.[15] The creation of a state requires *civic* space to be generated, transcending ascriptive identities, which are heavily contextual. Within citizenship debates (Turner 1990) this universalism is often taken for granted. However, in many countries of the global South culture and tradition still play a more dominant role than the modern state in people's livelihoods. In those countries, difference-blind citizenship has not yet been accepted. The argument has been for group rights and for differentiated citizenship rights (Young 1995). Thus, the nation state is struggling to exist with multiple voices and identities (Mathew and Pellissery 2010).

However, the members of the moral economy are in advantageous position because of their existence in the nation states: the rights that a nation state provides and the facilitating environment that ascriptive identities provide. This means that a bottom-up demand for 'rights' is absent. The absence of political mobilization for gaining rights in Marshall's (1950) sense of civil, political and social rights indicates the lack of a social contract for institutionalizing rights. This does not mean that politics of rights are non-existent: the discourse of rights is used abundantly in the global South.[16] Agarwala (2008) contends that informal workers are increasingly demanding welfare provisions directly from the state, bypassing employers. The state's granting of welfare rights is a symbolic gesture of recognition of the work status of informal labour. However, in the process the social contract between labour and the state is redefined.

The clash between the modern state and the moral economy was witnessed through a variety of policy responses. The earliest response to the informal economy was inaction. As elaborated above, it was expected that as modernity gained ground the informal economy would merge into the formal economy. Eventually, this inaction gave rise to impatience as the informal economy persisted. Thus, across the globe there were attempts to suppress the informal economy. Urban informal settlements were subjected to demolition drives, squatters in slums were forcibly evicted, traffic authorities 'cleared' the streets of vendors for the public good, and food inspectors challenged vendors in the name of public hygiene. Tax regimes attempted to register informal businesses for accounting purposes. Needless to say, each time informality was suppressed it bounced back like a ball.

Organizing Informal Workers

Historically, labour resolved its problem with capital through self-organization. Similarly, one of the important ways to address the problems of the informal economy was to organize informal workers and to help them to articulate their needs. One of the early attempts to organize informal workers dates back to 1972, when India's textile industry began to collapse. The Self Employed Women's Association (SEWA) in Ahmadabad, Gujarat, organized vulnerable women engaged in home-based work, waste picking, street vending, domestic service, and other types of casual work. It also provided a variety of services such as banking, health care, education for the children of workers, legal advice, and skill development. It also organized the employers for whom informal labourers often worked and facilitated a meaningful dialogue between employers and labourers for wage increases, improving the work environment, and so on. SEWA has also acted as an advocacy organization to influence government policies at a national level. Often, such advocacy measures have resulted in stricter implementation of the Minimum Wage Act or international decent-work principles.

In the 1990s the SEWA model attracted international attention. Some institutional responses that emerged as a spin-off are worth mentioning here. Women in Informal Employment: Globalizing and Organizing (WIEGO) is a policy network that seeks to improve the working conditions of informal workers, especially women. In many countries this research and generation of data have influenced policymakers and planners. Similarly, SEWA facilitated an international alliance of organizations working with street vendors (StreetNet) and home-based workers (HomeNet). In India, the National Association of Street Vendors of India (NASVI)[17] has been influential in the drafting of a national-level bill,[18] which in turn has resulted in state governments providing hawking zones in urban areas. NASVI has also spread legal awareness among street vendors, and won important law cases through litigation. These organizational activities have given recognition to the work status of people living on the margins of society. Without such a status the workers used to perceive themselves as 'unemployed', 'unskilled', or even as a nuisance in the city.

The residents of informal settlements were organized along similar lines in the city of Mumbai by the Alliance of Slum Dwellers.[19] By federating among themselves, the slum dwellers could explicitly state their preferences for location and type of house and even how they would achieve them. By actively networking with different political parties in Mumbai, the World Bank, NGOs and various levels of bureaucrats and municipal corporation, the Alliance has ensured decent housing for many street dwellers in Mumbai.

Broadening the Scope of Social Protection

Apart from trade unions, two types of collective institution have emerged to improve the conditions of informal-sector workers: labour cooperatives and welfare funds. In the two south Indian states of Kerala and Tamil Nadu, experiments with these institutions have taught important lessons that should be heeded elsewhere. Labour cooperatives were set up in response to demands from the unions. However, poor labourers lacked the capacity and skills to manage such institutions, which required intervention in the whole commodity chain (production, marketing and distribution). Welfare funds were set up in response to this deficiency, with strong intervention by the state (Pillai 2004). The first welfare fund was set up for toddy tappers in 1969. This was followed by the Labour Welfare Fund for workers in small-scale factories and shops in 1977. In the early 1980s welfare funds were set up for head-load workers and fishermen. Eventually, different occupational groups in the informal economy began to demand welfare funds as of right. In a significant way, in the state of Kerala a considerable number of the workers in the informal economy are covered by the social security provided by a welfare fund.[20] The fund is modelled on social insurance, with contributions from workers, government and employers.[21] Though the benefits from funds vary as between occupational categories, general benefits include pensions, provident funds, retirement benefits and gratuities, disability benefits, funeral expenses, educational support, housing loans, unemployment benefits and maternity benefits.

However, this model has not been successful in most other locations where the informal economy is booming. One important intervention in such a context has been to broaden the scope of social security through a framework of social protection. The framework of social protection takes into account the fact that poverty in the global South is a structural factor rather than an effect of individual incapacity. Thus, the World Bank specifies three types of social protection strategies: preventive (relief from deprivation), protective (*ex ante* management of risks) and promotional (improving income and human capital). In India, following the recommendations of the National Commission for Enterprises in the Unorganised Sector, comprehensive legislation was introduced for providing subsidized and targeted health insurance for unorganized workers. Since its implementation in 2009, 40 million people have become insured for hospitalization.[22] Most of them belong to the category of the very poor. In China a similar strategy of expanding social protection was adopted through the introduction of the Minimum Living Standard Scheme (MLSS).[23] By 2006, a total of 76 per cent of urban poor were covered through MLSS (Chen and Barrientos 2006). Both these programmes are examples of preventive social protection.

Since 2005 an experiment for promotional social protection has been conducted in India through the National Rural Employment Guarantee Act (NREGA). The Act provides up to 100 days of guaranteed employment for each household in rural areas, in exchange for work improving community infrastructure. Such work includes the construction of new roads which have increased market access, the revitalization of traditional water bodies, which has made it possible to plant a second crop, and similar efforts. Since its inception, 45 million rural households (33 per cent of the rural population) have been provided with jobs every year.

Still another approach to broadening social protection has been pioneered by the International Labour Office to achieve decent work standards. The ILO's guidelines for decent work go beyond the issues of secure employment, job protection or labour rights. The decent work agenda argues for cessation of 'unemployment solutions ... being used as an excuse to deprive employed persons of reasonable working conditions' (Sen 2000, cited in ILO 2001, p. 19). For this purpose Amartya Sen's concept of ensuring education, training and lifelong learning is adopted along with labour rights. Thus, the very right to work is understood to include vocational training, whether on or off the job.

Involving Informal Livelihoods in Planning

Often, development planning is undertaken by the state with a futuristic vision that poverty will disappear. Thus, the clearing of informal settlements, which are regarded as eyesores, has been a contentious issue in development planning. Human rights discourse has re-emphasized the priority of natural rights over the legal titles to property that poor people may be holding. To some extent this has given poor people a tool with which to fight forcible evictions demanded by city planning. Such evictions have often been either stopped or delayed through the intervention of the courts.

This eventual recognition of informality as a way of seeking a livelihood has changed the perceptions of planners. The population in the formal sector has often found the services provided by informal labourers to be not merely cheap but reliable and satisfactory. Examples include street food and buying fresh vegetables from a vendor rather than in a mall. The tacit knowledge of informal workers cannot be replicated by professionally trained skilled persons. Thus, city planners have attempted to allocate spaces to informal businesses. A recent innovation has been to create hawking zones in cities. In a similar way, eateries are provided near cinemas and or similar places of entertainment. Some examples of such planning are Durban Metropolitan Local Government (South Africa), where street traders are incorporated into town planning (Becker 2004) and Ahmadabad Municipal Planning (India).

Such innovative planning has revealed the close connection between two different types of rights: the right to a livelihood and the right to housing. Most informal workers have their informal housing arrangements close to their place of work, necessarily so because the goods they sell are frequently produced at home (with the help of family members) and conveyed to the selling point. When cities were redesigned and poor labourers in informal settlements (on public land such as river banks) were resettled, the labourers in effect lost their livelihoods. This realization has not brought immediate solutions.

Similarly, in dealing with street food vendors across the globe, the Food and Agricultural Organization (FAO) has realized that it is impossible to remove them in the name of providing safe food, since the variety that street vendors provide cannot be matched by the hotels. Therefore, FAO has worked with many local governments to provide adequate training for street vendors so as to maintain quality and improve food safety. However, the reach of this programme has been very limited. For instance, Kolkata has over 130,000 street food vendors, yet training has been provided only for 3,500 workers. Meanwhile in Sri Lanka the government has facilitated training for informal labourers. Artisans and food producers are encouraged, with the support of donors, to update their technical skills at both private and public training institutions.

CONCLUSION

Ignoring the informal economy has often resulted in policies that disproportionately benefit the formal sector. Nation states in the global South have learned this lesson after desperate attempts over decades to remodel their economies on industrialized lines. The recognition of the informal economy is an important lesson not only for the welfare state but for economic theory in general. The performance of firms is often discussed in a dichotomous framework that treats the 'economic' and the 'social' as an abstract duality (Elson 2004). Paradoxically, in non-Western countries where poverty is often very widespread, economic actions are 'carried out through relationships that have been conventionally cast as "non-economic"' (Kabeer 2004, p. 1). Devising policies for labourers in the informal economy is to pay attention to non-economic exchanges within larger market forces.

One of the arguments in favour of the informal economy is that it can integrate less resourceful individuals as citizens.[24] Often, less resourceful individuals cannot integrate as citizens through the market mechanisms of production, consumption and exchange. The informal economy and its overarching shadow state in practice play an integrative role, but through the principle of differential rather than universal citizenship (Lake and Newman 2003). However, integrating poor individuals into the economy comes at the cost of exposing them to serious risks and vulnerabilities. Institutionalizing the risk-mitigating mechanisms discussed in this chapter is the long-term challenge for stabilizing welfare systems in the global South.

NOTES

1. It is interesting to note that in some countries informal labourers continue to be called 'unorganized' workers. However, it has been realized that though there is no formal structure, the informal economy is organized organically and dynamically, though the system of such organization is opaque.

2. Legality is an issue that pertains directly to informality. Though perception has changed such that not all exchanges in the public sphere need be backed by the legal framework, 'legal status' is important to identity. In Mumbai (India) alone there are over 200,000 street vendors, yet only 14,000 licences have been issued by the municipal authorities. No new licence for street vending has been issued since 1978, since the legal provisions for issuing licences are very stringent, and the licensing process is so elaborate that illiterate and poor vendors find it difficult to access it (Bhowmik 2005; Anjaria 2006). This situation is replicated in most cities in India, and so street vending is often deemed an illegal activity.

3. It is worth noting that the Western welfare states emerged after the formalization of labour market in this Polanyian sense (see Esping-Anderson 1990).

4. Some scholars (e.g. Elyachar 2003) regard the related argument of downsizing of firms by informalizing their operations, in the context of economic crisis in the 1970s, as the key route to informality from an economic perspective. This aspect is elaborated in the next section since it deserves detailed treatment in the context of economic globalization.

5. In fact, the unrecorded nature of transactions (absence of official accounting systems or of receipts given to customers) is one of the key features of the informal economy.

6. The state's intervention in markets creates an array of institutions such as property rights, credit facilities, avenues for private trade and rules for exchange.

7. What is at stake here is the contention that there is an inherent connection between democratic forms of government and liberal capitalism. Some scholars have, however, dismissed this claim, arguing that crony capitalism could coexist with a full-blown democracy.

8. The absence of a working legal environment leads to corruption since extra-legal or illegal methods are required to fill the enforcement gap.

9. Often, the informal economy in developed countries has been explained by the survivalist strategies of immigrants. Against this, Sassen (1994) contends that the decline of mass production as the engine of national growth and the shift towards services changed the employment relationship in institutional frameworks and thus informalization became inevitable. In developing countries, too, there is no single, common definition of the informal economy. See Becker (2004, appendix 4) for a comparison of some of the definitions used by Southern countries when measuring the informal economy.

10. These calculations are based on data for the late 1990s, since when the informal economy has grown in all OECD countries.

11. There is increasing evidence from across the globe to show that labour disputes are on the wane.

12. In its international convention (No. 102) the ILO characterizes informality as exposed to nine types of insecurity. For instance, a study among street vendors in Mumbai showed that a quarter of them were illiterate (Bhowmik 2005). The same study showed that incomes varied but most women earned between Rs 30 and Rs 60, whereas the men earned between Rs 50 and Rs 150 (much lower than the minimum wage levels in the country). The nine insecurities specified by the ILO are sickness, maternity, employment injury, unemployment, invalidity, old age, death, the need for long-term medical care and for help supporting families with children (ILO 2002a).

13. It is important to understand the limitations of the moral economy argument by juxtaposing it against political economy approach (Popkin 1979). The focus of this chapter does not require a comparative treatment of these views. But see Platteau (1991) for a balanced evaluation of both approaches.

14. Since risk sharing within ethnic community does not require a tax-supported mechanism.

15. Such ethnicized accumulation structures frequently have their own paralegal procedures. In important ways, when the state permits private laws (customary laws of religion and ethnic groups) to exist alongside secular laws, a group-specific existence acquires some legitimacy.

16. Whether this demand for rights is for redistribution in the spirit of the liberal welfare state or for the transformation of societal relationships (which was marked by historical injustice) is a matter for debate. Nancy Fraser (2008) calls this 'the redistribution–recognition dilemma', involving two distinct analytical approaches to justice.

17. A similar federation of street vendors exists in Korea (the National Federation of Korean Street Vendors). The Korean federation has put up stiff resistance to the state, which used the mafia to remove the street vendors.

18. Kenya had similar policy dating back to 1992. In Kenya the informal economy is known as 'Jua Kali' (hot sun), referring to micro-enterprises working without shelter. Under its policy for Jua Kali, the government began to provide flexible credits for informal workers, subcontracting certain assignments and organizing group purchasing and marketing.

19. This Alliance is a result of a merger of three NGOs that had been working in Mumbai since 1970s. See Appadurai (2002) for more details on its workings.

20. About 13 million workers are included in 19 different boards, though the informal labourers' target is 8 million.

21. Exactly how the contributions are shared varies between occupational categories depending on the resource base of workers and employers. However, in all funds employers' contributions are significant. For instance, in the construction sector, where the financial situation of the employers is better, a mandatory levy of 1 per cent of the cost of construction is contributed to the construction workers' welfare board.

22. In India, out-of-pocket expenses for health care account for 83 per cent of total health expenditure, in the context of limited insurance coverage.

23. The scheme began on a pilot basis in Shanghai and by 1998 it had expanded to 581 cities and 1,121 counties in China.

24. Rawls (1993, p. 18) defines a person as 'someone who can be a citizen, that is, a normal and fully cooperating member of society'.

REFERENCES

Agarwala, R. (2008), 'Reshaping the social contract: emerging relations between the state and informal labour in India', *Theory and Society*, **37**, 375–408.

Anjaria, J.S. (2006), 'Street hawkers and public space in Mumbai', *Economic and Political Weekly*, **27**, 2140–46.

Appadurai, A. (2002), 'Deep democracy: urban governmentality and the horizon of politics', *Public Culture*, **14** (1), 21–47.

Becker, K.F. (2004), *Informal Economy: A Fact Finding Study*, Stockholm: SIDA.

Berry, S. (1993), *No Condition Is Permanent: Social Dynamics of Agrarian Change in Sub-Saharan Africa*, Madison, WI: University of Wisconsin Press.
Bhowmik, S.K. (2005), 'Street vendors in Asia: a review', *Economic and Political Weekly*, 28 May, 2256–64.
Bromley, R. (1978), 'Introduction: the urban informal sector: why is it worth discussing', *World Development*, **6** (9–10), 1033–9.
Carr, Marilyn and Martha Chen (2002), 'Globalization and the informal economy: how global trade and investment impact on the working poor', Working Paper on the Informal Economy, Working No. 1 INTEGRATION, Geneva: International Labour Office.
Castells, M. (1999), *The Information Age: The Power of Identity*, Oxford: Blackwell.
Chakravarty, D. (1999), 'Labour market under trade liberalization in India', *Economic and Political Weekly*, **34** (48), 163–8.
Chandrasekhar, C.P., J. Ghosh and A. Roychowdhury (2006), 'The demographic dividend and young India's economic future', *Economic and Political Weekly*, 9 December, 5055–64.
Chen, J. and A. Barrientos (2006), 'Extending social assistance in China: lessons from the minimum living standard scheme', CPRC Working Paper 67, Manchester: Chronic Poverty Research Centre, School of Environment and Development, University of Manchester.
de Soto, H. (1989), *The Other Path: The Invisible Revolution in the Third World*, London: I.B. Taurus.
de Soto, H. (2001), *The Mystery of Capital*, London: Bentham Press.
Elson, Diane (2004), 'Social policy and macroeconomic performance: integrating "the economic" and "the social"', in T. Mkandawire (ed.), *Social Policy in a Development Context*, Basingstoke: Palgrave Macmillan.
Elyachar, J. (2003), 'Mappings of power: the state, NGOs, and international organizations in the informal economy of Cairo', *Comparative Studies in Society and History*, **45** (3), 571–605.
Esping-Anderson, G. (1990), *The Three Worlds of Welfare Capitalism*, Cambridge: Polity Press; Princeton, NJ: Princeton University Press.
Eyck, K.V. (2003), 'Flexibilizing employment: an overview', SEED Working Paper No. 41, Geneva: International Labour Office.
Fraser, N. (2008), *Scales of Justice: Reimagining Political Space in a Globalizing World*, Cambridge: Polity Press.
Gambetta, D. (1993), *The Sicilian Mafia*, London: Harvard University Press.
Gereffi, Gary (1994), 'The organization of buyer-driven global commodity chains: how U.S. retailers shape overseas production networks', in G. Gereffi and M. Korseniewicz (eds), *Commodity Chains and Global Capitalism*, Westport, CT: Praeger, pp. 95–117.
Granovetter, M. (1985), 'Economic action and social structure: the problem of embeddedness', *American Journal of Sociology*, **91** (3), 481–510.
Harriss-White, B. (2003), *India Working: Essays on Society and Economy*, Cambridge: Cambridge University Press.
Held, D., A. McGrew, D. Goldblatt and J. Perraton (1999), *Global Transformations: Politics, Economics and Culture*, Stanford, CA: Stanford University Press.

Holston, J. (2007), *Insurgent Citizenship: Disjunctions of Democracy and Modernity in Brazil*, Princeton, NJ: Princeton University Press.

Huiltfeldt, H. and J. Jutting (2009), 'Informality and informal employment', in *Promoting Pro-poor Growth: Employment*, Paris: OECD, pp. 95–108.

ILO (International Labour Office) (1972), *Employment, Incomes and Inequality: A Strategy for Increasing Productive Employment in Kenya*, Geneva: ILO.

ILO (2001), *Training for Decent Work*, Montevideo: Cinterfor, International Labour Organization, available at http://www.cinterfor.org.uy/public/english/region/ampro/cinterfor/publ/t_dw/ (accessed 13 May 2011).

ILO (2002a), *Decent Work and the Informal Economy*, Geneva: ILO.

ILO (2002b), *Women and Men in the Informal Economy: A Statistical Picture*, Geneva: ILO.

Kabeer, N. (2004), 'Re-visioning "the social": towards a citizen-centred social policy for the poor in poor countries', IDS Working Paper No. 191, Brighton: Institute of Development Studies.

Kohpaiboob, A., P. Kulthanavit, P. Vijitnopparat and N. Soonthornchawakan (2009), 'Global recession and labour market adjustment: evidence of Thai automotive industry', paper presented at a conference on the 'Impact of the Global Economic Slowdown on Poverty and Sustainable Development in Asia', Hanoi, 28–29 September.

Lake, R.W. and K. Newman, (2003), 'Differential citizenship in the shadow state', *GeoJournal*, **58**, 109–20.

Lewis, W.A. (1954), 'Economic development with unlimited supplies of labour', *Manchester School*, **22**, 139–91.

Maddison, B. (1998), 'From "moral economy" to "political economy" in New South Wales, 1870–1900', *Labour History*, **75**, 81–107.

Maloney, W.F. (2004), 'Informality revisited', *World Development*, **32** (7), 1159–78.

Marshall, T.H. (1950), *Citizenship and Social Class and Other Essays*, Cambridge: Cambridge University Press.

Mathew, L. and S. Pellissery (2010) 'Enduring local justice in India: an anomaly or response to diversity?', *Psychology in Developing Societies*, **21** (1) 13–31.

McKinsey Global Institute (2003), *Offshoring: Is It a Win–Win Game?*, San Francisco: McKinsey & Company.

Mohanakumar, S. and S. Singh (2011), 'Impact of the economic crisis on workers in the unorganized sector in Rajasthan', *Economic and Political Weekly* (28 May), 66–71.

Myrdal, G. (1968), *Asian Drama: An Inquiry into the Poverty of Nations*, London: Penguin Press.

North, D. (1990), *Institutions, Institutional Change and Economic Performance*, Cambridge: Cambridge University Press.

North, D. (1991) 'Institutions', *Journal of Economic Perspectives*, **5** (1), 97–112.

OECD (Organisation for Economic Co-operation and Development) (1996), *Pushing Ahead with the Strategy*, Paris: OECD.

Pfeifer, C. (2005), 'Flexibility, dual labour markets, and temporary employment: empirical evidence from German Establishment Data', *Management Revue*, **16** (3), 404–22.

Pillai, R.P. (2004), 'Kerala Construction Labour Welfare Fund', ILO Sector Activities Working Paper No. 219, Geneva: ILO.

Platteau, J. (1991), 'Traditional systems of social security and hunger insurance: past achievements and modern challenges', in E. Ahmad et al. (eds), *Social Security in Developing Countries*, Oxford: Clarendon Press, pp. 112–70.

Polanyi, K. (1944), *The Great Transformation*, London: Beacon Press.

Popkin, S.L. (1979), *The Rational Peasant: The Political Economy of Rural Society in Vietnam*, Berkeley and London: University of California Press.

Portes, A. and R. Schauffler (1993), 'Competing perspectives on the Latin American informal sector', *Population and Development Review*, **19** (1), 33–60.

Rawls, J. (1993), *Political Liberalism*, New York: Columbia University Press.

Rodrik, D. (2002), *Getting Institutions Right*, DICE Report 2-2004, Munich: CEAifo.

Sassen, S. (1994), 'The informal economy: between new developments and old regulations', *Yale Law Journal*, **103**, 2289–304.

Schneider, F. and D.H. Enste (2000), 'Shadow economies: size, causes and consequences', *Journal of Economic Literature*, **38** (March), 77–114.

Scott, J. (1979), *The Moral Economy of the Peasant: Rebellion and Subsistence in Southeast Asia*, Yale: Yale University Press.

Scott, J. (2005), 'Afterword to "moral economies, state spaces and categorical violence"', *American Anthropologist*, **107** (3), 395–402.

Sinha, A. (2005), 'Impact of reforms on the informal sector: poverty analysis through CGE Approach', Paper no. 2 of Expert group on informal sector statistics during the workshop of Nadi, Fiji Islands, 29–31 March.

Sundar, S.K.R. (2005), 'Labour flexibility debate in India: a comprehensive review and some suggestions', *Economic and Political Weekly*, 28 May–4 June, 2274–85.

Tilly, C. (1995), 'Globalisation threatens labour's rights', *International Labour and Working Class History*, **47**, 1–23.

Turner, B. (1990), 'Outline of a theory of citizenship', *Sociology*, **24** (2), 189–217.

Uzzi, B. (1997), 'Social structure and competition in interfirm networks: the paradox of embeddedness', *Administrative Science Quarterly*, **42** (1), 35–67.

Varcin, R. (2000), 'Competition in the informal sector of the economy: the case of market traders in Turkey', *International Journal of Sociology and Social Policy*, **21**, 3–4.

Varese, F. (2001), *The Russian Mafia*, Oxford: Oxford University Press.

Verick, S. (2010), 'Unravelling the impact of the global financial crisis on the South African labour market', Employment Working Paper No. 48, Geneva: ILO.

Vijayabaskar, M. (2011), 'Global crises, welfare provision and coping strategies of labour in Tiruppur', *Economic and Political Weekly*, 28 May, 38–46.

Weber, M. (1978), *Economy and Society: An Outline of Interpretive Sociology*, Berkeley: University of California Press.

Young, I.M. (1995), 'Polity and group difference: a critique of the ideal of universal citizenship', in R. Beiner (ed.), *Theorizing Citizenship*, Albany, NY: State University of New York Press, pp. 175–208.

6. Addressing the failings of public health systems: should the private sector be an instrument of choice?

Jane Doherty and Diane McIntyre

INTRODUCTION

Arguments about an increased role for the private sector in the health systems of low- and middle-income countries (in terms of both the funding and the provision of health services) have been taking place since the 1990s. The debate intensified in 2007 with the release of a report by the International Finance Corporation of the World Bank Group. Titled *The Business of Health in Africa: Partnering with the Private Sector to Improve People's Lives*, the report remains one of the most fervent expositions to date in favour of the commercial sector. It went as far as to suggest that, in order to strengthen their health systems, African governments and donors should facilitate private sector expansion through more business-friendly policies and even subsidize private sector initiatives.

This chapter uses the example of the health sector to highlight some of the issues that confront analysts of social policy when thinking through how to harness the strengths of the private sector in the service of social objectives. It also reflects on the contextual differences between low- and middle-income countries (LMICs) on the one hand, and high-income settings on the other, that affect the policy choices in this area. Examining these issues is important because of the current international focus on universal health systems. The 2010 World Health Organization report, titled *Health Systems Financing: The Path Towards Universal Coverage*, defines the core of universal coverage as providing financial protection from the costs of health care, as well as access to needed health services, for the entire population. It argues that while voluntary (also termed 'private') health insurance is unable to achieve universal coverage objectives, privately provided health services can contribute to achieving this goal.

This chapter begins by clarifying the structure of the private health sector and explaining why the focus of the chapter is on the formal, for-profit component of this sector. It then presents the argument in favour of expanded commercial activity in the health system. It goes on to comment on the track record of commercial health service providers (especially hospitals and general practitioners) and private health insurance in addressing the health needs of country populations, especially the most disadvantaged. Before concluding, the chapter presents the case of South Africa as a means to understand the system-wide impact of an expanding for-profit sector. The chapter ends by reflecting on whether it is indeed appropriate for governments – and other proponents of public policy (especially donors and international agencies) – to promote the commercial sector as a credible solution to the failings that currently beset public services in low- and middle-income countries.

THE STRUCTURE OF THE PRIVATE SECTOR

The private sector is made up of for-profit entities, social enterprises[1] (or 'not-for-profits') and non-profit organizations. Altruism is not the only incentive that drives the behaviour of the latter two components: religious or ideological beliefs may also play a part, for example. However, it is the incentive of profit-making that is of most concern to policy analysts as it has the potential both to increase the price of services and to distort patterns of service provision. For this reason, the rest of this chapter focuses on the for-profit health sector.

The for-profit sector has both formal and informal components. Among the latter are traditional healers, drug sellers, unlicensed doctors and midwives, and small shops selling public health products such as family planning methods and bed nets that protect against malaria-carrying mosquitoes. Informal for-profit providers are often distributed widely throughout countries and deep into even the remotest communities. This is one of the reasons why they are an attractive health care resource for disadvantaged communities: thus, for many low-income countries, 'the private sector' is predominantly informal in nature (Limwattananon 2008; Berer 2011). However, informal providers pose enormous challenges for governments around quality assurance as they operate outside the ambit of government regulation and often in isolation. Developing appropriate policy on this sector is an urgent priority, especially in health systems where the public health sector is very weak.

This chapter, however, focuses on the formal for-profit sector. This is partly because it is impossible to do justice to the entirety of the private health sector in one chapter. More important, some of the recent discourse on the role of the private sector (particularly that emanating from the World Bank) revolves around the types of formal enterprise associated with high-income countries – efficient, high-quality, complex and attractive to investors seeking business opportunities in new markets (see, for example, Preker et al. 2010). Thus, according to the International Finance Corporation, 'for health care companies looking for markets in which to expand, and for investors looking to invest in health care businesses, this [projected] $11–$20 billion in private health care expansion [in Sub-Saharan Africa] represents a significant opportunity', with about 60 per cent of these expansion opportunities predicted to attract for-profit investors (International Finance Corporation 2007, p. 15). There is already some evidence of expansion of this nature taking place in Africa, Asia and Eastern Europe (Drechsler and Jutting 2005; Preker et al. 2010; Doherty 2011). This may signal a future shift in the emphasis of public policy on the private sector from encouraging small-scale and often non-profit initiatives that are embedded within communities to promoting large-scale initiatives that seek greater returns on investment and are answerable to investors from communities – and even countries – much further afield. A change of this nature and scale would require careful consideration and certainly justifies the focus of this chapter.

The structure of the formal, for-profit health sector has five main sub-components. As Table 6.1 shows, these are health services provision (outpatient and inpatient), risk-pooling arrangements,[2] life sciences-related activities (pharmaceuticals and medical products), retail and distribution, and medical and nursing education. The first category, health services provision, represents around half of the current investment opportunities, at least in Africa (International Finance Corporation 2007); hence the selection of this sub-sector for special exploration later in this chapter. Private (voluntary) health insurance (a form of risk-pooling arrangement) is selected as the second area of focus because, in contemporary debates around financing health systems in LMICs, it has been suggested as an important precursor or complement to other forms of financing (such as mandatory social health insurance and tax-based financing). Also, the growth of private-for-profit provision is strongly dependent on the growth of private health insurance, as most residents in LMICs are unable to afford to pay for private health care, particularly private hospital inpatient care, on an out-of-pocket basis.

Table 6.1   The structure of the formal private sector, focusing on promising investment opportunities

Investment opportunity	Description
Health services provision	
Small, high-end hospital	'Boutique' hospital located in urban area, providing high-quality care and targeting the wealthy and expatriates
Network of primary and secondary clinics	Integrated set of facilities extending into lower-density areas, sharing overhead costs, management expertise and procurement systems; economies of scale allow specialized services to be delivered
Hospital offering in-house insurance	Offers own insurance scheme to families where the catchment population is uninsured; requires reinsurance or donor subsidies to manage risk
High-volume, low-cost hospital	Located in high-density area, providing basic care and targeting low-income people (patient throughput can be up to 100 patients per doctor per day); sometimes specializes in one type of service (e.g. cataract surgery)
Hospital with cross-subsidization model	Fees differentiated by patient income, with better hotel services provided to patients paying higher fees; quality of care supposedly not differentiated by fee level
Large diagnostic laboratory	Diagnostic laboratory providing diagnostic services to geographic area that can be quite wide-ranging
Telemedicine	Doctors in urban area provide advice to clinic nurses by phone or internet, particularly in rural areas where there is a shortage of doctors
Specialized doctors covering network of hospitals	Group of specialists travels between facilities with equipment to treat pre-booked patients in areas where there is a shortage of specialists
Risk-pooling arrangements	
Indemnity insurance within general insurance	Health insurance offered by general insurers with a fee based on risk profile
Health maintenance organization integrated with service providers	Organization providing insurance coverage together with access to selected providers, using managed-care principles
Micro-health insurance associated with micro-finance institution	Health insurance sold together with micro-finance products

Investment opportunity	Description
Life-sciences related activities (pharmaceuticals and medical products)	
Generics manufacturing	Formulation of generic medicines (prescription and over-the-counter)
Medical supplies manufacturing	Manufacturing of medical supplies (e.g. long-lasting mosquito nets, medical gauzes, medical furniture)
Life sciences innovation (South Africa)	Financing innovation and commercialization of local research outputs
Commercialization of infectious and neglected disease research	Financing commercialization and local application of research conducted globally
Retail and distribution	
Pharmacy chains (most profitable opportunity)	Consolidation of individual outlets into chains that compensate for lower margins (usually as a result of government regulation) with volume
Multi-sector distribution platforms	Shared transport of pharmaceuticals (especially over-the-counter medicines) with soft drinks and consumer goods
Multi-brand, vertically integrated platforms	Integration of different components of the supply chain, sometimes paired with distributing several different brands
Pharmacy accreditation programmes for informal retail operators	Private company managing accreditation programme
Supply-chain management programmes for donors or governments	Private company managing supply chain
Medical and nursing education	
Large, multidisciplinary university	(self-evident)
Schools for nurses, midwives and lab technicians	(self-evident)
Distance learning: nurses	(self-evident)

Source: Doherty (2011), adapted from Section III and Annexes 1–5 of International Finance Corporation (2007).

WHY IS THE PRIVATE SECTOR PROMOTED AS AN INSTRUMENT FOR TRANSFORMING HEALTH SYSTEMS?

The International Finance Corporation 2007 report noted that, at least in Sub-Saharan Africa, already 60 per cent of health financing was from private sources while 50 per cent of health expenditure was on private providers. It projected that rapid economic growth is set to expand the African middle-class, increasing the capacity to pay for care and consequently the demand for good-quality services. Demand is also increasing due to new developments in the health sector, such as the emergence of generic drugs, low-cost insurance and medical tourism. The International Finance Corporation forecast that public health systems would be unable to meet this demand because of shortfalls in capital and human resources and problems with efficiency and quality. Given that donor funding is also stagnating, the private health sector appeared to be the only component of the health system that had the wherewithal to address the health care gap. In addition, it has the potential to offer private investors good returns on investment, particularly as political stability and good governance practices emerge on the continent. The International Finance Corporation report concluded, therefore, that both populations and businesses can benefit from a stronger private sector.

While this argument in favour of the private sector is laid out with most conviction in the International Finance Corporation's 2007 report, some elements of the argument are supported by other policy analysts and applied to countries outside Africa (see, for example, Preker et al. 2007; Hanson et al. 2008; Dimovska et al. 2009). It is becoming increasingly clear to most analysts – whether or not they favour the private sector – that the private sector exists in one form or another in most countries and, in many of them, appears to be expanding (see, for example, Lagomarsino et al. 2009; Balabanova et al. 2011). In addition, there are high levels of out-of-pocket expenditure in many countries, meaning that people frequently pay directly for services and health products, and do not enjoy the financial protection – and sharing of risk – characteristic of tax- or insurance-based systems.

HOW SIGNIFICANT ARE FORMAL, FOR-PROFIT PRIVATE PROVIDERS TO THE POPULATIONS OF LOW- AND MIDDLE-INCOME COUNTRIES?

While expenditure on the private sector may be high, this does not necessarily mean that for-profit private provision is meeting the needs of country populations in a significant way. First, figures on the size of the private sector seldom differentiate between for-profit and non-profit, or between formal and informal, providers. This is the case in the International Finance Corporation report, for example. Marriott (2009) estimates that almost 40 per cent of private provision is in the informal sector, and the African Religious Health Assets Programme (2007) estimates that between 30 and 70 per cent of the health service infrastructure in different African countries is owned by faith-based organizations. Significant out-of-pocket expenditure goes to public sector providers and the purchasing of drugs (Hanson et al. 2008). Further, Berer (2011) emphasizes that, in developing countries, the formal private sector is by and large not made up of the well-qualified practitioners and impressive facilities one associates with high-income countries but is mainly comprised of poorly trained, widely dispersed and uncoordinated practitioners or single-proprietor facilities that are often in poor condition.

Second, high levels of private spending may not represent people's preferences but indicate lack of access to public services. The international experience is that, as countries' income levels increase, so does the proportion of government spending (and the availability of public services), leading to a decline in the percentage of expenditure accounted for by the private sector and out-of-pocket payments (see Figure 6.1).

Third, high expenditure is not a good proxy for utilization of, or population 'coverage' by, private providers because of the high prices prevalent in the commercial sector. In South Africa, for example, only 15 per cent of the population has private health insurance; yet private schemes account for 44 per cent of total health expenditure in the country, almost all of this on for-profit providers (McIntyre 2010).

Fourth, utilization of private care tends to be far higher in high-income than in low-income households, aggravating inequity in the health system. An Oxfam report noted that 'comparable data across 15 sub-Saharan African countries reveals that only 3 per cent of the poorest fifth of the population who sought care when sick actually saw a private doctor' (Marriott 2009, p. 3). Hanson et al. (2008) note, too, that it is poor people who are more likely to use the lower-quality and fragmented end of the private provision spectrum.

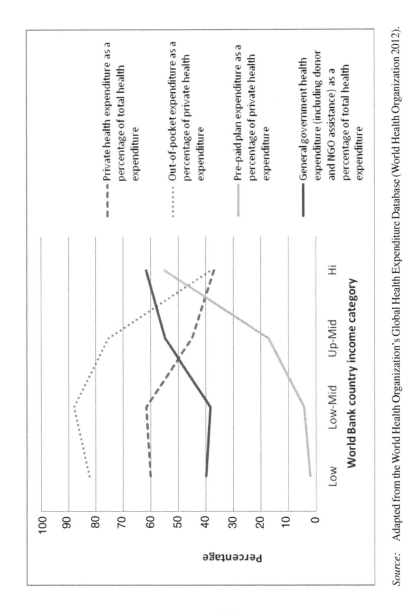

Source: Adapted from the World Health Organization's Global Health Expenditure Database (World Health Organization 2012).

Figure 6.1 Health expenditure by country income category, 2009

Fifth, while the for-profit private sector may serve some segments of the population well, it can have negative impacts on the health system overall, even with respect to the dimensions of quality, efficiency and sustainability, the very reasons put forward for involving the commercial sector in health care in the first place (these impacts are outlined in Table 6.2). These impacts have been investigated particularly well in the field of sexual and reproductive health (Ravindran and de Pinho 2005; and two issues of the journal *Reproductive Health Matters* in 2010 and 2011).

Such problems arise because provider performance is influenced by the profit motive which, especially when providers are paid a fee for each service rendered, shapes treatment according to the ability to pay (rather than need) and discourages the provision of inexpensive services. These tendencies are not counteracted by market forces because of the imbalance in information and power between patients and providers (which results in the well-described 'market failure' in health care), and are particularly evident in countries with weak regulatory systems and limited competition between private providers.

Despite these problems, the for-profit private sector clearly offers some patients advantages over public services. Balabanova et al. (2011) found that, even in countries with recent successes in meeting the needs of their populations – such as Bangladesh, China, Costa Rica, India (the states of Kerala and Tamil Nadu) and Sri Lanka – real and perceived quality advantages (including accelerated treatment and privacy) in the private sector seem to attract patients away from cheaper and more accessible services. Private provision must therefore remain a policy option for governments, provided that the distortions induced by this sub-sector can be circumvented.

IS COMMERCIAL HEALTH INSURANCE AN ATTRACTIVE FINANCING OPTION FOR DEVELOPING COUNTRIES?

Proponents of private health insurance for LMIC countries argue that, especially where public health systems are weak, it draws extra resources into health care and improves coverage, thereby supplementing the existing health system (Sekhri and Savedoff 2005; Preker et al. 2007; Preker et al. 2010). Out-of-pocket payments – which in 2009 averaged 83, 88 and 76 per cent of total health care expenditure in low, low-middle and upper-middle income countries respectively (World Health Organization 2012) – are widely acknowledged as a regressive form of financing and, together with the loss of income due to ill-health, can

*Table 6.2   Negative impacts of for-profit private providers on national
health care objectives*

Impact	Reasons
While private provision enhances access to care for some segments of the population (especially the better-off), it can worsen inequity, especially where public services are not readily available to other segments of the population.	• Serve only those able to pay • Concentrated in urban areas • Differentials in quality between public and private patients • Catastrophic financial impact on poor households
While some private providers render high-quality services, many are of poor quality, particularly where regulation is weak.	• Poor at following national guidelines • Neglect critical services (e.g. pregnancy and child-birth services, sexually transmitted infections, screening and follow-up services) • Misuse pharmaceuticals (inappropriate choice of drugs, over-prescribing and failure to inform patients of side effects) • Medicalize health issues, thereby skewing the uptake of services (e.g. recommending oral and injectible contraceptives as opposed to condoms which are better at preventing sexually transmitted infections) • Difficult to work with regarding quality improvement programmes • No quality control over illegal services (such as back-street abortions)
While private providers are often efficient in the business sense of maximizing profits, they are often inefficient from the health systems perspective, especially when there is little competition between providers or where providers are paid a fee for service (as this incentivizes over-servicing).	• Over-servicing, especially with respect to pharmaceuticals, diagnostic tests and costly procedures (e.g. Caesareans) • High prices and inflation • Corruption and fraud (e.g. theft, under-the-counter payments and diversion of patients into private practices where public health workers also work in private practice, fraudulent submissions to health insurers) • Subsidized private programmes not viable once donor or government subsidies withdrawn
While private provision can satisfy the needs of some portions of the population, often a large private sector undermines the integrity and sustainability of the health system overall.	• Fragment preventive, diagnostic and curative services • Brain drain from the public sector • Not coordinated • Little community participation

Sources: Ravindran and de Pinho (2005), Hanson et al. (2008), Berer (2011).

induce further impoverishment. Private health insurance, in contrast, offers households financial protection against the risk of future ill-health by pooling of risks faced by members (although in many cases private insurers charge risk-rated contributions, which undermines risk-pooling). Private health insurance also gives insurers the opportunity to bargain down the prices charged by providers and to control some of the negative behaviours described earlier. Proponents of voluntary private insurance argue, too, that it can act as a transitional form of insurance along the way to mandatory social health insurance.

The experience of the Netherlands is worthy of particular attention as its financial protection system was built on the foundation of private (albeit not-for-profit) health insurance schemes and because it is being advocated as a model for LMICs to follow. The Netherlands is a country in which social health insurance (for low- and middle-income earners), mandatory insurance for long-term illness (for the whole population) and voluntary private insurance have been combined to achieve almost universal coverage without leading to the two-tiered health system so characteristic of the United States, where high-income earners enjoy better access to health care through shorter queues, a higher standard of care, a greater choice of providers and improved 'hotel' services. The Dutch experience has inspired experiments in private health insurance in some African countries under the guidance of Dutch funding and expertise (Doherty 2011). As Box 6.1 shows, however, the achievements of the Netherlands were founded on a unique set of circumstances and policy choices – including risk equalization mechanisms, package speci-fication, strong price controls, outcome and quality measurement, strong governance structures and competition policy – that are unlikely to be easy to replicate elsewhere in the world. Even in the Dutch system, some inequities and anti-competitive features remained in the first decade of the twenty-first century, prompting further regulation of private insur-ance.

Box 6.1   Factors accounting for the positive impact of private health insurance in the Netherlands

- A strong tradition of private insurance and private provision, together with a strong culture of taking out financial risk protection

- Strong public policy on the role and size of the private sector
- Almost three quarters of the population covered by social health insurance
- Long-term care and care for the chronically ill financed by a separate, obligatory scheme that covers the majority of catastrophic costs for the whole population
- Only a small percentage covered by private health insurance (accounting for around 15 per cent of expenditure)
- Benefit packages largely prescribed
- State-regulated uniformity of access to providers and services for those insured under social and private insurance (including speed of access)
- Several mechanisms to achieve cross-subsidization on the basis of health risk between private and social health insurance, and within private insurance
- Most insurers are non-profit organizations
- Most providers are non-profit or faith-based
- A multi-payer system so that no company has more than 15 per cent of market share
- Strong global cost controls that limits cost escalation, including state-determined maximum tariffs for providers and even limits on total income

Sources: Colombo and Tapay (2004), Tapay and Colombo (2004), van de Ven and Schut (2008).

The experience of other OECD countries is more representative than the Dutch example of the problems associated with commercial insurance. Table 6.3 suggests that, on average in OECD countries, private health insurance increased choice and the responsiveness of the health system, but at an increased cost and often to the detriment of equity. It appears, too, that the quality and efficiency gains expected from private insurance did not materialize. Further, private health insurance accounted for only 6 per cent of total health care expenditure with most services still rendered by the public sector (OECD 2004). Indeed, no middle- or high-income country uses private health insurance as the primary method for insuring populations who are poor or at high risk, while the governments of high-income countries tend to intervene significantly in private health insurance markets to protect equity and quality (Sekhri and Savedoff

2005). Moreover, in countries where private health insurance coverage is relatively high, insurance plans tend to be employer-based as employers are able to negotiate prices more successfully and benefit from larger risk pools than insurance plans based on individual membership (Preker et al. 2007). Thus, in the United States and Canada around 90 per cent of private health plans are employer-based (Colombo and Tapay 2004).

In the past, private health insurance in LMICs accounted for a very small percentage of total health expenditure, but more recently it has become slightly more prevalent, accounting for more than 5 per cent of health expenditure in almost 20 LMICs by 2001 (Sekhri and Savedoff 2005). In 2005, Drechsler and Jutting (2005) estimated that the growth in the size of total premium payments had been more than twice as fast as in high-income countries. The impact of commercial insurance in LMICs has, in the main, not been evaluated systematically, especially with respect to equity, although there are some emerging case studies (see, for example, Preker et al. 2010). One could foresee, however, that the problems commonly associated with commercial health insurance in industrialized countries – such as small risk pools and weak incentives for cost-effectiveness – are likely to be more intense in LMICs because of weak (or absent) regulatory frameworks. The fact that LMIC governments tend not to have the capacity or experience to withstand the influence of powerful commercial providers is likely to aggravate this problem, as shown by the experience of Argentina, Brazil and Mexico (Marriott 2009; Victora et al. 2011).

Thus, an assessment of health insurance in Zimbabwe, a low-income country where private insurance accounts for as much as 20 per cent of total health expenditure, found that commercial schemes had reduced competition by indulging in vertical and horizontal integration, failed to meet regulatory reporting requirements, provided segmented benefit packages that reduced cross-subsidies between risk groups, encouraged hospital development in urban rather than rural areas, employed restrictive practices regarding consumer choice, practised tax avoidance and perpetuated high health-care costs and co-payments (Shamu et al. 2010). The Ministry of Health's regulatory office had very little capacity to deal with these problems because of a shortage of trained personnel, limited information and ambiguities in the legislation. Even in Brazil, a middle-income country with a longer history of insurance and a strong Ministry of Health, there is evidence of concentration of insurance plans, price increases well above inflation, exclusion of costly disorders and stagnant coverage, so that the insured still rely on public services for complex conditions while enjoying large tax deductions on their insurance premiums (Victora et al. 2011).

Table 6.3   The experience of private health insurance in OECD countries

Indicator	Description of impact	Impact rating
Does it improve coverage?	This depends on the size of the private sector and the size of the risk pool it covers. Historical reasons as well as affordability concerns have prevented significant financial protection through private health insurance in Korea, Mexico, Greece and Turkey, for example. In some other countries where the private sector is larger and public cover is not comprehensive or universal, private health insurance has improved access to health care for higher-income groups (through shorter queues – especially for elective surgery – more services and greater choice).	±
Does it improve equity?	While providing increased access to health care for the wealthy and healthy, private health insurance tends to leave the overall health system inequitable with higher-risk individuals facing high premiums or being excluded altogether. In response to this, some governments have introduced regulations to promote the availability and affordability of private health insurance for these groups. However, there is no clear evidence that the presence of a private sector reduces waiting times in the public sector, while there is some evidence that the presence of a private sector undermines public sector provision through its ability to attract away skilled staff through higher salaries. All in all, private health insurance tends to result in a 'two-tiered' health system, the Netherlands being a clear exception through regulations preventing the privately insured from enjoying better services and level of choice.	☹ (except the Netherlands)
Does it promote high-quality care?	It is only in the United States that the introduction of 'managed care' has changed the clinical process in a significant way. In other OECD countries, private health insurance has had very little impact on the quality of care. This is because insurers have had few regulatory or financial incentives to influence provider behaviour. In addition, there has been resistance to interventions by providers who do not want their treatment decisions questioned as well as by consumers who do not want their choices restricted. Even in the United States, reimbursement mechanisms do not reward quality improvements while reporting systems to monitor quality improvement are inadequate.	± (except the US)

Does it create more choice and responsiveness?	This has been improved by private insurance in many countries. First, private cover provides an alternative to using poorly performing public health services or paying out-of-pocket for private care. Second, it provides consumers with a greater choice of providers, services and the timing of care. Whether this choice translates into greater responsiveness to consumers' needs depends on whether insurers' product materials are clear and allow consumers to make meaningful comparisons between insurers. Product materials are often of poor quality; and in Switzerland and the United States, for example, the governments have had to address this by publishing comparative information on the cost, quality and characteristics of different plans. For the poorer segments of society, however, the improved choices offered by private insurance are often unattainable due to cost, which has led some governments to regulate insurers through requiring standardized benefit packages and preventing insurers excluding high-risk consumers or weighting their premiums for risk.	☺
Does it relieve cost pressures on the public sector?	Private health insurance has not significantly reduced public financing burdens. This is partly because people who are privately insured still rely on the public sector for certain services, especially as private hospitals tend to focus on a limited number of elective (and cheaper) services. In addition, many of those relying on the public system – such as the elderly, chronically ill and long-term disabled – tend to require more costly services. Private health insurance, therefore, does not relieve the public sector of expensive services, while sometimes it has added to health costs through increased utilization or, as in the case of Australia and the United States, through public subsidies to private insurance.	±
Does it make health systems more efficient?	Efficiency improvements are limited because of the high administrative costs associated with private insurers. These costs are incurred through efforts to attract and retain clients, offer a diverse set of insurance plans, and negotiate multiple contractual relationships with providers. Further, in several countries competition between private insurers is limited as consumers seldom move between insurers; this leads to high prices and shields insurers from pressures to improve cost-effectiveness and quality. This behaviour is reinforced by the fact that managing care cost-effectively is expensive and faces resistance from both providers and consumers. As a result, insurers tend not to compete on the basis of efficiency but through risk-avoidance and cost-shifting strategies.	± or ☹

± = neutral impact; ☹ = negative impact; ☺ = positive impact

Source: Adapted from OECD (2004).

In conclusion, Bassett and Kane (2007) note that, for private voluntary health insurance to have more positive effects, insurers have to practise active purchasing in order to reduce prices and control provider behaviour; but unfortunately active purchasing has been slow to develop, even in industrialized countries. Further, small and fragmented risk pools are inefficient and make it difficult to move towards equity: success depends on making insurance compulsory so that low-risk individuals do not opt out, and implementing mechanisms that link different risk pools (World Health Organization 2010). Unfortunately ministries of health in LMICs often have limited capacity and little information on the private sector to inform decision-making, or do not prioritize stewardship of this sector (Lagomarsino et al. 2009).

THE IMPACT OF EXPANDING COMMERCIAL HEALTH CARE: THE CASE OF SOUTH AFRICA

Unusually for Africa, South Africa is a middle-income country. What is more, it is the country which has the largest proportion of total health care finances channelled through private insurers in the world (Drechsler and Jutting 2005). While these features do not make South Africa a typical LMIC, trends in the for-profit private sector have been analysed since the early 1990s, including from a health systems perspective, providing a rare opportunity to track the behaviour of different elements of this sector in response to changing contexts and government policy. In addition, it serves as an example for other LMICs of what can happen if the private health sector is aggressively promoted. The South African experience is therefore described here in some detail to illuminate the issues described in broad terms above.

By way of background, health care resources in South Africa during its apartheid years were concentrated in the hands of the white community, allowing the development of a strong for-profit private health sector that served this community. In the mid-1980s, successful unionization of black workers led to the negotiation of employer-based health insurance as part of workers' benefit packages, also giving this sector access to commercial health care. In line with global trends, however, the late 1980s and early 1990s saw spiralling health-care costs that led to pressure on the apartheid government to relax regulations on health insurers (known as 'medical schemes' in South Africa), who complained that they were no longer able to offer affordable premiums. Consequently, deregulation occurred shortly before the election of the first democratic government in 1994.

Until then, health insurers had mainly been 'closed', employer-based schemes. Membership had usually been a condition of employment, with premiums shared between employer and employee and adjusted according to income but not to the risk of ill-health (i.e. premiums were 'community-rated'). Benefit packages were also standardized. In combination, these features allowed cross-subsidization of the ill, old and poor by the healthy and rich. Schemes themselves were non-profit entities, with surpluses channelled back into the scheme. Although scheme administrators might themselves be profit-making entities, they were often part of the employer organization and overseen by a board consisting of employer and employee representatives keen to keep costs down. Schemes were aided in this by the setting of nationally negotiated tariffs for providers by the association of schemes. Even so, in 1992/93 the for-profit health sector captured 60 per cent of total health expenditure while only 23 per cent of the population had secure access to private services, and medical scheme contributions amounted to 15 per cent of average salaries (McIntyre et al. 1995).

In this context, deregulation was supposed to allow greater cost control by permitting schemes to differentiate benefit packages and risk-rate members (i.e. set higher premiums for members more likely to be ill). By allowing schemes to offer low-risk members cheaper packages, it was intended that private sector coverage would expand, relieving some of the health-care burden on the state.

Deregulation did, in fact, change the nature of the private sector fundamentally. The 1990s saw the proliferation of medical schemes, including the advent of a new type of scheme, the 'open' scheme. Unlike closed schemes, open schemes accepted individual members and were not linked to particular employers. They also offered differentiated benefit packages, with cheaper premiums for more limited packages and for low-risk members. These developments did not expand coverage, however (Doherty and McLeod 2003; Doherty and Steinberg 2003). Instead, existing members were 'churned' between schemes. The new open schemes aggressively 'cherry-picked' low-risk members, excluding high-risk (and expensive) members. This eroded the membership base of closed schemes, which were left with disproportionate numbers of older, sicker members. Financial incentives offered to brokers also encouraged the poaching of existing members from one scheme to another. Scheme administrators became adept at excluding risky beneficiaries rather than managing schemes efficiently, and costs continued to rise. This was aggravated by the fragmentation of risk pools, which reduced income and health risk cross-subsidies and led to rising premiums for the ill, old and poor. Increasingly, some form of co-payment became the norm, reducing the financial protection afforded by prepayment. This led to members 'buying down' to smaller benefit packages, the exclusion of poor or high-risk patients and the increasing 'dumping' of privately insured patients on the public sector when their benefits had expired.

In this climate of minimal regulation, some open-scheme administrators were able to strip surplus from their schemes through unethical reinsurance practices and kickbacks. Another mechanism for extracting surplus was to charge high administrative and managed care fees. All of these practices became easier as the vertical integration of reinsurance companies, medical scheme administrators and managed care organizations grew. Scheme reserves were also allowed to run dangerously low, putting members at risk.

Throughout this period providers were largely unregulated. Hospitals and specialists began to charge above the recommended medical scheme tariff and there were large markups on pharmaceuticals (especially by private hospitals) as well as instances of over-prescribing (particularly by dispensing doctors). The number of hospital beds doubled in the decade 1989–98, despite a government moratorium on the building of new hospitals (Doherty et al. 2002). Increasingly these beds fell under the aegis of three private hospital networks which were suspected of colluding on prices. There was also increasing vertical integration of providers, such as the ownership of private ambulance services and medical scheme administrators by private providers (McIntyre 2010).

As a result of these features of the deregulated environment, between 1996/97 and 1998/99 per capita expenditure grew ten times more quickly in the medical schemes industry than in the public sector (Doherty et al. 2002). By 1999 per capita expenditure on medical scheme beneficiaries was nearly four times that spent per public sector patient. Furthermore, the private sector increasingly captured government subsidies through a variety of mechanisms, including contracts with the public sector, undercharging of private patients using the public sector, tax relief to employers contributing to their employees' premiums (amounting to 20 per cent of the public sector health budget) and high premiums paid by government for its civil servants belonging to medical schemes (in the 1990s, government spent 12 times as much per civil servant for private insurance membership as it did on public sector dependents).

At the same time, high private fees and the expansion of the private sector attracted skilled health professionals away from the public sector. At the end of the 1990s, around 75 per cent of specialists, between 50 and 70 per cent of GPs and around 40 per cent of nurses were estimated to work in the private sector (Doherty et al. 2002). Doctors working in academic hospitals were allowed to engage in limited private practice, a strategy which undermined the provision of care at academic hospitals.

In the early 2000s new legislation was introduced to combat some of these negative effects. There were some hard-won achievements in regulating the practice of dispensing doctors, setting single exit prices for pharmaceuticals, enforcing generic substitution, controlling dispensing fees and reintroducing community rating and standardized (minimum) benefit packages in the medical schemes industry. As a result of these measures, spending on medicines as a proportion of total medical schemes expenditure decreased from 32 per cent in 1992 to 17 per cent in 2009 (McIntyre et al. 2012). However, cost containment in the rest of the private sector was disappointing (McIntyre et al. 2012). By 2010 medical scheme contributions per beneficiary reached a figure double that of 1996 (after the effects of inflation are removed) and expenditure on private hospitals and specialists as a proportion of total medical scheme expenditure had escalated sharply. The richest 40 per cent of the population paid more towards medical schemes than they paid in tax and out-of-pocket expenses for health-care services combined. The equity impact of re-regulation was also disappointing, with medical schemes covering only 16 per cent of the population, less than in 1994 (McIntyre and Ataguba 2012; McIntyre et al. 2012). Meanwhile, health service benefits from both private and public services were preferentially enjoyed by higher-income earners despite lower-income groups' greater need for health care, while private sector expenditure per beneficiary had risen to six times that on public sector dependents.

This is a worrying situation for a country that sees equity in health care as one of its primary objectives and has invested considerable resources in attempting to regulate the private sector in line with this objective. Obstacles include fragmented risk pools (both within the private sector and between the private and public sectors), increasing concentration of the ownership of hospital beds, pharmaceutical companies and medical scheme administrators and, very important, the third-party, fee-for-service payment mechanism that encourages providers to over-service. Powerful provider interest groups are resistant to interference in these issues on the part of government as well as medical scheme administrators, making it difficult for policymakers to move towards health-care coverage patterns that are more affordable and equitable.

It is in no small part due to the challenges arising from the growth of the private health sector, particularly the inequitable public–private mix, that the South African government has put forward a proposal for National Health Insurance (NHI) with the goal of achieving universal coverage (National Department of Health 2011). While primarily tax funded, a critical design component of the policy is the establishment of an NHI Fund, which will serve as a single, active purchaser of health services from both public and private providers. This is seen as a means of drawing on the human and other physical health-service resources located in the private sector through 'holding the purse strings', influencing the fees charged by private providers and ensuring that these providers serve the public good. Private voluntary insurance would continue, but in all likelihood would take the form of complementary (or 'top-up') cover. It is of interest that other LMICs with substantial private health sectors, such as India, are proposing very similar reforms in order to pursue universal coverage and 'manage' private providers through purchasing arrangements rather than through frequently ineffective regulatory mechanisms (High Level Expert Group 2011).

CONCLUSION

What does the evidence assembled in this chapter teach us about the relevance of the private sector for social policy in LMICs, especially in the domain of health care? First, the private sector is complex and diverse. Its different sub-components need to be analysed separately and treated differently because of the varying incentives that operate in its formal, informal, non-profit and for-profit sub-components. Opportunities for regulation are also different.

Second, the extent and quality of information on the impact of the private sector is woefully inadequate for making definitive judgements on the rightful place of private provision and private health insurance in LMICs. As with commercial enterprises elsewhere in the world, and in other sectors, this is partly because some secrecy surrounds pricing and the quality of services. Further research is required to better inform policymaking: this research should take a health-systems perspective to ensure that the wider impacts of the private sector are fully understood.

Third, country governments need to exercise greater stewardship over the private sector because it appears to be growing, often in a completely unregulated manner. There is enough evidence to suggest that, despite the excellent services rendered by some private providers, unregulated provision tends, overall, to lead to worsening inequity and inefficiencies, poor quality of care and a fragmented and destabilised health system. Key to regulation is incentivizing appropriate treatment and pricing behaviour in providers and enforcing risk-pooling within, and between, insurance plans.

Fourth, high-income countries generally have a relatively small commercial private sector, providing health-care cover mainly through publicly funded systems. At the same time, their regulatory frameworks are strong and complex, while private sector provision is subject to a long tradition of employer-based insurance. In developing countries, in contrast, the public sector tends to be weak and unable to compete effectively with private providers, normally a key driver of quality in the private sector. In LMIC ministries of health, capacity and experience in regulation tend to be limited: even where there is expertise and other resources behind regulatory efforts, the power of private-sector interest groups makes regulation very difficult, especially as competition tends not to be very vibrant in these countries. Neither is there a strong tradition of prepayment by individuals or involvement of employers in workplace-based insurance. All of these contextual differences suggest that stewardship of the private sector will be that much harder in LMIC settings and that reforms requiring intense stewardship should not be embarked upon lightly.

Fifth, in the context of human resource shortages in LMICs, the brain drain of skilled personnel from the public sector into the private sector is potentially disastrous, undermining prospects for strengthening the public sector in the long term. This phenomenon does not appear to be nearly as big a concern in high-income countries.

Finally, the fundamental challenge for policymakers in high-income and LMIC countries alike is that the profit motive underpinning the private sector means that commercial insurance and health-care provision are unlikely to ever become a sustainable option for poor communities, unless mediated by a system of universal coverage that ensures income and risk cross-subsidies and strictly controls prices. As the growing literature on universal coverage, particularly the 2010 World Health Report, clearly indicates, providing financial protection and access to needed health care for all cannot be achieved through voluntary health insurance. An integrated pool of public funds (including tax funding and possibly also mandatory health insurance) is required to ensure the necessary income and risk cross-subsidies. This pool must be used to actively purchase health services from public and private providers. 'Holding the purse-strings' and the use of strategic purchasing (through benefit package specification and payment mechanisms that create appropriate incentives for providers) are essential for ensuring that good-quality and appropriate health services are available to the whole population where and when they are needed.

NOTES

1. Social enterprises are businesses whose social purpose is central to their operation. Profits are used more to further social aims than to maximize shareholders' returns on investment.
2. Risk pooling refers to all the members of a group combining and sharing the financial risks associated with seeking health care in the event of future illness, so that individual members are not unduly burdened financially at the time of experiencing ill-health.

REFERENCES

African Religious Health Assets Programme (2007), *Appreciating Assets: Mapping, Understanding, Translating and Engaging Religious Health Assets in Zambia and Lesotho*, Cape Town: African Religious Health Assets Programme.

Balabanova, D., M. McKee and A. Mills (2011), *Good Health At Low Cost' 25 Years On: What Makes a Successful Health System?*, London: London School of Hygiene and Tropical Medicine.

Bassett, M.C. and V.M. Kane (2007), 'Review of the literature on voluntary health insurance', in A.S. Preker, R.M. Scheffler and M.C. Bassett (eds), *Private Voluntary Health Insurance in Development: Friend or Foe?*, Washington, DC: World Bank, pp. 335–98.

Berer, M. (2011), 'Privatisation in health systems in developing countries: what's in a name?', *Reproductive Health Matters*, **19**(37), 4–9.

Colombo, F. and N. Tapay (2004), *Private Health Insurance in OECD Countries: The Benefits and Costs for Individuals and Health Systems*, Health Working Papers No. 15, Paris: OECD.

Dimovska, D., S. Sealy, S. Bergkvist and H. Pernefeldt (2009), *Innovative Pro-Poor Health Care Financing and Delivery Models*, Washington, DC: Results for Development Institute.

Doherty, J. (2011), 'Expansion of the private health sector in East and Southern Africa', Discussion Paper 87, Harare: EQUINET.

Doherty, J. and H. McLeod (2003), 'Medical schemes', in P. Ijumba, A. Ntuli and P. Barron (eds), *South African Health Review 2002*, Durban: Health Systems Trust, pp. 41–66.

Doherty, J. and M. Steinberg (2003), *Priority Health Care Information Needs for Reform: What Role for BHF?*, Johannesburg: Board of Healthcare Funders.

Doherty, J., S. Thomas and D. Muirhead (2002), *Health Financing and Expenditure in Post-Apartheid South Africa, 1996/97–1998/99*, Pretoria: National Department of Health.

Drechsler, D. and J. Jutting (2005), *Is There a Role for Private Health Insurance in Developing Countries?*, Berlin: German Institute for Economic Research.

Hanson, K., L. Gilson, C. Goodman, A. Mills, R. Smith R. Feachem, N.Sekhri Feachem, T. Perez Koehlmoos and H. Kinlaw (2008), 'Is private health care the answer to the health problems of the world's poor?', *PLOS Medicine*, **5**(11), e233.

High Level Expert Group (2011), *High Level Expert Group Report on Universal Health Coverage for India*, New Delhi: Planning Commission of India.

International Finance Corporation (2007), *The Business of Health in Africa: Partnering with the Private Sector to Improve People's Lives*, Washington, DC: International Finance Corporation, the World Bank Group.

Lagomarsino, G., S. Nachuk and S. Singh Kundra (2009), *Public Stewardship of Private Providers in Mixed Health Systems*, Washington, DC: Results For Development Institute, The Rockefeller Foundation.

Limwattananon, S. (2008), *Private–Public Mix in Woman and Child Health in Low-income Countries: An Analysis of Demographic and Health Surveys*, Technical Partner Paper 1, Washington, DC: Results for Development Institute, The Rockefeller Foundation.

Marriott, A. (2009), *Blind Optimism: Challenging the Myths about Private Health Care in Poor Countries*, Briefing Paper 125, Oxfam International.

McIntyre, D. (2010), *Private Sector Involvement in Funding and Providing Health Services in South Africa: Implications for Equity and Access to Health Care*, EQUINET Discussion Paper Series 84, Harare: Health Economics Unit (UCT), ISER (Rhodes University), EQUINET.

McIntyre, D. and J.E. Ataguba (2012), 'Modelling the affordability and distributional implications of future health care financing options in South Africa', *Health Policy and Planning*, **27**, i101–i112, available at http://heapol. oxfordjournals/org/ (accessed 18 October, 2012).

McIntyre, D., G. Bloom, J. Doherty and P. Brijlal (1995), *Health Expenditure and Finance in South Africa*, Durban: Health Systems Trust and the World Bank.

McIntyre, D.E., J.E. Doherty and J.E. Ataguba (2012), 'Health care financing and expenditure –post-1994 progress and remaining challenges', in H.C.J. Van Rensburg (ed.), *Health and Health Care in South Africa* (2nd edn), Pretoria: Van Schaik Publishers.

National Department of Health (2011), *Green Paper on National Health Insurance in South Africa*, Pretoria: National Department of Health, Republic of South Africa.

OECD (Organisation for Economic Co-operation and Development) (2004), 'Private health insurance in OECD countries: policy brief', available at http://www.oecd.org/dataoecd/42/6/33820355.pdf (accessed 28 August 2011).

Preker, A., R. Scheffler and M. Bassett (eds) (2007), *Private Voluntary Health Insurance in Development: Friend or Foe?*, Washington, DC: World Bank.

Preker, A., P. Zweifel and O. Schellekens (eds) (2010), *Global Marketplace for Private Health Insurance: Strength in Numbers*, Washington, DC: World Bank.

Ravindran, T. and H. de Pinho (eds) (2005), *The Right Reforms? Health Sector Reforms and Sexual and Reproductive Health*, Johannesburg: Women's Health Project, School of Public Health, University of the Witwatersrand.

Reproductive Health Matters (2010), 'Privatisation', **18**(36), 4–234.

Reproductive Health Matters (2011), 'Privatisation', **19**(37), 4–226.

Sekhri, N. and W. Savedoff (2005), 'Private health insurance: implications for developing countries', *Bulletin of the World Health Organization*, **83**(2), 127–34.

Shamu, S., R. Loewenson, R. Machemedze and A. Mabika (2010), *Capital Flows Through Medical Aid Societies in Zimbabwe's Health Sector*, EQUINET Discussion Paper 82, Harare: Training and Research Support Centre, SEATINI, Rhodes University, EQUINET.

Tapay, N. and F. Colombo (2004), *Private Health Insurance in the Netherlands: A Case Study*, Health Working Papers No. 18, Paris: OECD.

van de Ven, W.P. and F.T. Schut (2008), 'Universal mandatory health insurance in the Netherlands: a model for the United States?', *Health Affairs*, **27**(3), 771–81.

Victora, et al. (2011), 'Health conditions and health-policy innovations in Brazil: the way forward', *The Lancet*, **377**, 2042–53.

World Health Organization (2010), *Health Systems Financing: The Path to Universal Coverage*, Geneva: World Health Organization.

World Health Organization (2012), Global Health Expenditure Database, available at http://apps.who.int/nha/database/DataExplorerRegime.aspx (accessed 10 August 2011).

PART III

Instruments and mechanisms

7. Social security: risks, needs and protection

Robert Walker*

Social security is a basic human right and has been recognized as such internationally since 1919 when it was included as one of the core pillars of the constitutional mandate of the International Labour Organization (ILO). Article 22 of the 1948 *Universal Declaration of Human Rights* further lays down that:

> Everyone, as a member of society, has the right to social security and is entitled to realization, through national effort and international cooperation and in accordance with the organization and resources of each State, of the economic, social and cultural rights indispensable for his dignity and the free development of his personality.

The reality, however, is that the majority of people who enjoy this right live in the global North, while the mass of individuals living in developing countries generally have no or limited access to any social security other than that provided by family and friends. Twenty per cent of people in developing countries live in abject poverty, which is arguably the antithesis of social security (ILO 2010a).

It should be recognized that social security is both a goal and the mechanism (increasingly a range of mechanisms that offer cash and cash-like provisions) by which the goal of social security is achieved. The goal of social security, it is usually argued, requires provision to protect persons against inadequate income caused by sickness, disability, maternity, employment injury, unemployment, old age, the death of a family member, or by insufficient family support, leading to the risk of poverty. The mechanisms include contributory benefits paid on the basis of prior contributions, universal schemes available to all residents, categorical benefits available to persons with prescribed demographic characteristics, occupational benefits that accrue as a consequence of employment contracts, conditional benefits dependent on recipients fulfilling certain obligations or accomplishing specific tasks, and social assistance benefits which require persons initially to have no more than a threshold level of resources.

It is important to note, however, that the above formulation of social security is premised on the existence of a labour market that can generate incomes sufficient for most people of working age and also create sufficient surplus to enable many people in employment to save against the contingencies of ill health, old age and unemployment. In many developing countries, of course, no such labour market exists. Instead, one finds extensive unemployment and underemployment around an informal labour market predominantly offering poverty level wages. Rather than social security being required as a response to short periods of inadequate income or at the end of working life, many people in developing countries confront a lifetime with inadequate incomes. This situation has generated additional forms of social security including employment guarantee schemes, various forms of mutual benefits provided by neighbourhood and other kinds of collective such as micro-insurance, and livelihood benefits, such as micro-credit, that are intended to facilitate people to generate an ongoing income stream on the own account. There is also an unresolved debate about the viability of providing a basic income to all citizens without a means-test and irrespective of employment status (see Parijs [2002] and the journal *Basic Income Studies* for a flavour of these discussions since they are not pursued in this chapter).

It will be apparent that several of these mechanisms constitute the foci of other chapters in this volume and so are covered here only in passing. It should also be borne in mind that much discourse on social security provision includes that designed to offer protection against lack of access to affordable health care, a topic addressed in considerable detail in Chapter 6. Hence, this chapter deals with only a subset of the provision usually categorized as social security.

Since social security mechanisms typically involve simply a transfer of resources from less needy to more needy groups, rather than the actual production and consumption of resources, governments and societies should, in principle, be much more able to make social security provision than to deliver services even at low levels of economic development. However, as already noted, social security provision is a defining constituent of the welfare states that characterize the advanced economies of the OECD club of nations and is comparatively poorly developed elsewhere. But, if the dominant story is one of social insecurity among low- and some middle-income countries, this is not universally the case. Indeed, there is remarkable diversity in the extent and nature of social security provision in countries at ostensibly similar stages of economic development. Furthermore, since the early 1990s a rapid expansion has occurred in the coverage and quality of provision in a number of low- and middle-income countries; and new forms of provision have emerged that are now being replicated in the global North.

However, the global economy is changing fast. The legacy of the 2008 economic crisis, estimated in one year to have added 215 million to the 633 million already living and working in poverty with incomes of less than USD 1.25 per day, is still unclear. Likewise, continuing global financial uncertainty at the time of writing (November 2011) emphasizes the possibility of growing uncertainty and instability to which social security systems may need to adapt. The truth, though, is that social security provision can mitigate the social and personal consequences of new economic instability such that it is now increasingly argued, by the ILO among others, that the further development of social security is a social and economic imperative (ILO 2011). In contrast to the contestation about the merits of social security witnessed during the period characterized by the so-called Washington Consensus, the contention now is that, by protecting workers and families against the worst effects of economic, natural and personal crises, social security can simultaneously enhance the effectiveness and efficiency of market economies. It does so by empowering men and women to engage or re-engage in entrepreneurial activity, facilitating productive employment, aiding structural change through reducing the associated personal and social risk and fears, and by simultaneously stabilizing demand and maintaining social harmony during times of economic downturn. Rather than global economic uncertainty leading to a slowdown in the development of social security, the argument is that it should act as a stimulus towards improved provision.

While acknowledging current global insecurities, the chapter seeks first briefly to review current provisions and then to consider the structural constraints that must be negotiated if social security is to be further developed in low- and middle-income countries. It next draws attention to innovative ways of implementing social security in conditions that categorize many developing economies, before finally engaging, by way of conclusion, with the recent concern that promoting social security may be a further example of cultural and economic imperialism.

SOCIAL SECURITY PROVISION AND COVERAGE

There are various ways of characterizing social security provisions. A simple but still useful approach is to distinguish between the range of risks covered by a jurisdiction, the proportion of the population at risk that is covered and additionally the proportion of those people actually experiencing the risk who receive benefit, the generosity of the provision received and the mechanisms through which social security is provided (Walker 2005).

The ILO recognizes eight risks (or branches) of provision: sickness; maternity; old age; invalidity; survivors' benefits; family allowances; injury at work; and unemployment (ILO 2010b). Almost all developing countries, including over 95 per cent of low income ones, have employment injury cover and some benefits to meet the needs of old age, survivors and the costs of disability, although in many cases the coverage is highly restricted applying only to persons in the formal labour market and frequently only to those in privileged sectors such as civil servants and the military (Figure 7.1).

Around 55 per cent of the economically active population is covered by mandatory employment injury schemes in Latin America and the Caribbean (a region with a long history of social security provision), 21 per cent in Asia and the Pacific, and 17 per cent in Sub-Saharan Africa; this level of coverage compares with 67 per cent in North America and 62 per cent in Western Europe. It should be stressed that these regional averages mask considerable differences; for example, 42 per cent of the economically active population in Zimbabwe are covered against employment injury but less than 10 per cent in Gambia and no more than 3 per cent in Burundi, Zambia, Tanzania, Niger and Chad (ILO 2010b).

The almost 100 per cent availability of old age pensions – 97 per cent in low-income countries – is similarly misleading when the focus shifts to coverage (Figure 7.2). Sixty-four per cent of economically active people are legally covered by pensions in Latin America and the Caribbean, 32 per cent in Asia and the Pacific, and 26 per cent in Sub-Saharan Africa where 12 per cent of people are covered by non-contributory schemes; in the Middle East and North Africa comparable proportions are 40 per cent and 34 per cent respectively. The effective as opposed to the legal coverage is lower still since contributions are not always paid and the legal coverage for groups such as the self-employed is often restrictive. Hence, effective coverage is only 37 per cent in Latin America, 18 per cent in Asia and the Pacific region, 10 per cent in North Africa and just 5 per cent in Sub-Saharan Africa. By comparison, effective coverage is 72 per cent in North America, 65 per cent in Western Europe and 50 per cent in Central and Eastern Europe.

If actual pension receipt is considered, numbers can drop still further since provision is often a product of policies introduced some time ago to which rights may have been lost, or of new policies that have not

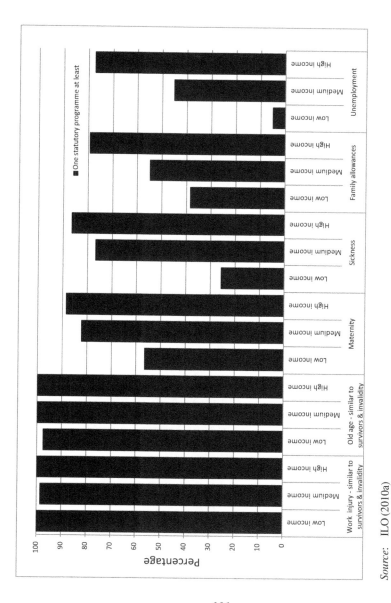

Source: ILO (2010a)

Figure 7.1   Percentage of countries with statutory programmes, latest available year

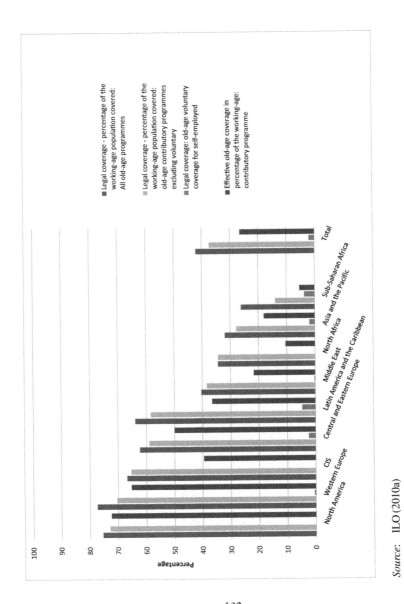

Source: ILO (2010a)

Figure 7.2 Coverage of old-age pensions by region, 2008–09

132

matured or from which earlier generations are excluded. In Latin America as a whole, where the early introduction of schemes means that they have had time to mature, actual coverage is largely constrained by the size of the formal labour market to between 30 and 60 per cent. It is, though, higher in Bolivia (69 per cent) as a result of the provision of 'universal' (if small) pensions, in Brazil (85 per cent) where a contributory system is supplemented by tax-funded social pensions, and in Uruguay (87 per cent). In Africa, it is typical for less than a tenth of the elderly population to receive pensions, the exceptions being Mauritius, Namibia and Lesotho where, as in Brazil, contributory pensions are complemented by universal social pensions, and South Africa where nominally means-tested provision achieves coverage of over 90 per cent. Pensions in most Asian and Pacific countries reach less than 40 per cent of the elderly population; the only exceptions are Nepal, Hong Kong and the minute Micronesian island of Naura.[1]

Comprehensive provision (in the sense that all eight risks are covered) is rare in the developing world, in marked contrast with OECD countries. Only Algeria and Tunisia in the whole of Africa have comprehensive systems whereas in Europe solely Turkey (with no family allowances) does not. Other African countries omit a single risk: Cape Verde, Equatorial Guinea, Guinea, Morocco and Namibia have no unemployment benefit; Egypt and the Seychelles have no family allowances; and South Africa provides no survivors benefit (ILO 2010b). Five countries in the Latin American and Caribbean region (Argentina, Brazil, Chile, Colombia and Uruguay) have comprehensive systems, while in Asia, leaving aside former Soviet countries, only Iran, Hong Kong, Mongolia and Thailand can lay claim to comprehensive provision, although, as in every case, this does not mean that all persons experiencing a risk are covered either legally or in practice. Thirty per cent of African countries have what the ILO considers to be very limited statutory coverage of risks (four or fewer branches) and another 48 per cent have limited provision (five to six) (ILO 2010b). The corresponding percentages for Asia and the Pacific region are 25 per cent and 28 per cent respectively, and 3 per cent and 53 per cent for Latin America and the Caribbean.

If coverage is one criterion for assessing provision, level of benefits is another. Assessing the relative generosity of benefits is exceedingly difficult especially given the diversity of the developing world. Table 7.1 presents social security spending, net of that on health, as a percentage of gross domestic product (GDP). Globally, the average country spends 7.1 per cent of its total wealth on social security transfers: among low-income countries the corresponding value is 2.0 per cent; in Latin America and the Caribbean it is 4.0 per cent, in Asia and the Pacific 3.6

per cent, and in Sub-Saharan Africa 2.3 per cent. A better measure takes account of differences in the size of countries and is interpretable as the proportion of GDP that the average resident might receive through social security payments; values of 2.8 per cent, 3.6 per cent and 7.1 for Sub-Saharan Africa, Asia and the Pacific, and Latin America and the Caribbean respectively, compared with 18 per cent for Europe, underline the contrasts between the global North and South in terms of the overall generosity of their social security systems.

Table 7.1 Social security spending by region and national income level

	Total social security expenditure as a percentage of GDP		
	GDP-weighted	Simple average	Population-weighted
Region			
Western Europe	17.9	16.7	18.0
Central and Eastern Europe	14.5	13.9	14.1
North America	9.0	9.3	9.0
North Africa	10.5	9.5	11.0
Commonwealth of Independent States (CIS)	9.0	8.2	9.9
Asia and the Pacific	7.9	3.6	3.6
Middle East	8.8	6.6	7.6
Latin America and the Caribbean	6.6	4.0	7.1
Sub-Saharan Africa	5.6	2.3	2.8
National income			
Low income	2.1	2.0	2.3
Middle income	6.2	6.6	4.8
High income	12.7	12.9	12.8
Total (138 countries)	11.3	7.1	5.7

Source: ILO (2010b)

To turn finally to the mechanisms of provision, it is usual to distinguish between financing, allocation and delivery. Financing can be achieved through direct taxation, contributions variously apportioned between government, employers and individuals (either in the role of employees or as members of collectives), and via donors. Allocation can be universal or selective whether based on a shortage of resources, conditional on some behavioural change, or accessed through previous contributions or membership of a collective. Delivery can be made in cash or in kind through a government agency, private company or an NGO.

Unfortunately, a lack of systematic evidence makes it impossible to adequately characterize the range of mechanisms employed in the developing world, but some observations are in order. First, the relative importance of social insurance and social assistance benefits differs markedly between developing countries, but generally social insurance is less important than in the developed world. This is partly because of the difficulties of administering insurance within an informal labour market and without a sophisticated administrative capacity. However, it is also because social security provision in the developing world is more often targeted at poverty relief rather than income maintenance or the production of social cohesion. The figures presented in Table 7.2 should be treated with caution since they are not based on a comprehensive set of countries but suggest that reliance on social assistance is particularly great in some African countries – reaching 72 per cent of social protection spending in Malawi and 56 per cent in Mauritius. It is also substantial in parts of Asia (51 per cent in India and 53 per cent in Bangladesh), in certain Middle Eastern countries (especially Iran, Yemen and possibly Iraq where the amount of assistance payments exceeds social insurance) and in a number of Caribbean states (less so in Latin America). Nowhere in Europe, except for Ireland, does social assistance account for more than a fifth of total spending and in the vast majority of countries it much less than 10 per cent (ILO 2011).

The implication of the above reliance on social assistance is that the state, possibly with the help of external donors, directly funds a greater proportion of social security spending in many developing countries than in Europe, where contributions from employers and employees help to allay the costs. However, such evidence as there is equally suggests that governments in Europe contribute to social insurance to a greater degree than those in the developing world. On average, European governments meet over a quarter of the contribution cost of retirement pensions, whereas in the developing world government contributions are generally negligible (ILO 2011). Indeed, the state or sovereign provident fund is a form of social security that is more prevalent in the global South than in the North, and is a system of either compulsory or voluntary personal saving, usually with no state contributions and only occasionally contributions from employers. Unlike social insurance schemes, there is no

*Table 7.2   The relative importance of social insurance and social
            assistance by region, 2005 or earlier*

	Social insurance expenditures as a % of GDP	Social assistance expenditures as a % of GDP	Total social protection expenditures as a % of GDP	Social assistance as a % of social protection
Sub-Saharan Africa (n = 9)	1.5	3.1	4.3	61.9
East Asia Pacific (n = 9)	2.6	0.9	2.5	27.2
Eastern Europe and Central Asia (n = 25)	8.0	2.0	10.2	21.4
Latin America Caribbean (n = 25)	3.8	1.3	5.0	33.0
Middle East North Africa (n = 14)	3.0	3.6	6.6	45.0
South Asia (n = 5)	1.4	0.9	2.3	38.3
OECD (n = 23)	13.2	2.5	15.7	15.9

Source: World Bank (2008)

pooling of risk or redistribution among participants in the fund, although the aggregate funds are often invested in government activity such as housing provision. Examples include the Central Provident Fund in Singapore, the Employees' Provident Fund Organisation of India and Malaysia's compulsory Employees Provident Fund.

Social security, notably social assistance, is more often delivered in kind in developing countries than in the global North and takes a number of forms, such as public works schemes or food and seed distribution (see Chapter 9). Developing countries have similarly pioneered conditional cash schemes that are beginning to be experimented with by economically advanced countries, such as Mayor Bloomberg's programme in New York (Riccio et al. 2010). Under such schemes benefits are paid conditional on beneficiaries participating in socially desirable activities, such as the immunization or education of offspring, thereby achieving multiple social objectives often with the intention of tackling the intergenerational persistence of poverty (Chapter 8). Comparatively recently developing countries have also developed community-based initiatives, albeit often orchestrated by NGOs and initiatives from the UN and the World Bank, such as the micro-finance schemes pioneered by Professor Muhammad Yunus and the Grameen Bank in Bangladesh (see Chapter 10). These in some respects resemble the local and trade union-based mutual associations that tended to be supplanted by government institutions as welfare states took hold in Western Europe. Some, such as the 'savings and credit cooperative organizations' in Africa, are direct derivatives of the credit unions first established in Germany in the 1850s, which emphasize the need to save before members can borrow. Credit unions are particularly significant in the Caribbean region, where penetration exceeds 50 per cent of the economically active population; but there are 20 million members in India and about four million each in Kenya and Brazil (WCCU 2011). Credit unions, of which there are some 53,000 in 100 countries, are owned by their members, who have exclusive rights to save and borrow from their unions, whereas micro-finance, more broadly defined, allows investment from beyond the pool of members.

To summarize, while social security provision is widespread in the developing world, actual coverage, though varied, is generally low; it is frequently exceedingly low, contributing to the perpetuation of high rates of poverty. Social insurance is largely confined to the formal labour market sector and therefore social assistance, delivered as categorical or means-tested provision, is typically more important than in the global North. While the ILO aspiration that social security should be a fulfilled right is rarely achieved, there are positive developments and striking innovation in some countries.

CHALLENGES TO THE EXTENSION OF SOCIAL SECURITY

Set against the human rights framework referred to in the opening section of this chapter, the level of social security provision is clearly inadequate in many parts of the developing world. Factors that help to explain this situation – limited economic development, informality of production, corruption – are in part the challenges that have to be addressed if provision is to be improved.

Resources

The popular view is that without reasonable per capita income, social security is a luxury that cannot be afforded (Dicke 2012; Hagemejer 2009). Indeed, many governments seem similarly to have presumed that social security is not an option in low-income countries, fearful that it would undermine prospects for growth and might foster resentment and social instability. However, the fact that systems have been successfully implemented in some low- and middle-income countries suggests that resources may be less of a barrier than expectations, a lack of political will and of the preparedness to create the necessary fiscal space.

Recent estimates from the ILO suggest that probably even the poorest countries could sustain a minimum social security package comprising basic child benefits, an employment guarantee scheme (100 days) for the persons of active working age, and a universal basic old-age and disability pension (ILO 2008).[2] The projected cost ranged from around 2.2 per cent for Viet Nam and Pakistan to 5.7 per cent for Nepal, and around 5 per cent for Kenya and Tanzania. While this level of provision, together with universal access to essential health care, would in some cases mean more than a doubling of expenditure and might need some initial donor support, it would generally be sustainable from domestic resources by 2030, given reasonable growth rates, and could already be supported by countries such as India, Pakistan and Viet Nam.

At the technical level, there are numerous strategies available for creating the fiscal space required to implement a basic social security package. Given past history and current global finances, deficit funding, a strategy used to kick-start provision in many OECD countries following World War II, may not be generally available. In contrast, development assistance from international donors is probably essential for most of the very poorest countries, but it is unpredictable in the long term and runs the risk of creating aid dependency and even of recipient countries losing control over their domestic policy. Moreover, given that the cost of providing an income floor across all less developed countries would cost 112 per cent of the total official global aid budget, it is unlikely to be a strategy available to all (ILO 2011). (Targeting just the least developed countries, which would be sufficient to lift 442 million people out of poverty, would reduce costs to just 38 per cent of official global aid, a target that might not be beyond reach.) More sustainable, and necessary in the longer term, is domestic revenue generation through a combination of taxes on individual and corporate incomes, property, wealth, trade and sales (though this can be regressive if imposed on basic necessities), and individual and trade, and individual and corporate contributions to funded insurance systems. While tax administration requires an appropriate infrastructure, the evidence is that efficient tax collection is possible in most settings. Taxing the informal sector, as already noted, presents challenges, but in addition to value-added taxes, associational taxation entailing a bargain between government and business associations (as introduced in the informal transport sector in Ghana as long ago as 1987), and 'forfeit' systems whereby small businesses pay taxes in relation to directly observable characteristics such as rent paid or size of business premises, have proved viable (Joshi and Ayee 2009; Thirsk, 1997).

At a political level, the challenge is one of commitment to raising funds or redistributing expenditure. Evidence of the benefits of social security provision listed above together with the political momentum generated as social security provisions spread across the developing world may help to incentivize laggard governments.

Informal Economy

An undoubted constraint on the development of social security is the dominance of informal economic activity in much of the developing world; indeed, the definition of informal employment often includes lack of access to social security (ILO 2010b). The nature of informal labour markets is discussed in detail in Chapter 5. Therefore, suffice it to say that, as in other regards, the experience of developing countries is very varied. Moreover, while informal employment is apparently falling according to the narrow definition of own-account workers and their family members, more comprehensive measures suggest a more variegated picture with falls in Africa, little change in Latin America and rises in Asia after a period of decline during the 1990s (Figure 7.3) (Bacchetta et al. 2009).

An important driver of the informal economy is the existence of abject poverty in the context of a labour supply that exceeds demand (Pellissery and Walker 2007). Without social security the labour market is unable to clear this poverty, since the point at which labour demand matches labour supply generates wages that are so low that they are at or below subsistence level. Faced with the need to make ends meet, jobs take the edge off destitution, but skilled workers are forced to accept jobs requiring less skill, while others involuntarily work less than full time. In such settings, employers tend to minimize employment costs by paying low wages, evading taxes and refusing to meet social security contributions or to contribute to provident schemes; and they compensate for their lack of capital investment by overstaffing. Productivity is typically low. This reinforces the pattern of low wages and many workers directly sell their labour to employers on a daily or even hourly basis, or else they create their own work or supplement low wages through self-employment. In sum, therefore, the lack of social security perpetuates the

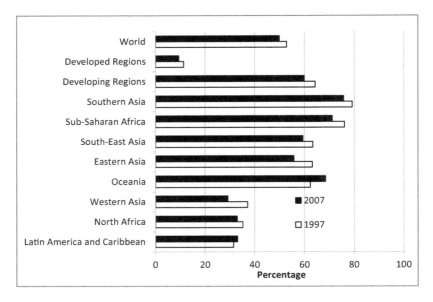

Source: Bacchetta et al. (2009)

Figure 7.3 Own-account and contributing family workers, 1997 and 2007

dominance of the informal economy the characteristics of which inhibit the introduction of social security provision.

Furthermore, the informality appears to increase some of the risks that social security would protect against. It prevents developing countries from fully benefiting from open trade and globalization because it inhibits countries from developing a sizeable, diversified export base due to the limited capacity of companies to grow. Workers find it difficult to acquire generic transferable skills, and firms lack the ability to generate sufficient profits to reward innovation and risk taking and hence fail to grow and/or to develop high-quality products and services. Hence wages remain low and casual employment is perpetuated. Moreover, economies with above average-sized informal economies are more than three times as likely to experience adverse effects of global economic crises as those with lower rates of informality. This is due to their chronic inability rapidly to respond to events and an associated lack of protective infrastructure, including social security, that could enable governments to implement counter-cyclical fiscal and monetary policies (Bacchetta et al. 2009).

The more pragmatic definitions of informality point to activity that falls de facto or de jure outside the reach of law (ILO 2010a). They highlight that, both by definition and in practice, social security legislation cannot easily have purchase on informal activity. The task of collecting contributions and linking them to payments requires employers and employees to be visible and reachable by governmental agencies, levels of compliance to be high so that trust in the system can be sustained, and employment relationships to be sufficiently stable for records to be established and satisfactorily maintained. Traditional social security is a lifetime activity, requiring a vision of, or hope for, collective and individual futures in which it is both appropriate and possible to set resources aside in the present to provide enhanced incomes in the future. Not surprisingly, therefore, it has often proved difficult to extend social security in settings characterized by subsistence-level incomes and without formal structures that facilitate outreach to employers and workers. Strategies discussed below have largely sought, first, to extend the boundaries of formal employment, and more recently to adapt social security to the demands of informality.

Limited Administrative Capacity

A further, not unrelated, challenge is that of the administrative capacity to design and deliver social security systems. Apart from the important requirement of political will, there is typically an additional need for policy coordination, design and delivery. Political priority needs to be established, resources raised, targeting principles determined and delivery mechanisms developed, implemented and monitored. For the most part, political mobilization and design will necessarily be located in government even if delivery is undertaken or assisted by NGOs or the private sector. Therefore, there is the requirement that government has the institutional capacity to manage policy development often involving cross-departmental working, which in turn requires the acumen and concentration of political influence necessary to secure adequate resources and to overcome competing institutional interests.

Delivery, particularly if any form of contributory system is entailed, requires the collection as well as the dispersion of funds, associated systems of accounting and accountability and some registration mechanism that facilitates identification of claimants. It is sometimes suggested that a centralized 'single registry' management information system, similar to that pioneered by Brazil's *Bolsa Familia* cash-transfer programme and adopted by countries as disparate as Ghana, Zambia and Pakistan, is preferable, although a centralized scheme normally needs to be accompanied by a decentralized delivery system that makes direct contact with beneficiaries and/or contributors (Samson et al. 2006). Given this, capacity building is typically required at the local level involving staff training as well as significant capital investment in office equipment, information and communications technology and probably vehicles for outreach activities.

Different social security mechanisms place varying demands on government capacity. While means-tested systems hold out the possibility of targeting resources on the most needy, they require sophisticated systems for identifying and assessing eligible recipients, especially when operated at the individual or household level as is the norm in the global North. Household resources, including income in kind and self-production, need to be assessed, which typically demands a degree of literacy on the part of the applicant and site visits by officials. Even neighbourhood-level assessment, as adopted by Mexico's *Oportunidades*, requires high-quality spatial data, while in the Mexican case this is supplemented in urban areas with individual data due, in part, to the heterogeneous composition of neighbourhoods. Moreover, a conditional cash transfer, such as *Oportunidades*, in which receipt is made conditional on behavioural change, requires further levels of infrastructural development and administrative sophistication given the need to make available the educational and protective health services that recipients are required to use and systems to monitor such usage. In contrast, universal benefits, such as Child Support and Disability Grants in South Africa and the Basic Retirement Pension in Mauritius, that are available to everyone in broad demographic groups, are much easier to deliver in jurisdictions with limited administrative capacity.

Not implementing a social security system because of limited administrative capacity may, of course, serve to delay the development of administrative infrastructures. Governments have therefore variously employed a number of strategies to circumvent limited capacity including contracting with private sector companies, such as Maximus and Serco, to deliver systems, partnerships with NGOs and staged introduction, which allow for the gradual and iterative build-up of expertise and experience that facilitates a gradual expansion of coverage. Each approach necessarily has attendant advantages and disadvantages, including the profit motive, which can result in creaming – that is, servicing easy-to-reach clients ahead of others; the commitment of some NGOs to particular models of implementation; and sometimes the limited ability of NGOs to scale up and to manage delivery in the long term.

Corruption

Corruption, defined to include bribery, nepotism and the evasion of tax and social security payments, is reported to be widespread in much of the developing world, often being linked to economic informality, low wages, high inequality, tribal and ethnic differences and collectivist cultures that prioritize the well-being of group over the behaviour of individuals (TI 2011). There is evidence that corruption reduces economic growth (Lambsdorff 2005), results in less social expenditure, ostensibly because it offers fewer rent-seeking opportunities (Mauro 1998), adds to administration costs and inefficiency and effects a transfer of resources away from poorer people thereby further increasing inequality (Gupta et al. 2002). The failure of employers to register employees, or to make contributions on their behalf, undermines the public's trust in social security institutions, while collusion in non-payment by employers and employees prioritizes short-term wants above long-term security and understates the true value of social security. Furthermore, the failure to collect revenues means, with funded schemes, less finance to invest, higher premiums or lower benefits and, for pay-as-you-go designs, lower benefits, more subsidy or the need for greater targeting.

Pellissery (2006) has documented how access to income maintenance and employment creation schemes in rural India is mediated by an intermediary class, comprising state officials and local elites, that determines programme entry through systems of 'patronage' fuelled by social, economic and political pay-offs. Proof of eligibility almost always requires the intervention of a member of the local elite that favours its own casual employees. Claimants, often the casual employees of members of the local elite, are 'engineered for a fit' (Houtzager 2003) often by means of petty corruption and forged documents, resulting in uptake by ineligibles and the exclusion of often poorer eligible applicants aligned with weaker factions and/or drawn from minority ethnic communities.

The scale of abuse and evasion of contributions can be substantial. It has been estimated that, as recently as 2005, the social security system in the Philippines collected only 26 per cent of contributions due for employees working in the formal sector. Moreover, revenues could have been almost doubled had the estimated 5.1 million informal workers been brought into the scheme (Ortega 2006). Improved enforcement in India in 2001 resulted in the addition of almost 116,000 enterprises and 11.5 million workers to the Employees' Provident Fund, 5.79 million of them first-time members (Viswanathan 2006).

This last example, of the Indian Employees' Provident Fund, demonstrates that the problem of corruption need not be insuperable. Reducing corruption nevertheless requires the institutional commitment and administrative infrastructure to implement greater monitoring, improved management and internal security systems and better enforcement. Often cheaper and more effective are programme designs and delivery systems that are resistant to corruption. Cash payments are easier to monitor precisely than payments in kind. Simple eligibility criteria with limited discretion minimize scope for bribery. Direct delivery eliminates intermediaries and limits the potential for diversion, while the imposition of conditionality can guard against 'ghost' beneficiaries (van Stolk and Tesliuc 2010). It has also been suggested that streamlined atomistic systems which establish a direct relation between the government office (typically at national or federal level) and the recipient are also robust to corruption because they create no space, opportunity, or incentive for local communities to promote sectional interests illicitly (Grimes and Wängnerud 2010).

Demographics

Finally, it might be argued that demographic trends combined with low income have prevented the further development of social security in developing countries. Certainly demographic circumstances in the global South have not generally fostered growth in social security over recent decades. In particular, dependency ratios, that is, the number of children and old people as a proportion of the working-age population, have remained very high. However, future trends look much more auspicious. A low ratio indicates that the burden of support is shared between a large number of potentially economically active persons; and whereas at the turn of the century the dependency ratio in developing countries was much higher than the world average, by 2050 it is projected to be noticeably lower (Table 7.3). This is because the rise in old-age dependency will be more than offset by falling fertility and a consequent decline in youth dependency. This change is particularly marked in Sub-Saharan Africa, and in the least developed countries more generally, where dependency ratios are predicted to fall from 88.5 per cent and 84 per cent to 52.4 per cent and 52.5 per cent respectively. As always the situation is not everywhere the same. The legacy of the one-child policy in China means that the cohort born before the policy was introduced is becoming economically dependent as it ages on the much smaller cohorts born later. In the least developed countries, however, noticeable declines have already been registered since 2000, and the challenge ahead is to ensure productive occupations for those of working age.

A further consideration that needs to be taken into account is migration. Even though it may not directly impede the development of social security in developing countries, the scale – estimated globally at 105.5 million in 2010 – within and between developing countries and out to the generally more prosperous North – necessarily affects the economies and tax base of the exporting countries (ILO 2010c). While migrants often add to the incomes of their countries of origin through remittances, they generally lie beyond the reach of domestic taxation and insurance contributions. Moreover, migrants are often denied access to social security in destination countries due to eligibility criteria based on periods of employment and residence, coverage being restricted to nationals or permanent residents, and the exclusion of workers in the informal economy (in which migrants are often concentrated) from mainstream social security provision. At the same time, migrants risk losing entitlement to social security benefits in their countries of origin due to their absence, leaving them with little protection in periods of sickness or during old age. They also encounter additional risks in the employment market, with occupational accidents being twice as high for migrants to Europe as for the local workforce.

There have been, and remain, substantial obstacles to the development of social security provision in the global South: lack of financial resources, irregular and informal employment, limited administrative and sometimes policymaking capacity. However, despair and inaction are entirely inappropriate. Social security arguably represents an investment in human capital that is as important as, if not more so than, the economic capital investment of which it may be, in many situations, a necessary precursor. Moreover, the demographic concerns of the global North, accompanied by somewhat hysterical talk of a demographic time bomb, are generally not replicated in the global South despite a growing population of elders. There is much to play for and considerable innovation to be learned from.

INNOVATION IN SOCIAL SECURITY PROVISION

Despite structural challenges, global spending on social security (net of health) in low-income countries has increased from 1.3 of GDP in 2000 to 2.3 per cent, a rise of 76 per cent; it increased by 37 per cent in middle-income countries and by just 5 per cent in high-income countries (ILO 2010b). The impact of the recession on this trend and of austerity

Table 7.3 *Total and old-age dependency ratios by region, 2000–2050*

	Total dependency ratio (%)					Old-age dependency ratio (%)				
	2000	2005	2010	2030	2050	2000	2005	2010	2030	2050
Sub-Saharan Africa	88.5	86.0	83.5	65.4	52.4	5.7	5.7	5.8	6.4	9.1
Africa	83.9	80.2	77.6	62.6	52.5	6.0	6.0	6.1	7.4	10.8
Asia	57.4	52.5	49.0	48.2	54.4	9.0	9.5	9.9	17.0	26.7
Europe	47.8	46.6	46.3	59.6	73.5	21.8	23.3	23.8	36.1	47.5
Latin America and the Caribbean	60.2	56.4	52.8	48.8	57.5	9.2	9.8	10.6	18.3	30.7
North America	50.9	49.2	49.1	60.9	63.6	18.7	18.6	19.5	32.2	35.9
Oceania	55.6	54.3	53.8	59.7	60.6	15.4	15.7	16.6	25.5	30.0
More-developed regions	48.5	47.8	48.1	61.1	71.3	21.3	22.6	23.6	36.2	44.9
Less-developed regions	61.9	57.2	53.8	50.8	53.8	8.1	8.5	8.8	14.6	22.5
Least-developed countries	84.0	80.0	76.0	61.8	52.5	5.8	5.8	5.8	7.3	11.3
Less-developed regions, excluding least-developed countries	58.9	53.9	50.4	48.6	54.1	8.4	8.9	9.3	16.1	25.6
Less-developed regions, excluding China	67.4	63.0	59.1	51.4	51.9	7.3	7.6	7.9	12.2	19.3
World	59.1	55.3	52.7	52.3	56.0	10.9	11.3	11.6	17.8	25.3

Source: ILO (2010b)

policies being pursued in Europe is not yet clear; but expenditures will have necessarily risen at least initially as they are deliberately counter-cyclical. While spending in the richest countries is still five times greater as a proportion of GDP than in the poorest, the established dynamics seem to be that of catch-up, helped in some low-income countries by more sustained economic growth.

In this environment it is appropriate to accentuate the positive and to focus on the innovation that is taking place in response to the challenges identified above. Mention has already been made of the advance of conditional cash transfers that are discussed in Chapter 8, the public work programmes described in Chapter 9, and the micro-finance programmes covered in Chapter 10, all of which are initiatives indigenous to the developing world and which have already been implemented with varying degrees of success. Van Ginneken (2009), concluding an extensive review of social security conducted under the auspices of the International Social Security Association, chose to focus on Sub-Saharan Africa. While, as noted above, coverage of social security in this region is low, van Ginneken nevertheless detected three important developments in a region that shares challenges common among developing countries: a small and hardy growing formal labour market, informal workers themselves prioritizing health care over pensions, and the limited capacity of informal workers to contribute to formal social security.

Penetrating the Informal Sector

Governments are beginning to plan for the extension of social security coverage with the goal of eventually attaining universal coverage. Senegal is an example where reform is being driven forward by the state supported, symbiotically, by a shared will to combat all forms of vulnerability fostered by social dialogue with workers, trade unions, and stakeholders that has built mutual understanding (Thiam 2009). Extension has required addressing numerous concerns to do with clarity of the link between contributions and benefits, limited trust of social security, and the burden of compliance for employers (large and small) and for workers (Fultz and Stanovnik 2004). In Senegal non-compliance was a major problem with, in 2002, more than half of legally covered private-sector salaried workers evading contributions. A special initiative has been established under the National Programme for Social Protection to extend membership in all social insurance institutions by strengthening and clarifying the incentives of contribution compliance through information, communication and education activities and strengthened monitoring of the affiliation of salaried workers. Attempts have been made to

extend social coverage to day-labourers, requiring adaptation of the
contribution system after earlier attempts failed as systems were
swamped by the number of salary declarations submitted by employers
for processing.

Ghana created its Informal Sector Fund in 2008 in an attempt to reach
the 80 per cent of the nation's labour force that were excluded from the
Social Security and National Insurance Trust. While the principal goal is
to provide resources for retirement, the scheme's success is built on
provisions that enable participants to use their savings as collateral,
enabling them to access microcredit to support more sustaining livelihoods (Samson 2009). Members can also withdraw part of their contributions to cope with financial shocks, to pay school fees or health
insurance premiums or to meet other urgent expenses. Zambia has also
sought to provide social insurance for some categories of informal
workers, including the self-employed, by reforming the National Pension
Scheme to allow workers to join the contributory system on a voluntary
basis. Uptake of voluntary initiatives can be much improved through
linkages with organized groups of workers who can promote the scheme
and foster class applications.

Unemployment benefit for the formal sector is a rarity in the developing world, and extending it to the informal sector poses great challenges.
In 2002/3 South Africa successfully imposed a requirement on domestic
workers and their employers to make contributions to the Unemployment
Insurance Fund, and in so doing extended provision of its contributory
scheme to the largest, but possibly most tractable, component of the
informal sector. Packaging provision to cover multiple risks arguably
makes registration more attractive, and so insurance against unemployment is combined with maternity or adoption benefits as well as benefits
in case of illness or death. In Brazil, *Bolsa Família*, a conditional cash
transfer that reaches over 60 per cent of the households in the four
poorest income deciles, has the effect of providing a form of unemployment assistance and, indeed, has been credited with reducing the number
of people in forced employment by providing an exit door (Uthoff 2009).
While Argentina has an unemployment insurance scheme, it does not
reach far into the informal sector, and so in 2009 the government
introduced by decree a means-tested family allowance scheme targeted
on the children of unemployed parents, those in the informal sector
including domestic workers, and those in rural areas with incomes below
the minimum monthly wage.

Universal Social Pensions

A second notable development is that countries such as Mauritius, Botswana, Lesotho and Namibia have determined to pay universal social pensions. Sub-Saharan Africa is, of course, not unique in this. Chile, Ecuador and Brazil have established fully tax-financed non-contributory pension schemes, while Mexico and Peru have such schemes for the neediest persons (Uthoff 2009). However, the Mauritian strategy of seeking to extend coverage by better integrating tax-financed non-contributory pensions into a three-tier retirement system has become a model for policy discussion and developments in South Africa, Kenya and Zambia. The first tier provides a universal non-contributory minimum income guarantee for older people (the Basic Retirement Pension). The second tier comprises mandatory income-related pension schemes – the National Pension Fund and the National Savings Fund – while the third tier is made up of various targeted voluntary schemes that seek to reach persons not covered by the first two tiers.

The non-contributory pension scheme implemented in South Africa, second only in size to that of Brazil, is not currently universal as in Mauritius, but is means-tested by assessment of the combined incomes of beneficiaries and their partners (Olivier 2009). Effective means-testing requires a sophisticated administrative infrastructure with exemplary financial control, which may restrict it as an option in some countries. In Brazil and Mexico the targeting of social pensions is geographic, such that in Mexico it is universal for persons living in rural communities of fewer than 2,500 persons whereas in Brazil eligibility is established by 12 years' work in agriculture. Universal non-contributory pensions are not only administratively simpler than means-tested ones, they can readily reach the informal sector and address poverty directly while avoiding disincentives for persons to add to their basic provision. Even the South African non-contributory pension has been shown to reduce child poverty because each pensioner's income helps five other people and the means test ignores the incomes of non-dependants in the household (Taylor 2002).

Micro-insurance

A third development is the growth of micro-insurance. Since microfinance is a topic covered in detail in Chapter 10, just three points are offered here. The first is that social insurance has to be sold rather than simply provided. Where compulsory, the 'sale' is political; where voluntary, prospective participants must see it as relevant and worthwhile.

Second, using agencies already close to the target population is often more effective than creating new organizations. Third, packaging risks together can reduce costs as well as appearing to be more attractive.

These points can be illustrated with reference to the Self-Employed Women's Association (SEWA) which was founded in Gujarat province in India in 1972 (Ranson et al. 2007). A trade union representing primarily self-employed women working in the informal sector engaged in activities such as head carrying, rubbish collecting (as 'pickers'), door-to-door sales, home-based work and sales, and small-scale commerce, it established a micro-insurance scheme, VimoSEWA, in 1992, used in 2008 by 214,000 members. The insurance provided is specific to the needs of the membership; it covers multiple contingencies including health and maternity care, death, invalidity and, importantly, insurance against the loss or deterioration of work equipment or the home. Female counsellors, known as *Aagewans*, usually recruited and trained from the membership, conduct home visits to explain the importance of the scheme and to assist with applications, claims and renewals. VimoSEWA was backed by the Life Insurance Corporation of India and the interest on a revolving fund (Chatterjee and Ranson 2003) but in 2009 it became officially the National Insurance VimoSEWA Cooperative Ltd – a multi-state co-operative society with areas of operation extended to the states of Rajasthan, Madhya Pradesh, Delhi and Bihar.

VimoSEWA is unique to the Indian context in that a trade union should represent workers in the informal economy and be officially recognized as doing so. It demonstrates, though, that informal workers, many illiterate and working in the most lowly of occupations, can be organized and can themselves organize collective forms of social security. This experience demonstrates once again that workers in the informal economy need not remain outside the reach of social protection.

CONCLUSIONS

It is impossible to adequately represent in mere words the phenomenon that is social security in the developing world. For billions of people it is effectively absent in any formal sense, and its absence reinforces the fear associated with a life lived at the edge of subsistence. For some, however, it makes retirement possible and, for a few, even financially secure and carefree. For yet others it reduces the risk of infanticide when families are faced with an extra mouth that cannot be fed; and for some it offers a way out of forced labour and financial slavery.

Such dramatic contrasts are the reality of the world, not typically the content of academic texts. This chapter has demonstrated a shortfall in provision in many developing countries; it has identified some of the reasons for this shortfall and certain constraints on the development of social security policy. It has also illustrated a small number of the plethora of innovative, interesting and variously successful initiatives that have been put in place to circumvent the constraints and offer social security to populations that need it.

The goal of collective security, of adequate resources for all in the community, is very probably universal, although the community is not necessarily viewed as synonymous with the nation state. The traditional mechanism for the delivery of social security payments made with respect to insured contingencies and funded by the contributions of employees and employers, and latterly by governments – is culturally and historically specific. It relates to Western Europe in the late industrial age, to Fordist and bureaucratic employment models and to single male breadwinner, nuclear families. It was a model exported through colonial channels and a post-colonial legacy of international agencies. However, it is not likely to be a model for the future in either the developed or developing world. Instead, new models have emerged such as micro-insurance, conditional cash transfers, multiple-risk insurance and universal social pensions and benefits that are targeted without recourse to individual means-testing and are well adapted to the diverse circumstances of developing countries. Some of these models have already been copied by OECD countries, and yet others may be copied if the trend towards increasingly flexible labour markets combined with calls for fiscal austerity continues.

NOTES

* The author would like to thank the guidance received from Timo Voipio but accepts full responsibility for the content of this chapter.
1. This is not true of states in the Asian and Pacific region that were formerly part of the Soviet Union or are members of the OECD. Hong Kong is also an exception.
2. The ILO package also included universal access to essential health care.

REFERENCES

Bacchetta, M., E. Ernst and J. Bustamante (2009), *Globalization and Informal Jobs in Developing Countries*, Geneva: International Labour Office and the Secretariat of the World Trade Organization.

Chatterjee, M. and M. Ranson (2003), 'Exploring the quality and coverage of community-based health insurance among the poor: the VimoSEWA experience', in L. Chen, J. Leaning and V. Narasimhan (eds), *Health and Human Security*, Cambridge, MA: Harvard University Press.

Dicke, V. (2012), 'Beyond charity', available at http://www.dandc.eu/articles/198244/index.en.shtml (accessed 5 June 2012).

Fultz, E. and T. Stanovnik (2004), 'Introduction', in E. Fultz and T. Stanovnik (eds), *Collection of Pension Contributions: Trends, Issues and Problems in Central and Eastern Europe*, Budapest: ILO, Subregional Office for Central and Eastern Europe, pp. 11–20.

Grimes, M. and L. Wängnerud (2010), 'Curbing corruption through social welfare reform? The effects of Mexico's conditional cash transfer program on good government', *American Review of Public Administration*, **40**(6), 671–90.

Gupta, S., H. Davoodi and R. Alonso-Terme (2002), 'Does Corruption Affect Income Inequality and Poverty?', *Economics of Governance*, **3**, 23–45.

Hagemejer, K. (2009), 'Can low-income countries afford basic social security?' in OECD, *Promoting Pro-Poor Growth: Social Protection*, Paris: OECD, pp. 89–110.

Houtzager, P.P. (2003), 'Introduction', in P. Houtzager and M. Moore (eds), *Changing Paths*, Ann Arbor: University of Michigan Press, pp. 1–31.

ILO (International Labour Organization) (2008), 'Can low-income countries afford basic social security?', Social Security Policy Briefings Paper No. 3, Geneva: ILO.

ILO (2010a), *Extending Social Security to All: A Guide Through Challenges and Options*, Geneva: ILO.

ILO (2010b), *World Social Security Report 2010/11: Providing Coverage in Times of Crisis and Beyond*, Geneva: ILO.

ILO (2010c), *International Labour Migration: A Rights-Based Approach*, Geneva: ILO.

ILO (2011), *Social Security for Social Justice and a Fair Globalization*, Labour Conference 2011, Report VI, Geneva: ILO.

Joshi, A. and J. Ayee (2009), 'Autonomy or organisation? Reforms in the Ghanaian internal revenue service', *Public Administration and Development*, **29**(4), 289–302.

Lambsdorff, J. (2005), *Consequences and Causes of Corruption – What do We Know from a Cross-Section of Countries?* Passau: University of Passau, Diskussionsbeitrag Nr. V-34-05.

Mauro, P. (1998), 'Corruption and the composition of government expenditure', *Journal of Public Economics*, **69**, 263–79.

Olivier, M. (2009), 'Informality, employment contracts and extension of social insurance coverage', Working Paper No. 9, Geneva: International Social Security Association.

Ortega, A. (2006), 'Administrative innovations to improve compliance and enforcement: the Philippines case', paper presented at the ISSA Regional Conference for Asia and the Pacific, New Delhi, 21–23 November.

Parijs, van P. (2002), 'Does basic income make sense as a worldwide project?' Paper presented at the IXth Congress of the Basic Income European Network International Labour Organisation, Geneva, 12–14 September.

Pellissery, S. (2006), 'The politics of social protection in rural India', doctoral thesis, Oxford University.

Pellissery, S. and R. Walker (2007), 'Social security options for informal sector workers: emergent economies and the Asia and Pacific region', *Social Policy and Administration*, **41**(4), 401–9.

Ranson, M., T. Sinha and M. Chatterjee (2007), 'Promoting access, financial protection and empowerment for the poor: VimoSEWA in India', in S. Bennett, L. Gilson and A. Mills (eds), *Health, Economic Development and Household Poverty: From Understanding to Action*, Abingdon: Routledge, pp. 203–24.

Riccio, J., N. Dechausay, D. Greenberg, C. Miller, Z. Rucks and N. Verma (2010), *Toward Reduced Poverty Across Generations: Early Findings from New York City's Conditional Cash Transfer Program*, New York: MDRC.

Samson, M. (2009), 'Good practice review: extending social security coverage in Africa', Working Paper No. 2, Geneva: International Social Security Association.

Samson, M., I. van Niekerk and K. Mac Quene (2006), *Designing and Implementing Social Transfer Programmes*, Cape Town: Economic Policy Research Institute.

Taylor, V. (2002), *Transforming the Present – Protecting the Future*, Report of the Committee of Inquiry into a Comprehensive System of Social Security for South Africa, Taylor Commission Report RP/53/2002, Johannesburg: Department of Social Development.

Thiam, B. (2009), 'Study on extending social protection in Senegal', Working Paper No. 3, Geneva: International Social Security Association.

Thirsk, W. (ed.) (1997), *Tax Reform in Developing Countries*, Washington, DC: World Bank.

TI (Transparency International) (2011), 'Corruption Perceptions Index 2011', available at http://cpi.transparency.org/cpi2011/results (accessed July 2012).

Uthoff, A. (2009), 'Social security for all in Latin America and the Caribbean will require integration of schemes and solidarity in financing', Working Paper No. 4, Geneva: International Social Security Association.

van Ginneken, G.T. (2009), 'Extending social security coverage: good practices, lessons learnt and ways forward', Working Paper No. 14, Geneva: International Social Security Association.

van Stolk, C. and E. Tesliuc (2010), 'Toolkit on tackling error, fraud and corruption in social protection programs', SP Discussion Paper 1002, Washington, DC: World Bank.

Viswanathan, A. (2006), 'Administrative innovations to improve compliance and enforcement: initiatives and innovations for re-assuring trust', paper presented at the ISSA Regional Conference for Asia and the Pacific, New Delhi, 21–23 November.

Walker, R. (2005), *Social Security and Welfare: Concepts and Comparisons*, Milton Keynes: Open University Press/McGraw-Hill.

WCCU (World Council of Credit Unions) (2011), *2010 Statistical Report*, available at http://www.woccu.org/publications/statreport (accessed July 2012).

World Bank (2008), *Spending on Social Safety Nets: Comparative Data Compiled from World Bank Analytic Work Database*, Washington, DC: World Bank.

8. The implications of conditionality in social assistance programmes

Paul Dornan and Catherine Porter

INTRODUCTION

Social protection measures as the cornerstone of social policy in low-income countries are riding high on the international development policy agenda. This has led to a rapid increase in the number of state-led schemes aimed at alleviating chronic poverty and vulnerability in lower-income countries since the turn of the twenty-first century with a growing focus on conditionality.

International policy attention to social protection is illustrated by the ongoing UN Social Protection Floor initiative, launched in 2009, focusing attention on social protection through the UN system (ILO and OECD 2011). The focus was sharpened by the recent global financial downturn (World Bank 2009a), with social protection positioned as a key tool to help countries and households both cope with the crisis and to deliver more 'inclusive development' (European University Institute and European Commission 2010). A key policy message is that countries with established social protection systems in place were able to react more quickly to the crisis (World Bank 2010). The Bank makes use of '3P' framework of Prevention, Promotion and Protection common in discussions about social protection (World Bank 2010), though it is perhaps worth noting that others have sought to introduce a 'transformative' element into the framework (see Devereux and Sabates-Wheeler 2004) to emphasize the potential of effective social protection in empowering marginalized groups. There is therefore an increasing and welcome recognition that one-off or patchwork solutions to social protection challenges are inadequate, and that more comprehensive systems are needed.

Alongside this international focus, national and nationally designed social protection schemes have been developed in low- and middle-income countries. Characterizing them as a 'development revolution from the Global South', Hanlon et al. (2010, p. 167) noted schemes in 45 countries covering 110 million families. Though positive, coverage of 110 million families in the global South implies that a very large number of very poor and vulnerable households are not covered. In 2001 France, Germany and the UK spent between 14.2 per cent and 17.9 per cent of GDPs on social security, compared with India (1.5 per cent), Ghana (2.1 per cent) and Kenya (0.3 per cent) of their (lower) GDPs (Townsend 2009a). A World Bank study on safety nets[1] using data from 2000 to 2004 showed that low-income countries spend on average 1.9 per cent of GDP on social assistance (Weigand and Grosh 2008).

Within this growing consensus about the importance of social protection per se, a series of interrelated and more practical questions has arisen: which groups are to be covered, how will these groups be reached, what benefits should they receive, and how will they be financed? Design issues then sit alongside political considerations which often receive little attention in technical debates (including financing and how support is to be delivered and sustained for a given scheme). Implementation and delivery concerns need to be addressed (if administrative systems are weak, how is need to be assessed and benefits distributed?).

There are different modes of delivering social protection policies in order to help reduce poverty, manage risk or replace income. Transfers tend to be categorized into social insurance, assistance and more categorical models. Insurance-based policies seek to replace income lost as a result of contingencies like old age or ill health), and have an element of prior contributions from beneficiaries. Social assistance refers to non-contributory policies, often directly aimed at poverty reduction. Some schemes also provide support to certain categories (for example, households with children or older people) usually in recognition of additional need or as a targeting method, and do so with or without an additional test of household need. These are broad distinctions since schemes often mix features of several categories. There are a number of examples of these mechanisms in developing countries; perhaps most prominent is the Child Support Grant in South Africa (Townsend 2009b). They are common in developed countries, and have considerable importance for reducing poverty rates (Bradshaw 2006), which may reflect more entrenched social provision and higher resources but also suggest a policy form (supporting families with children or with older or disabled members) regarded as an important element of the welfare contract by developed world populations.

The arguments in favour of unconditional categorical payments are that they can be relatively simple to administer, being primarily dependent on information about household membership (testing needs is likely to cause further complexity). Further, they can be a relatively efficient and effective way of targeting those in need (since households with children tend to be poorer) whilst keeping the targeting route simple. By not adding further conditions for receiving support, the payments also have the advantage of trusting poorer people to make their own decisions about how to bring up their children.

Access to a growing number of schemes in developing countries now includes a conditional element – a major focus of this chapter. Policymakers tend to use conditionality as a mechanism to meet objectives beyond the income needs of beneficiaries. In particular, recent debate has centred on requirements of conditional cash transfers (CCTs) that primarily target developing human capital development in children (through school attendance and health interventions). These may also serve a secondary purpose in building support for programmes by creating what may be seen as a 'something for something' relationship where 'redistribution is political feasible only when conditioned on "good behaviour"' (Fiszbein and Schady 2009, p. 11). This second justification for conditionality extends well beyond CCTs. Here we refer to the labour requirements within public works, to emphasize that these serve the dual function of employment creation and helping build public support for state intervention. Such conditions also have implications for children.

This chapter focuses on understanding the impact of conditionality within particular social protection instruments, drawing on a wider debate and citing evidence from the Young Lives longitudinal study of childhood poverty. The chapter draws substantially on Porter with Dornan (2010). We begin by considering some of the different types of schemes often used to deliver social protection, with a discussion of the conditionalities implied by each. In particular, we document the positive effects for beneficiaries but also possible unintended and negative consequences for vulnerable household members.

SOCIAL ASSISTANCE AND TYPES OF INSTRUMENTS

This section considers common types of mechanism adopted to meet social protection objectives, within the realm of social assistance (non-contributory) programmes. Within the broader focus on social protection, the question increasingly becomes not the appropriateness of social protection as an intervention by the state, but choices over the mechanisms used and how these suit objective(s) and context, together with effective implementation and sustained financing. The particular focus of this chapter is the implications for children of conditionality decisions with respect to social assistance.

We first consider some of the different instruments typically used. We make use of a definition from a recent joint statement of social protection and its effects on children: 'Social Protection is generally understood as a set of public actions that address poverty, vulnerability and exclusion as well as to provide means to cope with life's major risks throughout the life cycle' (DFID et al. 2009). Others have also argued recently for the particular importance of social protection measures for children (Handa et al. 2010). We assume that child sensitivity implies recognizing the need to think carefully about how children may experience household-based social protection measures, monitoring these effects, and adjusting policy accordingly.

Particular social assistance mechanisms are likely to vary depending on choices around several key parameters. Each choice requires trade-offs between objectives, so there is no clearly 'right' answer. Choices have to be made, first, about who is perceived to be in need, which will also affect the proportion of the population covered; and second, about how those targeted will be reached, including whether policymakers choose to extend entitlement to particular categories of households (for example, those with children), whether a scheme is area-based (for example, operating in only rural or poorer communities), and whether there is a test of means (perhaps judged in light of household circumstances, or through some community-based targeting mechanism). Schemes also vary with the conditions that recipients must meet, though most schemes contain some conditions (from work requirements in public works to health and education participation in typical CCTs). In many developing countries, the decisions are made in dialogue between governments and international development partners, who often finance a large proportion of social spending (for example, in Ethiopia social assistance represents 4.5 per cent of GDP, of which 4 per cent is contributed by international aid; Weigand and Grosh 2008).

CCTs have become the most prevalent type of social protection in Latin America (Rawlings and Rubio 2005). Much attention has been paid to this modality and examples such as the Mexican *Oportunidades* are well publicized. There has been some agreement in many respects that CCTs are politically more palatable as they target the 'deserving' poor who behave responsibly in order to receive the cash. Fiszbein and Schady (2009) summarize a large body of evidence (often generated by the World Bank) and make a strong case for CCTs as an effective poverty reduction strategy. The compelling argument is that CCTs provide both a safety net in terms of an income transfer in times of need and an investment in human capital through the conditionality that will help to break the intergenerational cycle of poverty. The explicit paternalistic assumption is that parents need to be encouraged to make the right choices over the health and education of their children. As with public work schemes, there is a risk this reinforces existing stereotypes. Hanlon et al. (2010), for example, quote a World Bank official and author of a widely cited review of CCTs as arguing at a meeting 'that there is a problem of "persistently misguided beliefs"' [i.e. not investing in human capital development] on the part of the poor that means their children remain poor' (2010, p. 128). This view seems to leave little room for understanding the weaknesses in the quality and availability of public services that poorer people are likely to encounter. We return to this point with empirical evidence from Young Lives in the following section.

It is also worth noting that it is often difficult to establish whether participation is driven by the effect of conditions or by the additional income provided through the scheme. Many evaluations have shown positive impacts on schooling and health, yet very few have actually compared a conditional transfer with an unconditional one. Rather, they have compared CCT beneficiaries with non-beneficiaries. One study managed to isolate the impact of conditionality in Mexico, due to some administrative errors that led to no conditionality being imposed on one particular group of people. The study found that school outcomes improved less for the group that was not monitored (de Brauw and Hoddinott 2008). However, a World Bank study of a programme in Malawi, using a randomized control trial (RCT) to target a subsidy to the families of adolescent girls, found that, in fact, conditionality does not reduce the probability of dropping out of school (Baird et al. 2009). However, the combination of an increase in the size of the transfer and imposing attendance conditions did improve both attendance and performance. A study of a pilot programme in Morocco reports similar findings on attendance (Benhassine et al. 2010, quoted in Banerjee and Duflo 2011, p. 80).

Hanlon et al. (2010) discuss the logical extension of CCTs to payment by results (conditioning, for example, not the use of clinics or attending school but child weight or test scores), and cite an example from Nicaragua which resulted in punishing the poorest households and encouraging perverse behaviour such as households having 'stuffed their children with food and water on growth monitoring days to avoid penalties' (2010, p. 132). There has also been criticism of this approach (e.g. Molyneux 2006) due to the pressure it puts on mothers; nevertheless, the popularity of CCTs is expanding quite rapidly in the African context.

Whether the paternalism implied by CCTs is more empowering in both the short term and long term is clearly somewhat contested within governments and international institutions.

CCTs both rely on the existence of a foundation of public services which households can access in order to meet conditions, and require good administrative records of participation to be kept. In principle, the existence of a CCT may help drive improvements in service quality or capacity, but both points suggest some caution in developing CCTs in lower-income countries where the public service environment may be weaker and where greater human capital improvements may be generated simply by redistributive methods.

An alternative modality with a conditional element is public works. Such schemes have a long history, in both the developed and the developing worlds. Del Ninno et al. (2009) review 20 years of evidence and show that public works have been used in response to one-off large shocks and repeated shocks, and also for poverty reduction. The main advantage of public works is arguably that participants are self-selecting, opting in themselves rather than having bureaucrats decide who is eligible. Ravallion (1991) outlines how labour-intensive rural public works projects have the potential to both screen and protect poor people, with the evidence suggesting few non-poor people want to participate,[2] while the direct and indirect transfer and insurance benefits to poorer people can be sizeable. Further, public works also have an element of 'beneficiary responsibility' by being conditional on the work done, and this may help make them more politically palatable as they are less likely to be seen as 'free handouts'. Equally, by running with the grain of this thinking, public works programmes fail to challenge, and may strengthen, assumptions that poorer people are somehow lazy and therefore need to be made to work, and perhaps by extension that lack of work ethic, rather than structured disadvantage, may be the explanation for their poverty (McCord 2008).

Public works are also thought to have a broader developmental impact if they create public assets (such as infrastructure); however, there is a tension between the objective of low wage rates to exclude richer groups from participation in targeted schemes and the creation of high-quality assets. McCord (2008) critically examines several problems with the use of public works as a safety net and argues that they are often used in an attempt to achieve more aims than are possible with one scheme – for example, offering one-off episodes of employment in response to structural unemployment (failure to deal with structural unemployment would therefore make graduation from such schemes difficult). In India the

Mahatma Gandhi National Rural Employment Guarantee Scheme (MGN-REG) scheme is self-selecting, but in Ethiopia administrators select participants in public work, although at a decentralized level that includes community leaders, since arguably demand would otherwise be too high even at very low wage rates. This leads to differing issues in the two countries.

The next section illustrates some key issues, drawing on empirical research from the Young Lives study, a rich and growing data set containing detailed information on many aspects of the lives of almost 12,000 children in four countries.[3] Since 2001, in Ethiopia, Peru, India and Vietnam children from two cohorts have been visited three times for quantitative surveys, and twice for qualitative studies. The 2,000 'index children' in each country were aged 6–18 months on the first visit, were resurveyed again at age four to five years and most recently aged seven to eight years. They will be followed until their 15th birthdays. The 'older cohort' children were aged seven to eight years in the first round of the quantitative survey, and in the third and most recent round were 15 years old.

DESIGN AND IMPLEMENTATION ISSUES IN PUBLIC WORKS

We first discuss the impact of conditionality in terms of a work requirement on the lives of children in Ethiopia and India. MGNREGS is now the largest public works programme in the world. It came into force in 2006 with the legislative backing of the National Rural Employment Guarantee Act (2005). It has been welcomed as a scheme which addresses weaknesses inherent in the earlier systems and is rights-based in its language.

In Ethiopia, the Productive Safety Net Programme (PSNP) is currently the largest public works in sub-Saharan Africa outside South Africa, and has attracted considerable policy and academic interest. The PSNP includes the provision of food or cash for work as well as direct support (DS) to poor households that are unable to participate in public works (around 20 per cent). This is complemented by the Other Food Security Program (OFSP), which provides households with access to a suite of improved agricultural technologies such as extension services, fertilizer, credit and other services (Government of Ethiopia 2004).

Some descriptive statistics on participation in MGNREGS for the Young Lives sample in 2006 show that the scheme is fairly well targeted at the poor. This echoes findings from some other studies to the effect that lower castes and holders of Antyodaya cards[4] were more likely to register for the programme (e.g. Jha et al. 2009; Shariff 2008). In the rural sample overall (just under 2,200 households with the two cohorts pooled), 45 per cent are participating in MGNREGS and 14 per cent worked more than ten days in the scheme. In terms of the wealth distribution in 2006, it was fairly well targeted – though with fewer participants in the bottom wealth quintile than in the second-bottom. This could be because poorer households have less labour available to work (because of disabilities or other health issues, or they may be further from a work site). In 2006 the MGNREGs scheme was still being rolled out in a limited number of districts; analysis of data from 2009 shows high coverage of job cards (four in five households in the sample). Coverage was highest for poorer households, but relatively few households were working the full 100 days possible (Galab et al. 2008, s. 5).

In the Young Lives sites in the Indian state of Andhra Pradesh, using 2006 data we found that the children of participants in both cohorts were significantly shorter than those of non-participants, which is a sign of long-term differences in nutrition. This could be an indicator that the participant households were poorer in the past, and thus that targeting is working. We do not find significant differences in between the two groups in per capita consumption or in school enrolment. By contrast, in the Ethiopia sample there are actually not many significant differences between PSNP participants and non-participants, which is partly due to the extremely low levels of consumption in the whole of Ethiopia. In fact, only household size is different (with participants coming from slightly smaller households). In terms of the wealth distribution, participation is quite similar in all of the wealth quintiles (as defined by an index of assets and services available to households).

In both India and Ethiopia, there is quantitative and qualitative evidence that households participating in public works benefit from it in terms of child outcomes, but that participation brings extra work responsibilities to children. Uppal (2009) finds different processes determining the incidence of child labour (which is defined in this case as paid work) among boys and that among girls as a result of MGNREGS. For boys, the incidence of drought seems to increase the likelihood of work by 14.8 per cent, while registration for the scheme has a negative effect that counteracts this, reducing the likelihood of work by 13.4 per cent, suggesting the scheme serves an insurance purpose. For girls, being in a rural area increases the chances of child labour by 10.1 per cent. However, girls in households taking up work under the scheme are 8.2 per cent less likely to participate in other paid work. This could be because of the income effect or, alternatively, because girls are substituting for household members in other activities such as on the household land or in housekeeping. Additionally, children of farmers with small plots have been shown to increase their workload if their parents can no longer afford to employ labourers (Morrow and Vennam 2010).

MGNREGS programme design includes the presence of child care facilities at all sites where more than five children under the age of six are present, a move especially important given that MGNREGS requires at least 33 per cent of beneficiaries to be women (Government of India 2008). This does not, however, seem to be reflected in the data, with only 8.7 per cent of registered respondents reporting the availability of childcare centres on site (Uppal 2009). Woldehanna (2009) examined hours of paid and unpaid work, domestic chores, schooling and childcare of 11–12 year olds in Young Lives Ethiopia. He finds that the public works component (PWP) of the PSNP increased the amount of time both girls and boys spent on paid work. However, it reduced the amount of time girls spent on childcare and housekeeping. The net effect was that children's total hours of work were reduced. The PWP also increased the time girls spent studying. Woldehanna also found that the Direct Support component (DSP) of the PSNP reduced child work in paid and unpaid activities and increased the grades completed by boys in both rural and urban areas. In rural areas, boys' hours of unpaid work outside the home and girls' hours of childcare and housekeeping declined. In urban areas, girls' hours of paid work and boys' hours of paid and unpaid work declined significantly. The DSP was found to increase the grades completed by boys in both rural and urban areas.[5]

Emirie et al. (2009), using qualitative methods in a subset of Young Lives sites, found that, as a result of income they receive from PSNP, participants in PSNP have started to send their children to school instead of sending them to rich farmers for farm wage employment. Members of some PSNP households, including children, are involved in other income-generating activities like collecting and selling cow dung to fill the income gap that is not covered by PSNP and farm earnings. This has particularly been the case in those sites where payment has been in cash rather than in food due to food price rises. Given the poor market and rising prices, almost all beneficiaries preferred PSNP payment in kind rather than in cash.

Respondents mentioned instances of labour substitution where they saw children (both boys and girls) carrying out domestic chores while their parents were away on safety-net work. In fact, some clearly felt that the labour demands of the PSNP mean that children need to sacrifice their time and energy for domestic work instead of studying or playing.

Furthermore, the practice of children labouring on public works was followed in at least three of the four research sites: Amhara, Oromia and SNNPR.[6] Also, some respondents, including teachers, stated that PSNP activities and increased household demand for child labour (as substitutes in domestic or public works) have negatively affected children's educational participation and performance.

CONDITIONS IN CONDITIONAL CASH TRANSFERS

We contrast these findings with those on conditional cash transfers, drawing on evidence from Peru. We note that Peru is classified as 'upper-middle income' in development terms; it has a significantly higher average national income than Ethiopia or India,[7] and has also higher inequality (World Bank 2009b). Within the Latin American region, however, Peru has performed economically less well than the average, and has higher levels of poverty and lower human development achievements that many other countries in the region. The number of people covered by (non-contributory) social assistance programmes in 2002 was high, but benefits were low (see below for specific information on Juntos, which was introduced in 2005). This is partly because Peru has a smaller tax base than average for the region, but spending on social assistance was also low in comparison even with health and education.

Peru's Juntos ('Together') programme is a CCT scheme, introduced in 2005, which currently covers around 430,000 households in 638 districts, making it the largest social programme in Peru.[8] The key objectives are to reduce poverty and increase human capital (as with most CCT programmes). The monitoring of Juntos (after the introduction of the programme) has been conducted by a number of donors in collaboration with government agencies,[9] and thus far it has not been subject to the charges of corruption and cronyism that have been levelled at other programmes in Peru.

Eligible households in Juntos receive 100 soles (around 30 US dollars) per month, regardless of household size. This is relatively modest compared with other similar programmes in the region. The conditionalities attached to the programme depend on the age of children: those under five years must attend regular health and nutrition checks (including for height and weight monitoring, vaccinations, parasite checks and vitamin supplements); children aged 6–14 years with incomplete primary education must attend school for at least 85 per cent of the year; pregnant/breastfeeding mothers must undergo a series of pre- and post-natal checks (including for vaccinations, vitamin supplements and parasite checks). Health campaigns are also operating in eligible regions, including sanitation and nutrition programmes.

As long as they comply with these conditions, families are eligible to receive the cash transfer for up to eight years; the full 100 soles a month during the first four years, and a reduced transfer in the final four years. The cash transfer is suspended for three consecutive months in the case of non-compliance and indefinitely if non-compliance is repeated. Every three months, Juntos local promoters are scheduled to visit the homes of beneficiaries to monitor their compliance, information that should be cross-checked with school attendance and health-care visit records.[10] According to the Juntos 2007 Annual Assessment, 95 per cent of beneficiary families complied with what it called 'health-related' conditionalities, 97 per cent ensured that their children attend school regularly, and 99 per cent participated in the National Nutritional Assistance Programme for children under the age of three (Juntos 2008).

A recent World Bank study (Perova and Vakis, 2009) found that Juntos reduces the depth of income poverty and increases food consumption (though it brings few households over the poverty line because the transfer is relatively small). Children in Juntos were less likely to have experienced illness in the month prior to the survey. Juntos beneficiaries more frequently sought medical attention for their under-fives in the event of illness, had more vaccinations and attended more health controls.

Qualitative studies in Young Lives communities have found effects that echo the World Bank quantitative study cited above, but add more depth on both intra-household and social dynamics in communities. Alcazar (2010) finds that considerable impacts can be attributed to Juntos, such as improved school attendance, especially for girls (and particularly in the last year of primary school), as well as improved attendance and performance of teachers.

Streuli (2009) finds that, even though children and parents recognize that the programme aims to benefit families living in poverty, they observed targeting errors and leaks. For example, a beneficiary girl said that 'some families appear with someone else's child' so as to fulfil the selection criteria. Parents also observed that the programme is supporting both 'poor' people and those who are 'not so poor'. Alcazar (2010) notes that a large number of women receiving the benefit seemed unclear about the conditions for their receiving the benefit, and there were some instances of communities being disgruntled due to perceived errors in within-community targeting.

Juntos's targeting process appears to have had a less positive impact on community dynamics. In a context of general poverty, when some families are included and others not and there is insufficient clarity about the reasons for this, the introduction of the programme has generated feelings of sadness, resentment and anger among some community members. Especially in the initial stages, the programme suffered from a number of weaknesses in identifying beneficiaries. Streuli (2009) finds that Juntos's emphasis on 'human capital' may be undermining people's 'social capital' and other crucial aspects such as participation, choice and power in decision-making. There are tensions between Juntos and non-Juntos families – non-beneficiaries believe that Juntos families are dishonest in their efforts to obtain the benefits and lazy as a result of participating. Some non-Juntos children are singled out for discrimination. This is of particular concern given that the areas where Juntos is being targeted have a long history of political violence and community tensions. Streuli does not, however, conclude that the community effects are solely negative. In some cases, the programme has also generated a feeling of solidarity among the beneficiaries, who seek to share with those who do not receive the cash transfers but who are obviously impoverished.

The evidence from Young Lives suggests that Juntos is 'child-oriented' but not yet child-centred; that is, the programme needs to fully recognize children equally, and not simply as passive recipients of services. From a policy point of view there is an important question about whether it is service improvement or conditionalities which drive improved service engagement, given that the answer ought to determine policy development.

CONCLUSION

Empirical evidence of social assistance programmes from a child's viewpoint show positive impacts on children. Public works schemes in India act as a cushion, which possibly proves the existence of insurance effects. There are particular benefits when drought hits the welfare of households; the poorest households benefit from this, including those of lower castes, but those of scheduled castes[11] are less likely to participate. In Ethiopia, we find that schooling outcomes are improved by certain components of the Productive Safety Net Programme, though there are different impacts on boys and girls. In Peru there is evidence that conditional cash transfers are mainly reaching the intended beneficiaries by providing a welcome boost to the poorest, as well as improving their capacity to attend school and the attendance and performance of their teachers.

However, research has also uncovered some of the unintended consequences of social protection for children. While children in Peru are attending school, there are concerns that increased demands on schools (through increases in class size) have not been adequately matched by investment in schools. While the inclusion of children with different needs is to be welcomed, this should be accompanied by the training of educators. There is also evidence from Peru, based on views that have been expressed by children and their communities in Young Lives sites, that programme placement has introduced some tensions into the community. A finding of particular significance from Young Lives research is that public works have both an income transfer and a household labour requirement; in India and Ethiopia household participation in public works may increase labour demands on children, possibly in different ways for girls and boys and for older and younger children. Since public works programmes by definition seek to increase the amount of work available, and since work is a daily reality for many children, it is perhaps unsurprising that these schemes increase the amount of work some children undertake (for instance, in housekeeping or other work that would have previously been undertaken by adults now working in the scheme). Boyden (2009), however, notes that work should not always be viewed as a risk. If supported and valued it can act as a protective mechanism. Combining work with school can be part of building child and family resilience. However, if work undermines schooling and/or a stigma is attached to work, this can increase children's vulnerability and distress.

Overall, child-focused research on social protection can provide important insights that can make social protection more inclusive of children's needs. This can improve programme design so as to make better use of scarce resources, and invest in the future of children in very poor communities. We conclude, therefore, that well-designed social protection has a major role to play in improving children's life chances. There is, however, a risk of unintended consequences within social protection, especially when conditions apply to beneficiaries. Such effects have important intra-household and gendered dimensions that must be incorporated within the policy design process. Finally, social protection schemes operate in a context, and policymakers need to consider both the schemes themselves and how other economic and social policies are able to foster graduation beyond social protection.

NOTES

1. Safety nets are also referred to as social assistance, or non-contributory transfers, in contrast with social insurance schemes.
2. A principle elsewhere named 'less eligibility' used to justify the harsh and demeaning conditions of the British workhouse to avoid the risk that anyone other than the desperate made use of them (see Brundage 2002, p. 54). In short, this argument, by definition, argues for social provision but set at a very low level of generosity.
3. See www.younglives.org.uk for data documentation, links to questionnaires and data sets, and technical notes describing sampling and methodology. The study is core-funded by UKAID from the Department for International Development (DFID) and the Netherlands Ministry of Foreign Affairs.
4. Households that are entitled to subsidized rations of food – a measure of destitution in India.
5. These results should be treated with caution given that the PSNP was both new in 2005 and in many cases replacing participation in one of the previous food or cash-for-work or transfer schemes.
6. Southern Nations, Nationalities and Peoples Region.
7. Peru's GNP per capita is over ten times that of Ethiopia as measured with current US dollars (World Bank 2010). There is an ongoing discussion on the merits of various comparison mechanisms between countries, but the difference in development terms overall (and especially in large urban areas) is clear. It is also notable that though Peru's per capita GDP is higher than those of the other countries, high levels of inequality mean there is much less of a difference in absolute poverty between Peru and Vietnam.
8. www.juntos.gob.pe, accessed 17 March 2010. Note also that approximately 20,000 households are suspended for conditionality reasons and around 60,000 others are in process.
9. World Bank, Inter-American Development Bank (IADB), United Nations Children's Fund (UNICEF), Grupo de Análisis para el Desarollo (GRADE), Consorcio de Investigación Económica y Social (CIES), Ministerio de Economía y Finanzas (MEF), Ministerio de Salud del Perú (MINSA), Ministerio de Educación (MINEDUC) and Instituto Nacional de Estadística e Informática (INEI).
10. But see below for qualitative evidence that these conditions are often not met.
11. 'Scheduled Caste' is a term used in the Indian Constitution since 1950 to specify those castes that are scheduled to receive economic and social protection, previously known as 'backward castes'. See several Young Lives papers that explore issues of caste in the sample under consideration here.

REFERENCES

Alcazar, L. (2010), 'El gasto public social frente a la infancia Análisis del programa juntos y de la oferta y demanda de servicios asociadas a sus condiciones', Working Paper, Lima: Young Lives/GRADE.

Baird, S., C. McIntosh and B. Ozler (2009), 'Designing cost-effective cash transfer programs to boost schooling among women in Sub-Saharan Africa', Policy Research Working Paper No. 5090, Washington, DC: World Bank.

Banerjee, A. and E. Duflo (2011), *Poor Economics: A Radical Rethinking of the Way to Fight Global Poverty*, New York: Public Affairs.

Benhassine, N., F. Devoto, E. Duflo, P. Dupas and V. Pouliquen (2010), 'The impact of conditional cash transfers on schooling and learning: preliminary evidence from the Tayssir pilot in Morocco', Mimeo: MIT.

Boyden, J. (2009), 'Risk and capability in the context of adversity: children's contributions to household livelihoods in Ethiopia', *Children, Youth and Environments*, **19** (2), 111–37.

Bradshaw, J. (2006), *A Review of the Comparative Evidence on Child Poverty*, York: Joseph Rowntree Foundation.

Brundage, A. (2002), *The English Poor Laws, 1700–1930*, Houndmills, Basingstoke: Palgrave Macmillan.

De Brauw, A. and J. Hoddinott (2008), 'Must conditional cash transfer programs be conditioned to be effective? The impact of conditioning transfers on school enrollment in Mexico', IFPRI Discussion Papers 757, Washington, DC: International Food Policy Research Institute.

Del Ninno, C., K. Subbarao and A. Milazzo (2009), 'How to make public works work: a review of the experiences', Social Protection Discussion Paper 0905, Washington, DC: World Bank.

Devereux, S. and R. Sabates-Wheeler (2004), 'Transformative social protection', Working Paper 232, Brighton: Institute of Development Studies.

DFID (Department for International Development) et al. (2009), *Joint Statement on Advancing Child-Sensitive Social Protection*, DFID, HelpAge International, Hope & Homes for Children, Institute of Development Studies, International Labour Organization, Overseas Development Institute, Save the Children UK, UNDP, UNICEF and the World Bank.

Emirie, G, W. Negatu and D. Getachew (2009), *Impacts of Productive Safety Net Programme on Child Poverty Reduction: Implications for Child Education*, Addis Ababa: Young Lives IDRC Paper.

European University Institute and European Commission (2010), *The 2010 European Report on Development: Social Protection for Inclusive Development*, Brussels: European Communities.

Fiszbein, A. and N. Schady (2009), *Conditional Cash Transfers: Reducing Present and Future Poverty*, Washington DC: World Bank Publications.

Galab, S., P. Prudhvikar Reddy and R. Himaz (2008), *Young Lives Round 2 Survey Report. Initial Findings Andhra Pradesh, India*, Oxford: Young Lives, Department of International Development, University of Oxford.

Government of Ethiopia (2004), *Productive Safety Net Programme, Programme Implementation Manual*, Addis Ababa: Ministry of Agriculture and Rural Development, Government of the Federal Democratic Republic of Ethiopia.

Government of India (2005), 'The National Employment Guarantee Act', *The Gazette of India*, 7 September.

Government of India (2008), *The National Employment Guarantee Act 2005 Operational Guidelines* (3rd edn), New Delhi: Ministry of Rural Development.

Handa, S., S. Devereux and D. Webb (eds) (2010), *Social Protection for Africa's Children*, London: Routledge.

Hanlon, J., A. Barrientos and D. Hulme (2010), *Just Give Money to the Poor: The Development Revolution from the Global South*, Sterling, VA: Kumarian Press.

ILO (International Labour Organization) and OECD (Organisation for Economic Co-operation and Development) (2011), 'Towards National Social Protection Floors', a Policy Note for the G20 Meeting of Labour and Employment Ministers, Paris, 26–27 September 2011, Geneva/Paris: ILO in collaboration with OECD.

Jha, R., S. Bhattacharyya, R. Gaiha and S. Shylashri (2009), '"Capture" of anti-poverty programs: an analysis of the National Rural Employment Guarantee Program in India', *Journal of Asian Economics*, **20** (4), 456–64.

Juntos (2008), *Informe de Evaluacion Anual 2007*, Lima: Programa Nacional de Apoyo Directo a Los Mas Pobres – 'Juntos'.

McCord, A. (2008), 'The social protection function of short-term public works programmes in the context of chronic poverty', in A. Barrientos and D. Hulme (eds), *Social Protection for the Poor and the Poorest*, Basingstoke: Palgrave Macmillan, pp. 160–80.

Molyneux, M. (2006), 'Mothers at the service of the new poverty agenda: Progresa/Oportunidades, Mexico's Conditional Transfer Programme', *Social Policy & Administration*, **40** (4), 425–49.

Morrow, V. and U. Vennam (2010), 'Combining work and school: the dynamics of girls' involvement in agricultural work in Andhra Pradesh, India', *Children and Society*, **24**, 304–14.

Perova, E. and R. Vakis (2009), *Welfare Impacts of the 'Juntos' Program in Peru: Evidence from a Non-Experimental Evaluation*, Washington, DC: World Bank.

Porter, C. with P. Dornan (2010), 'Social protection and children: a synthesis of evidence from Young Lives research in Ethiopia, India and Peru', Young Lives Policy Paper 1, Oxford: Young Lives, Department of International Development, University of Oxford.

Ravallion, M. (1991), 'Reaching the poor through rural public employment: arguments, evidence and lessons from South Asia', *The World Bank Research Observer*, 6 (2), 153–76.

Rawlings, L. and G. Rubio (2005), 'Evaluating the impact of conditional cash transfer programs', *World Bank Economic Observer*, **20** (1), 29–55.

Shariff, A. (2008), *Growth and Safety Net in Tandem: A Case of India's National Employment Guarantee Scheme*, New Delhi: IFPRI Asia.

Streuli, N. (2009), 'Children's and parents' views of Juntos: a conditional cash programme in Peru', Ph.D. thesis, University of London.

Townsend, P. (2009a), 'Social security and human rights', in P. Townsend (ed.), *Building Decent Societies: Rethinking the Role of Social Security in Development*, Basingstoke: Palgrave Macmillan, pp. 29–59.

Townsend, P. (2009b), 'Social security in developing countries: a brief overview', in P. Townsend (ed.), *Building Decent Societies: Rethinking the Role of Social Security in Development*, Basingstoke: Palgrave Macmillan, pp. 245–59.

Uppal, V. (2009), 'Is the NREGS a safety net for children?', Young Lives Student Paper, Oxford: Young Lives, Department of International Development, University of Oxford.

Weigand, C. and M. Grosh (2008), 'Levels and patterns of safety net spending in developing and transition countries', Social Protection Discussion Paper No. 0817, Washington, DC: World Bank.

Woldehanna, T. (2009), 'Productive Safety Net Programme and children's time use between work and schooling in Ethiopia', Young Lives Working Paper 40, Oxford: Young Lives, Department of International Development, University of Oxford.

World Bank (2009a), *World Bank Group Operational Response to the Crisis,* Washington, DC, available at http://www.worldbank.org/financialcrisis/pdf/ WBGResponse-VFF.pdf (accessed on 21.06.2012).

World Bank (2009b), *Peru at a Glance*, available at devdata.worldbank.org/AAG/ per_aag.pdf (accessed 31 August 2010).

World Bank (2010), *Building Resilience and Opportunity: The World Bank's Social Protection and Labour Strategy 2012–2022*, Concept note, Washington, DC: World Bank.

9. Work and welfare in the global South: public works programmes as an instrument of social policy

Anna McCord and Charles Meth

INTRODUCTION

Public works programmes (PWPs) have been implemented in the global North for five centuries at least, as a core component of social policy in response to the needs of the working age poor. The Elizabethan poor laws of 1601 enshrined the principle that the poor should work in return for support from the parish but as early as 1535–36 statutes had been passed in England to propose that the state should provide some form of work for the able-bodied poor in return for the receipt of 'relief', recognising, albeit implicitly, the inability of the market to provide sufficient employment (Leonard, 1900). Over the intervening centuries employment-based programmes to support the working age poor retained their popularity, and throughout the last half millennium PWPs have been adopted, in one form or another, as countercyclical responses during periods of significant labour market disruption and economic restructuring, particularly at times when the state has recognised elevated unemployment as either inherently undesirable, or potentially deleterious to public stability. PWPs reached their apogee during the massive US New Deal programmes of the 1930s, which consumed 4 per cent of GDP at their height, and absorbed up to 3–9 per cent of the labour force annually between 1933 and 1940 (McCord, 2012). Public Works' policy profile rose again in the North during the Reagan era, with the emergence of 'workfare' (known in the UK as 'welfare to work') presented as an alternative to ongoing cash transfer provision, and perceived as a component of both labour market activation and social protection provision.

The enduring popularity of PWPs in the north has also been transposed to middle income MICs and low income countries LICs in the developing world over the last half century, with large numbers of programmes implemented with support from donors, multilateral agencies and governments. In some instances this programming has built on long established indigenous traditions, with PWPs being implemented in Southern Asia over a millennium prior to any northern influenced initiatives (Das, 2010). At least 200–300 such programmes were implemented in sub-Saharan Africa between 2000 and 2010 (McCord and Slater, 2009), employing up to 9 million people each year (del Ninno et al., 2009). Over 100 PWPs have been implemented in Asia over the same period (McCord and Chopra, 2010), with the Mahatma Gandhi National Rural Employment Guarantee Scheme (MGNREGS) in India being the largest social protection programme in the world, employing 55 million workers each year.

In the past, PWPs were viewed as difficult to pin down conceptually, having a foot in both camps of the paid work/social protection dyad. This led some commentators to view them primarily as social protection mechanisms, to be invoked as short-term responses to crisis conditions, while others recognised the somewhat longer term usefulness of PWPs as anti-poverty measures. The work of McCord (2008) and of del Ninno et al. (2009) has brought clarity to the issues of the typology of PWPs, and the nature of the many uses to which they have been put. Abstracting from this variety of programming, it is possible to identify one essential characteristic that all PWPs share; namely putting income in the hands of the unemployed, be that seasonal, or cyclical or structural. It makes consumption possible, and also protects (if wage rates are adequate) the workers concerned against poverty. In that sense, it is clear that conceptually, they are identical to any paid employment activity.

In the social protection discourse the cash paid for working on PWPs is often referred to as a transfer payment, with the programme conceptualised as a form of conditional cash transfer. However, it is not clear that this is a useful or appropriate way to consider the cash paid. While a transfer is typically an unrequited transaction, the compensation made for participation in a PWP (whether cash or in-kind transfers, like food) is one side of an act of exchange, the other of which is work performed. It is important to stress this point because by implementing a PWP, government is acting, directly or indirectly, as an employer, and as such PWPs may be characterised as a form of government sponsored employment, with governments implementing PWPs in developing countries sometimes referred to as employers of last resort. Despite the growing emphasis on immediate poverty alleviation, these are interventions primarily designed to address major market failures.

In recent years donor interest in the potential role of PWPs in development has extended beyond basic social assistance to include productivity enhancement, graduation out of poverty and even economic

growth. This chapter explores the current role of public works programming in social policy in developing countries.

PUBLIC WORKS DURING THE LAST CENTURY

Public works have then been used by the state as instruments to support
the able bodied poor in various forms over many centuries. While
programmes have been used to assist the poorest during temporary
periods of labour market disruption, for example in response to flooding
or drought, here we focus on the role of public works as a social policy
instrument to address chronic unemployment.

Public works have been used historically in many instances represented
nationwide and systematic interventions implemented in recognition of
mass labour market failure and the inability of the poor to find adequate
remuneration to meet basic consumption needs. These programmes have
been shaped by concerns not to distort the functioning of the labour
market or diminish the work ethic of the poor, encouraging them to
withdraw from the labour market, and for this reason have entailed a
significant work requirement from the poor in return for support from the
state. Some programmes have focussed on the provision of work in return
for payment, by providing a form of state-sponsored employment, while
others have entailed a combination of short-term work, sometimes in
combinationg with training, with the objective of improving 'employability' by improving the skills of the unemployed in order to take up any
unfilled jobs within the economy – a response which is useful mainly in
contexts of structural unemployment, where jobs exist but workers lack
the relevant skills or experience to fill them.

In the last century a number of large public works programmes have
been implemented during periods of major labour market crisis, such as
the New Deal programmes implemented in the US during the Great
Depression of the 1930s, the workfare programmes initiated in that
country during the 1980s, and the employment creation programmes
implemented in Argentina during the economic crisis of the early 2000s.

RECENT CHANGES IN THE GLOBAL ECONOMY

Over the last two decades there has been a major restructuring in the
nature of the global labour market, resulting in the emergence of a
significant population which is surplus to the requirements of the
international economy, and excluded from the benefits of economic

growth. This restructuring has seen a period of growth throughout much of the developed and developing world, which has been accompanied by a rise in underemployment and also unemployment, resulting in a massive absolute increase in the number of working age poor. The distinction between underemployment and unemployment is no longer useful within this debate, as even those fully engaged in the labour market in many low and middle income countries are suffering from impoverishment due to their adverse incorporation into the global economy.

This period of economic transformation has resulted in GDP growth which has been associated with the creation of poor quality employment on a mass scale, being poorly paid, insecure, with poor working conditions, and only the extremely limited provision of jobs conforming to the ILO's conception of 'decent work'. At the same time processes of mass urbanisation and migration, largely driven by the search for a share of the benefits of growth have coincided with major changes in the agricultural sectors in many LICs, resulting in the breakdown of traditional rural livelihoods and traditional support mechanisms. Together this perfect storm of fundamental economic change nationally and internationally has resulted in the emergence of mass underemployment and unemployment on a global scale.

REASONS FOR CONCERN

The shift described in the previous section represents a major challenge from (at least) two perspectives. On the one hand mass labour market failure and the resultant impoverishment represents a significant moral challenge, requiring immediate policy responses to protect the basic social and economic rights of the poor. On the other hand, this situation also demands a response from the perspective of enlightened self interest on the part of government, as mass underemployment and unemployment are major drivers of social and political instability and civil unrest, particularly where different groups are competing for access to limited employment opportunities. The emergence of mass youth unemployment has been a major factor behind instability and civil conflict in many countries, and the Arab spring was largely driven by labour-market-related frustrations, and the issue of NEETS (youth 'not in education, employment or training') has been recognised as one of the major challenges of the coming decades (see for example the ILO 2013 World Development Report) with an estimated 11 million youths falling into this category in sub-Saharan Africa alone (McCord, 2012). It is interesting to note that many of the major public works initiatives of recent decades have been developed in response to situations of actual or potential political destabilisation, or as mechanisms to promote stabilisation in the wake of conflict in fragile states.

POLICY RESPONSE

There are two main policy approaches for addressing the emergence of mass underemployment. The one attempts to address the problem from a structural perspective, aiming to shift the nature of national integration into the global economy, for example through national economic and industrial policies, which will be likely to bear fruit in the medium to long term. The other approach aims to respond to the problem in the short term, pending the success of macro-policies, by actively intervening to compensate for labour market failure through the provision of some form of social protection provision. This can take the form of support to the working age poor directly through the provision of cash transfers, although fears of labour market distortion and dependency (neither well founded in terms of the international evidence base) result in a preference for state sponsored employment as the main compensatory approach, often implemented as part of a package in association with the provision of cash transfers for the 'deserving poor' (typically considered to include children, the aged and the disabled).

THE PREFERENCE FOR PWP RESPONSES TO POVERTY

The preference for the public works–cash transfer package response to poverty and underemployment in part reflects the influence of the donor community on programming in many developing countries, particularly those without the resources to finance (and hence design) their own social policy responses. The package of support based on a work requirement rather than unconditional support for the working age poor reflects donor traditions, preferences and ideologies. These are informed by the conservative concept of the deserving and undeserving poor, the dignity of work and fears relating to labour market distortion, rather than the tradition of redistributive justice and rights. The latter tradition would recognise a responsibility of the state to provide for its citizens directly in recompense for its inability to provide adequate employment for all through the functioning of the market.

PWPs are also popular as they are perceived as carrying with them the promise of 'productive safety nets', investment in social protection which is also an investment in growth; with the wage and physical assets created combining to enable the diversification of livelihoods and increased productivity at the household level, and potentially also stimulating productivity and growth dividends at the local and national levels. This aspiration has been promoted in recent years by the implementation of the mass 'productive safety nets programme' (PSNP) in Ethiopia, which includes a PWP component supporting on average 7 million people each year, and anticipates 'graduation' out of poverty as a result of programme participation.

This prevalent vision of PWPs is one in which they represent a form of 'treatment' for poverty and unemployment, with participation resulting in graduation, rather than one in which ongoing sponsored employment is required. This is true where PWPs are implemented as a response to a temporary labour market disruption (for example after a flood or cyclone) but is unlikely to hold true in the context of ongoing mass unemployment and adverse incorporation.

This vision of PWPs as a means of promoting graduation is, however, attractive for a number of reasons; it implies a reduction of the ongoing fiscal burden implied by ongoing cash transfer based social protection support, which renders it attractive to both donors and governments facing significant resource constraints, particularly given the current global economic recession. It also links social protection provision with increases in productivity and potentially also growth, rather than presenting it as essentially consumption expenditure. The graduation, productivity and growth potential of public works programming has been promoted by those eager to promote PWP-based approaches to support the poor internationally, as a way to 'sell' social protection provision to states otherwise reluctant to sponsor social protection provision of any kind for the working age poor.

As well as responding to governmental preferences for social protection interventions with the potential to contribute to productivity and growth, PWPs also respond to the fear of promoting dependency on the state on the part of the working age poor which is prevalent in relation to cash transfer programming. Unsurprisingly, given the low levels of most cash transfer provision in developing countries relative to the poverty gap in poor households, there is little evidence to indicate working age poor withdrawal from the labour market upon receipt of state support, and research suggests that cash transfer receipt may actually promote re-engagement with the labour market by enabling increased job search activity. PWPs also match well with many government preferences to provide employment and honour the dignity of work rather than provide 'hand outs' and cultural norms which may not easily accommodate the provision of state support without a contribution of some kind from beneficiaries.

RESOURCE CONSTRAINTS TO EFFECTIVE PROGRAMMING

However, the above approach to social protection provision carries with it resource implications which can serve to limit performance significantly and so constrain effective support for the majority of the working age poor, with the major resource implications being costs and institutional capacity. The renowned Mahatma Gandhi National Rural Employment Guarantee Scheme (MGNREGS) in India, one of the few programmes internationally to be implemented on a national scale and provide significant employment benefits for participants costs between 0.5 and 1 per cent of GDP per annum to employ 55 million workers, which is financed domestically. The programme also requires significant administrative capacity from national to district level to enable the mass provision of employment, and also major technical inputs during both design and implementation stages to ensure that appropriate quality assets are constructed. Such resource mobilisation is possible in the Indian context given the strength and local level permeation of state structures, and is facilitated by the fact that the requirement for mass employment provision under the programme has a legislative basis, (the National Rural Employment Guarantee Act (NREGA) of 2005) and as such is a mandatory function of both national and state government.

The other programme which manages successfully to overcome many of the major resource demands implied by a PWP-based response to mass poverty is the aforementioned Ethiopian PSNP. The PSNP also benefits from the existence of a strong state and institutional structures, but crucially depends on the NGO sector and international community for support in implementation and financing respectively.

Both the MGNREGS and the PSNP manage to meet the significant requirements for the provision of mass employment on an ongoing basis required to address structural underemployment and unemployment and thereby provide a credible response in terms of alleviating widespread poverty. Most LICs and many MICs, however, do not have the capacity to meet the significant fiscal and institutional requirements of employment provision on such a scale, rendering the preferred social policy response to mass unemployment inherently problematic in many developing contexts.

THE LIMITS TO PREVAILING PUBLIC WORKS PROGRAMMING

Policies that are seen to work well in one setting (or one set of circumstances) can, and often have been, less successful when transferred to another. Public works programmes, developed in the North, are among the many policies about which concerns have been expressed, in particular in relation to their transferability, relevance and appropriateness for developing countries.

Given the appropriate institutions and sufficient resources, PWPs can and have been successfully implemented in the developing world (del Ninno et al., 2009). There have, however, also been many failures. The conditions for success and sustainability are similar in both the North and South in several regards. As in advanced economies, they can only succeed if there is sufficient demand for labour of the relevant type. It is also a requirement that appropriate institutions exist to implement the policies and to carry out the programmes. Although these need not necessarily be government bodies, whoever does the work has to be competent enough to perform a difficult task in a sustainable way. These human resource and institutional capacity challenges are well acknowledged in the context of development. There is, however, one major additional difference between the attempted applications of PWPs in developing, as opposed to developed economies, namely, the absence in most of the former of other types of formal social protection against the contingency of unemployment. Social insurance and assistance in the context of more expansive Northern welfare states has the consequence that the unemployed and economically inactive are less able to be coerced into taking part in such programmes which rely (to varying degrees) on voluntary participation. However, the severity of unemployment and underemployment in so many developing countries, together with the absence of alternative social protection, means that participation in PWPs in developing countries is likely to be enthusiastic. As a consequence, the fiscal resources to accommodate all of those desirous of finding employment will generally not be available. This, in turn, means that places in the programmes will have to be rationed.

As a result of the constraints faced by many governments selecting PWP implementation as the primary policy response to the challenge of the working age poor, many, if not most programmes tend to be small scale with low coverage and offering only a single short-term period of employment. This alternative model of PWP provision is more fiscally and institutionally realistic in many developing countries, and also favoured by donors who are reluctant generally to finance sponsored employment on a large and sustained scale, but it is far from the NREGA, PSNP or New Deal vision in terms of the recognition of the need for the provision of significant scale state-sponsored employment in the face of chronic under- and unemployment. The more common approach is reliant on the realisation of the somewhat aspirational graduation, productivity and growth assumptions relating to programme implementation, if it is to offer any meaningful social policy response to chronic labour market failure and the realities of the globalised economy in the 21st century.

The main PWP interventions in developing countries, particularly in sub-Saharan Africa, are often high profile but tend to be at least in part symbolic, providing very limited direct social protection benefits and covering only an extremely small proportion of those in need. They rest in part on the assumption that the employability of workers after programme participation will be significantly enhanced, but given the demand deficient characteristics of chronic unemployment in most developing contexts it is unlikely that PWP participation will result in increased employment, but at best worker substitution in the absence of complementary programming to directly increase labour demand. The symbolic importance of PWP implementation should not, however, be underestimated, and may have an impact on political stability inasmuch as the state is signalling its engagement directly with the challenge of chronic employment, however inadequately.

Hence, much public works programming in developing contexts is limited by capacity and resource constraints such that the social protection package of cash transfers for the deserving poor and public works employment for the working age poor tends to offer extremely low coverage overall, with the public works component often being particularly limited, and support for the working age poor being contingent on extent to which the state is able and willing to provide temporary employment opportunities.

This programming is driven by the same impetus which governs social protection provision in the North in terms of the need for the provision of state support for the working age poor. However, it fails to take into account the context of structural economic transformation and chronic labour market failure, and the fact that the market-based employment which is available may be provided on terms which are inimical to the satisfaction of even basic household income security, and is in need of supplementation by state employment. The provision of public works-based support for the working age poor is limited by binding resource and capacity constraints and in most instances, with the notable exception of Ethiopia, donors are not willing to compensate with recurrent financing contributions. This in effect renders the execution of the preferred model for supporting the working poor on any meaningful scale politically, and hence also fiscally, unfeasible in many developing countries.

LIMITS TO STATE CITIZEN RESPONSIBILITY

This is linked to a more fundamental issue, namely the lack of political interest in the provision of support for this group on a mass scale. This lack of interest can be explained by the fact that there is not a recognition in most developing countries of the state's responsibility to compensate its citizens for the consequences of mass labour market failure and the resulting underemployment and unemployment and poverty among the working age poor. Hence, in the absence of either a perceived moral imperative to address this issue, or other political incentives such as mass mobilisation by civil society in favour of support for the working age poor, there is little political urgency to develop adequate social policy provision in support of this group in many countries, despite the fact that chronic underemployment and unemployment, particularly among the youth, is likely to be a major contributor to future social and political instability in the developing world.

Finally, it is worth noting some fundamental tensions in the constraints governing the use of PWPs. In developing countries, PWPs are one of the few instruments that can be used to address directly, the problem of insufficient demand for labour. However in a climate of general hostility to the expansion of the 'size' (number of employees) and scope of government, particularly on the part of the international financial institutions, PWPs are likely to be limited both in the form that they can take, in the duration of work opportunities made available, as well as in the wage offered. There is considerable pressure for the work opportunities offered by PWPs to be of short duration and provide only minimal remuneration. While this to a large extent may reflect concerns about state fiscal capacity, in part it may also be related to the fact that PWPs in general, and long-term PWPs in particular, where they exist, serve as a silent reproach to a labour market that cannot absorb all who wish to work (Meth, 2010, 2011).

REFERENCES

Das, M. (2010), *Employment Programs By Any Other Name* ..., available at http://blogs.worldbank.org/endpovertyinsouthasia/blog/39 (accessed August 2010).

del Ninno, C., K. Subbarao and A. Milazzo (2009), 'How to Make Public Works Work: A Review of the Experiences', SP Discussion Paper No. 0905, Social Protection and Labour. Washington DC: World Bank.

Leonard, E.M. (1900), *The Early History of English Poor Relief*, Cambridge: Cambridge University Press.

McCord, A. (2008), 'Recognising Heterogeneity: A Proposed Typology for Public Works Programmes', Southern Africa Labour and Development Research Unit (SALDRU), Working Paper no. 26, SALDRU, School of Economics, University of Cape Town, South Africa, December.

McCord, A. (2012), *Public Works in Sub-Saharan Africa: Do Public Works Work for the Poor?*, Cape Town: Juta Press.

McCord, A. and D. Chopra (2010), 'Review of public works programmes in the South Asia Region', Overseas Development Institute, unpublished.

McCord, A. and R. Slater (2009), 'Overview of Public Works Programmes in Sub-Saharan Africa', available at http://www.odi.org.uk/resources/download/4700.pdf (accessed May 2009).

Meth, Charles (2010), '"Active" Labour Market Policies: Lessons for South Africa?', Research Report No. 86, School of Development Studies, University of KwaZulu-Natal, November 2010.

Meth, Charles (2011), 'Employer of Last Resort? South Africa's Expanded Public Works Programme (EPWP)', SALDRU Working Paper 58, Southern African Labour and Development Research Unit, University of Cape Town, March 2011.

10. The social entrepreneurship–social policy nexus in developing countries

Alex Nicholls

1. INTRODUCTION

Over recent years there has been growing practitioner, policy and academic interest in a set of organizational activities and outputs characterized as 'social enterprise' and – more recently – 'social innovation' (Nicholls and Murdock 2011). United by a common definitional haziness under the umbrella of 'social entrepreneurship',[1] these terms have, nevertheless, entered the normative lexicon of organizations as diverse as Citibank, the World Economic Forum, the United Nations' Development Programme, the Gates Foundation and the British Conservative Party, among many others. The advocates of social entrepreneurship suggest that its combination of boundary-spanning organizational forms with a strong mission focus allows it to address 'social' market failures equally well across the private, civil society and public sectors. Thus, from a commercial perspective social entrepreneurship can create new market opportunities at the 'bottom of the pyramid' (Prahalad 2005; Karamchandani et al. 2009) as a natural extension of socially responsible investing practices (Freireich and Fulton 2009). In this context, social enterprises are 'businesses with a social purpose' (DTI 2002) that can overcome the free-rider issues associated with the creation of social and public goods[2] by reconfiguring commercial markets to capture economic value as a by-product of creating social value. Within civil society, social entrepreneurship can offer a new arena for hybrid partnerships (Austin 2004; Austin et al. 2006), a model of political transformation and empowerment (Alvord et al. 2004), or even a driver of systemic social change (Nicholls 2006; Martin and Osberg 2007). In this sector, social entrepreneurship can generate innovation in circumstances where conventional charitable models have become sclerotic around normative frames of action that fail to deliver mission outcomes effectively. Finally, with respect to government, social entrepreneurship can be conceptualized as a solution to the inefficiency and ineffectiveness of conventional welfare models in developed countries (Leadbeater 1997; DTI 2002). Moreover, and of particular relevance here, in developing country contexts social entrepreneurial organizations can address market failures in the provision of basic welfare services, even acting as a 'shadow state' in some cases (Nicholls 2006): that is, in the absence of well-functioning states and/or incomplete or distorted markets, social entrepreneurship is gaining increasing attention as an innovative means by which to address unmet welfare needs and mitigate welfare risks. From this perspective, social entrepreneurship offers new models to tackle policy gaps and fill institutional voids in welfare service provision.

However, a more critical analysis of social entrepreneurship has also emerged in parallel with the more optimistic framings of the field. From the perspective of the conventional not-for-profit/charitable/non-governmental sector, social entrepreneurship has been seen as evidence of ongoing processes whereby private interests can capture the traditional structures and mechanisms of social provision without the community embeddedness or democratic accountability of the civil society systems they typically replace (e.g. Salamon et al. 2003). This has been strongly evidenced by the public debate concerning the role and legitimacy of the so-called 'new' philanthropy sometimes characterized revealingly as 'philanthro-capitalism' (Bishop and Green 2008; Edwards 2008). Else-where, private corporations have drawn attention to the potential for market distortions resulting from market entry by social enterprises that often have access to capital at low or zero cost (i.e. grants) whereas competing firms cannot access finance on such advantageous terms. While this analysis tends to ignore the fact that social enterprises typically have very different cost structures from those of conventional firms – usually with much higher internal costs – the accusation that they may create an 'unfair playing field' has resulted in some caution on the part of policymakers, even those that are actively supportive of social enterprise per se (see DTI 2002; OTS 2006). Finally, social entre-preneurship that either contracts with the state to provide services or replaces the state entirely in failed welfare markets is open to the criticism that it excuses and, thus, perpetuates state failure or com-placency rather than advocating against it. The relative absence of social entrepreneurship in highly corporatist countries such as Germany demon-strates such a cultural framing of social entrepreneurship – in that country there simply was no institutional logic for the field to emerge at all (although this is beginning to change following the financial crisis of 2008).

This chapter explores the implications of social entrepreneurship in developing-country contexts for the typical objectives of social policy and also tests how far it is challenging the boundaries of conventional policymaking and the responsibilities of policymakers. This chapter falls into six sections. Section 2 sets out the nature, scale and scope of global social entrepreneurship. Section 3 analyses the institutional drivers of the social entrepreneurship revolution in order to suggest some of the distinctive contributions that it can make in developing countries. Of particular importance here is a discussion of the institutional fluidity of this type of action and its tendency to blur conventional institutional boundaries and sectoral legitimacies. Section 4 presents case examples of social entrepreneurship in action in different social welfare contexts in order to explore its potential to address social policy objectives in the global South. Section 5 elaborates a range of challenges and controversies around social entrepreneurship and social welfare, specifically in terms of the interplay of public and private action and governance and accountability structures. In Section 6 the main arguments of the chapter are summarized and some closing observations made.

2. WHAT IS SOCIAL ENTREPRENEURSHIP?

Despite first appearing in public discourse many years ago (Nicholls 2006), 'social entrepreneurship' continues to be subject to definitional disputes, particularly in terms of: how broad or narrow its scope should be (Light 2008); how distinctive it really is from other entrepreneurial models (Dacin et al. 2010); and how systemic its effects may be (Martin and Osberg 2007). Furthermore, theoretical disputes are reinforced by the lack of a clear legal form for social entrepreneurship, in contrast to, say, the generally accepted charitable status of the not-for-profit sector. While bespoke organizational forms do exist for social entrepreneurship – for example, the Community Interest Company (CIC) form in the United Kingdom, Social Cooperatives (Types 1 and 2) in Italy, Social Solidarity Cooperatives in Portugal, and the L3C form in the United States – social entrepreneurship is also incorporated in conventional forms such as companies limited by guarantee, publicly limited companies (PLCs), cooperatives, as well as hybrids that combine several of these forms (Nicholls and Murdock 2011). Nevertheless, although there is as yet no consensus on a single definition or a common legal form, there is broad agreement on three defining characteristics of social entrepreneurship (Nicholls and Cho 2006).

First, there is always evidence of sociality defined as a primary focus on achieving social or environmental outcomes in all strategic decision-making at the organizational level. Therefore, even in a commercial social enterprise, maximizing the effectiveness of achieving a social mission will always override other managerial considerations such as profit maximization (Dees 1998). It is also the case that social entrepreneurship typically separates value creation from value appropriation – the social and economic benefits of a social enterprise do not usually accrue to the owners or managers of the organization but to the clients or beneficiaries that are the focal point of their mission (see Santos 2009).[3] This excludes all conventional businesses that aim primarily to maximize returns to their owners from being categorized as social entrepreneurship, with the exception of cooperatives or mutual organizations where social ownership and profit distribution is the social outcome of the organization.

Second, social entrepreneurship always demonstrates innovation in terms of addressing its social mission. This can be evident in novel organizational processes and structures that create new social value – for example, hiring staff from disenfranchised or excluded populations (Nyssens 2006). Equally, there may be innovation in new and more effective products and services that address social needs. Some organizations achieve both types of innovation. Innovation also operates at different institutional levels in social entrepreneurship, from the macro (challenging normative conceptions of an issue) to the mezzo (changing the markets and institutional structures around a social issue) to the micro (in the new products and services that are actually delivered on the ground) (Nicholls and Murdock 2011).

Finally, and perhaps most distinctively, social entrepreneurship exhibits a clear market orientation demonstrated by an emphasis on performance measurement and enhanced stakeholder accountability, linked to a relentless focus on improving organizational impact and effectiveness. It is this that marks out social entrepreneurship as separate from the many examples of not-for-profit organizations engaging with various types of innovation. Market orientation also allows social entrepreneurship – as social enterprise businesses – to enter and compete in commercial markets (Alter 2006). However, a careful distinction needs to be drawn here between market orientation and marketization; many performance-driven social entrepreneurs do not aim to develop profitable businesses as part of their mission objectives, but rather adopt market-like strategies and models in pursuit of maximizing their social impact. In this way, many social enterprises remain not-for-profits.

Despite evidence of a marked increase in interest in social entrepreneurship (see, for example, the growth of published academic papers researching the subject: Nicholls 2010a), there is only limited data available concerning the scope and size of the field as a whole and patchy evidence of its particular impacts. Largely this is a consequence of the novelty of the sector as a whole and the difficulty of extracting data from national statistics given the multiple legal forms taken by social entrepreneurship.

The Global Entrepreneurship Monitor (GEM) survey of entrepreneurial activity attempted to capture the level of social entrepreneurial activity worldwide in 2010 (Bosma and Levie 2010). At a global level, the overall figures for direct engagement with social entrepreneurship averaged between 1.6 per cent and 1.9 per cent of the total population depending on the region concerned and its level of economic development. At the individual country level several surveys carried out in the UK suggest that the number of social enterprises could be anywhere between 15,000 and 232,000 (Lyon et al. 2010), with policymakers generally citing the Annual Small Business survey average figure of 62,000 (IFF Research 2008; Cabinet Office 2011). The same surveys suggest that the sector may contribute up to £18 billion to the UK economy annually. Elsewhere, data on individual organizations or initiatives also provide some useful information as to the global scale and scope of social entrepreneurship. For example, in Bangladesh the Bangladesh Rural Advancement Committee (BRAC) runs more than 37,000 schools, provides microfinance products to over 8 million poor people, engages 80,000 health volunteers, employs 120,000 workers and serves over 100 million people (Dees 2010). Another example of social entrepreneurship on a global scale is Fair Trade: the movement now generates more than £3 billion of sales from certified products worldwide and benefits more than seven million people across more than 60 countries (Nicholls 2010b). Finally, evidence from organizations that support social entrepreneurship also suggests a vibrant and growing community: Ashoka's Global Fellowship now has over 2,000 members; and since 2001 UnLtd in the United Kingdom has supported more than 3,000 social entrepreneurs to initiate projects and take them to scale, and is now operating in India as well. However, while such data does suggest social entrepreneurship is both growing as a field and achieving a global scale in some cases, it is still the case that mapping and measuring the scale and impact of social entrepreneurship remains a challenging work in progress.

3. POLICY VOIDS

As noted above, social entrepreneurship often addresses market failures or institutional voids (Mair and Marti 2009), where the demand for public or social goods is not being met by supply-side organizations. These institutional voids are highly context-specific and are typically the consequence of complex socio-political and political-economic factors, as well as historical traditions and trajectories (Kerlin 2009). In many cases, social entrepreneurship has developed to fill policy voids where state action has failed to devise effective interventions to address key welfare challenges either alone or in conjunction with the private or civil society sectors. Such voids tend to emerge either because of particularistic ideological or economic agendas – such as reducing public spending or the 'role' of the state – or as a consequence of demographic or structural dynamics that challenge the capacity of the state to provide sufficient public goods and services. The way a government chooses to frame and confront minority or niche issues within its democratic mandate may also create 'winners' and 'losers' and consequent policy voids for the latter group.

With respect to government and policy agendas, social entrepreneurship first responded to the consequences of a series of significant shifts in the political landscape of developed economies in the 1980s and 1990s that led to new institutional voids and market failures emerging in welfare provision. Subsequently, in the 2000s social entrepreneurship became institutionalized within policy agendas, notably in the UK, but latterly also in other developed economies.[4]

The neoconservative ideological agenda that became dominant in the 1980s in the UK and the United States sought to 'reinvent government' (Osborne and Gaebler 1992) by reducing and reforming the state, cutting taxation and rolling back state provision of social and public goods (Grenier 2009). This policy agenda promoted more enterprising and entrepreneurial public-sector structures and behaviour, and reached its logical conclusion with the introduction of internal 'quasi-markets' within public welfare systems (Le Grand 1991). At the same time, a broader focus on enterprise and individualism across society in general lionized entrepreneurs as both economic heroes and strategic management 'gurus' (Dart 2004). One consequence of these changes was a blurring between notions of commercial performance and success and policy effectiveness such that a range of private sector leaders were invited to chair or direct public policy reform committees.[5] Later, in the 1990s, as a 'third way' (Giddens 1998) ideology came to dominate

Anglo-American political discourses, market action and enterprise became further decoupled from commercial business and allowed a new language of welfare provision to emerge that re-imagined social and public goods as best delivered by innovation outside of, but commissioned by, the state. These changes in the political landscape were evident across many countries and fundamentally altered the dynamics of the relationships between the state and other sectors in the production and consumption of social and public goods. As a result, there emerged both a range of new market failures in the provision of welfare services and a variety of new opportunities for social innovation in addressing them. However, while social entrepreneurship developed in response to changes in the scope and structures of state provision of welfare and social and public goods, it did not evolve homogeneously across the United States and Europe (Kerlin 2009). In the former, a slowdown in the economy from the mid-1970s led to a reduction in funding of the not-for-profit sector, particularly state funding. The consequence was innovation in the sector and a range of new sustainability strategies, often taking the form of earned income models. In Europe, on the other hand, the UK and Continental Europe went different ways. Although the economic context was similar in both, the UK followed a similar trajectory to the United States, while Continental Europe was more focused on unemployment with the emergence of a new Work Integration Social Enterprise sector as part of a broader social solidarity economy (*l'économie sociale et solidaire*).

Outside of the United States and Europe social entrepreneurship emerged as a consequence of different political-economic contexts (see Kerlin 2009; Table 10.1). For example, in the transition countries of eastern Europe after the fall of communism, weak market structures, significant injections of international aid, and a rejection of centralized organizational forms led to the development of social entrepreneurship focused on creating small businesses. These took two forms, paralleling the Italian Type 1 and Type 2 cooperatives, though rejecting this legal form for cultural–political reasons: employment models designed as economic regeneration; welfare services social enterprises that were self-sustainable in the absence of effective state funding (though often funded by international aid). In Latin America, after the financial crisis of the late 1990s, market, state and international aid structures were severely weakened. In this context, social entrepreneurship evolved, first, as a mechanism of social solidarity built from the grass roots up (Klein 2002) that engaged with communities in organizing the provision of their basic needs. Second, social enterprises emerged that aimed – as in the transition economies – to rebuild jobs and regenerate economies (see e.g.

NESST 2005). In Africa, on the other hand, the context for the emergence of social entrepreneurship was created by the intersection of state and market failures (sometimes bordering on actual collapse), high levels of extreme poverty and large inflows of international development aid. As Chabal and Daloz (1999) noted, the focus of aid-financed nongovernmental organizations on non-state actors became an important driver of the development of social enterprises in Africa. Particularly significant here was the provision of microcredit for small businesses, as well as the emergence of innovative organizations in health, education and farming. More recently, there has been a strong focus on environmentally sustainable businesses and enterprises, particularly in green technology, often funded by international investors. Finally, in parts of South and South East Asia – notably Bangladesh and India – social entrepreneurship emerged to address a combination of minimalist state welfare structures and growing welfare failures. This did not reflect state failure or welfare crises on an African scale, but rather was the product of a context in which the relationship between the private individual and the state was often remote and problematic. In the case of the Grameen Bank and BRAC in Bangladesh, social entrepreneurship reached a national scale, with these two organizations functioning as a shadow state delivering financial services, employment, health, and education to many more citizens than the elected state. The problems such models create for democracy are considered below. Across all developing country contexts three basic models of social entrepreneurship can be discerned:

- Economic generation/employment social enterprises resembling conventional businesses (often funded by microcredit and sometimes set up as cooperatives)
- Innovative service delivery organizations resembling non-governmental organizations or the state (often funded by international aid)
- Sustainable energy enterprises focusing on solar or other green technologies (often funded by local or international investment capital)

Section 4 illustrates the range of social entrepreneurship models addressing policy voids and fulfilling welfare objectives with seven short case studies.

Table 10.1 Typology of social entrepreneurship–policy contexts across regions (after Kerlin, 2009)

	United States/UK	Continental Europe	Transition economies	Latin America	Africa	South East Asia
Policy context	Reinventing government	L'économie sociale et solidaire	Ideological disruption	State and market collapse	State and market failure	Minimalist state
Strategic objectives	i. Address state failures (in lieu of state) ii. Reform state provision (with state)	i. Build social solidarity ii. Address state failures (in lieu of state)	i. Market reform ii. Economic development	i. Build social solidarity ii. Rebuild economy	i. Sustainable economic development	i. Operate as a shadow state
Main programme focus	Welfare services	i. Employment ii. Welfare services	i. New business development ii. Employment	i. Employment ii. New business development	i. Employment ii. New business development	i. Welfare services ii. New business development
Organizational form	Social purpose business	Cooperative	i. Small business ii. Social purpose business	Cooperative	i. Small business funded by micro-credit ii. Environmentally sustainable business	i. Social purpose business ii. Small business
Primary sectoral focus	State	Civil society	Private market	Civil society	Private market*	Private market

Note: *Historically, the primary sectoral focus has been on civil society as embodied in non-governmental organizations funded by international aid. However, despite weak market economies in many countries, market-driven development has become the dominant rationale for social entrepreneurship since the turn of the twenty-first century, perhaps reflecting disillusionment with aid-based models (Kerlin 2009).

4. WELFARE CONTEXTS

As noted above, the sociality, or social and environmental focus, of social entrepreneurship can be identified in three aspects of its operation: the macro-level institutional context in which it operates; the organizational micro-processes it employs; and the focus and nature of its impacts and outcomes. In developing country contexts, social entrepreneurship has evolved in response to a range of policy voids in traditional social policy sectors such as: health services; education and training; social care; economic development via employment; financial services; housing; security. Examples of each of these are considered in turn.

4.1 Health Services: Aravind Eye Care System (India) (www.aravind.org)

It is estimated that there are over 300 million people in the world with visual impairments, of whom approximately 45 million are blind. Of these, 90 per cent per cent live in developing countries, with 12 million blind people in India alone – more than in any other single country. Most of the blind patients are easily treatable with simple cataract surgery, but the majority of the poor cannot afford the operation. Furthermore, for the poor curing blindness is particularly critical since it often excludes them from working and supporting themselves and their families. In many cases cataracts can, as a consequence, be fatal for the poor and their dependents.

Following his retirement in 1976, Dr G. Venkataswamy ('Dr V'), a trained ophthalmologist, established the GOVEL Trust under which Aravind Eye Hospitals were founded. The first hospital was built in Madurai in southern India. Dr V's objective was to address the problem of the lack of avoidable treatments for blindness in the poor, rural population of his home country. The model he developed aimed to be self-sufficient and to supplement state-funded eye care services that struggled to cope with the needs of the whole population. The project had a strong spiritual as well as a practical set of objectives. Aravind was named after Sri Aurobindo, one of India's most revered spiritual leaders, and Dr V insisted that the hospital's services contributed to transcendence into a heightened state of consciousness for its patients and staff, acting as an instrument through which the divine force might work.

Aravind was established as a non-profit institution dedicated to providing exceptional eye care to all patients irrespective of their ability to pay. To achieve this, the Aravind Eye Care System developed a high-quality, high-efficiency model of cataract surgery that allowed it to cross-subsidize roughly 55 per cent per cent of its services to the poor free of charge, or at a significantly reduced price, while maintaining overall profitability. Its high-quality services attracted full-fee patients while its 'production line' surgical model kept its unit costs low. For example, Aravind used its surgical equipment 24 hours a day with doctors performing only surgery, while nurses handled all other care. Other innovations – such as the development of low-cost intraocular lenses, in-house manufacturing, and establishing a network of Vision Centres using low-cost telemedicine technology to provide primary eye care in rural areas – also improved efficiency and effectiveness.

In 2011 the Aravind Eye Care System encompassed five hospitals (in Madurai, Theni, Tirunelveli Coimbatore, and Pondicherry), two surgical centres, four community eye clinics, 37 primary eye care centres, two managed eye hospitals, a manufacturing centre for ophthalmic products (Aurolab), an international research foundation, and a resource and training centre that supports new eye care programmes across the developing world. Aravind has grown from offering only 11 beds in 1976 to having over 3,600 in 2010. In 2009–10 Aravind carried out 2.54 million examinations, performed 302,180 surgeries and laser procedures, and had an annual budget of $16 million.

4.2 Education and Training: BRAC Village Schools (Bangladesh) (www.brac.net)

In 1972, shortly after the conclusion of the civil war, Fazle Hasan Abed established the Bangladesh Rehabilitation Assistance Committee (later the Bangladesh Rural Advancement Committee, BRAC) to offer emergency aid and relief. In 1974 BRAC began to focus more on long-term development issues and to offer microcredit to poor women in Bangladesh. During the next ten years it expanded its activities to include village-based development programmes, health initiatives, manufacturing units, retailing (via its own Aarong brand), and even – in 2001 – its own university. Across all its activities BRAC prioritized working with women and the very poorest and most disadvantaged members of society. It also focused on building the human potential and self-reliance of the poor.

BRAC is now the largest non-governmental organization in the world, with over 120,000 staff the majority of whom are women. By 2011 the organization was working in all 64 districts of Bangladesh, provided capital to over 7 million microcredit borrowers and supported more than 70,000 health volunteers. BRAC's tuberculosis programme alone covered 80 million people in Bangladesh. In addition, BRAC operated programmes in nine other countries across Asia, Africa and the Caribbean

(Afghanistan, Sri Lanka, Pakistan, Tanzania, Uganda, Southern Sudan, Liberia, Sierra Leone and Haiti), reaching more than 110 million people in total. The organization is 80 per cent per cent self-funded through a number of commercial enterprises that include a dairy and food project and its chain of retail handicraft stores. The organization maintains offices in 14 countries throughout the world. In 2009–10 BRAC's budget was $495 million, 70 per cent of which was self-financed from its social enterprises and 30 per cent coming from international grants.

In 1985 BRAC started a Non-Formal Primary Education programme based in village schools. The programme offers four years of primary education to poor rural children – and to others who cannot access formal schooling – aged 8 to 14 years. The typical village school is a one-room building designed for 30–35 students and one teacher. Core subjects include mathematics, social studies and English. By 2009 BRAC had established 37,500 primary schools enrolling over 3 million children, 65 per cent of whom were girls. The schools had a dropout rate of less than 5 per cent. BRAC pays particular attention to teacher training and encourages the creative development of children's communication, language and social skills via the use of multiple types of class-work, including arts and crafts.

In 1997 BRAC launched pre-primary education programmes to improve the impact of primary schooling for children whose parents are illiterate. By 2010 24,750 pre-primary schools had been set up serving 365,294 students, 62 per cent of whom were girls. Nearly 4 million children have so far successfully transferred from this programme to mainstream primary school education.

4.3 Social Care: Associação Saúde Criança (Brazil) (www.saudecrianca.org.br)

In 1991 Dr Vera Cordeiro, a paediatrician, set up Renascer (later Associação Saúde Criança) in Rio de Janeiro, Brazil. The organization was a coalition of professionals, including doctors and nurses, psychologists, lawyers, volunteers and families, established as a not-for-profit membership network. The twin drivers behind Associação Saúde Criança were the poorly functioning state health-care system that failed to offer timely or holistic treatment for poor children, and the difficult living conditions experienced by the poor in many cities' *favelas*. Associação Saúde Criança aimed to offer the families of children convalescing from an acute illness or with a terminal illness the support they needed to create the best home environment for the patient. The aim was to break the cycle that condemned many poor children in Brazil to repeated readmissions to hospital and, ultimately, to the deterioration of their overall health. Often this was because the children lacked the basic essentials for a healthy life, such as consistent post-operative care, adequate shelter and good-quality food.

Associação Saúde Criança's methodology was based on building close relationships between volunteers, hospital professionals and children's families to establish the key needs and best treatment for sustainable post-discharge health. This involved the provision of medicine and nutritional supplements via a network of contacts with pharmaceutical laboratories and food companies, as well as a range of other support including: transportation vouchers; psycho-therapeutic support; dissemination of health information; access to chemotherapy; help with parental drug and alcohol abuse problems; referrals to self-help groups; and help organizing work schedules so that parents could best attend to the health-care needs of their children. In exchange for this support, families promised to support the programme as volunteers in the future. Associação Saúde Criança aimed to empower parents to be fully responsible for the well-being of their children by making them aware of how they could help themselves to improve the family environment that ultimately determined the outcome of a child's physical health and life expectancy.

In regions where the Associação Saúde Criança's methodology has been implemented, the health status of effected children changed to 50 per cent in good health (up from 25 per cent) and 7 per cent in life-threatening conditions (down from 20 per cent). Furthermore, average family income increased by 32 per cent and the average number of days per year children spent in hospital fell by 66 per cent. By 2010, Associação Saúde Criança's model had been replicated in 23 other hospitals in six states across Brazil, helping approximately 40,000 people every month. Moreover, Associação Saúde Criança's approach has been incorporated into public policy in Belo Horizonte and Rio de Janeiro.

4.4 Economic Development via Employment (Work Integration Social Enterprise): Honey Care Africa (Kenya and Tanzania) (www.honeycareafrica.com)

In 2000 Farouk Jiwa established Honey Care Africa in Kenya as a social business that aimed to promote sustainable, community-based bee-keeping in East Africa. Honey Care Africa aimed to build village-level capacity and skills in apiary via training, locally focused extension services, and the provision of microcredit for start-up and growth. The social enterprise manufactures and supplies high-quality Langstroth

Hives and related bee-keeping equipment to small farmers and communities. Honey Care Africa also acts as a Fair Trade[6] wholesale intermediary and processor for small producers' honey, providing market access and branding, and guaranteeing a fair price for their product. Honey Care Africa has built strong local brands, such as 'Beekeeper's Delight', and now has a significant market share in East Africa. In 2004 it expanded its operations into Tanzania.

Honey Care Africa's operations are grounded in the core Fair Trade principles of fairness and transparency across the entire value chain of honey production. The social enterprise aims to work with all its stakeholders as equals in symbiotic partnerships that are beneficial for all those involved. It is strongly performance-driven, using a triple bottom-line approach that captures its economic, social and environmental value creation.

By 2011 Honey Care Africa was employing over 50 staff and helping over 9,000 small-scale beekeepers. This generated a positive impact for over 38,000 beneficiaries in total who typically earned an additional, Fair Trade, income of $180–250 each per year. Honey Care Africa is now the largest producer of high-quality honey in East Africa and is one of the largest exporters of beeswax in the area. This social enterprise is also a member of the World Fair Trade Organization.

4.5 Financial Services: Grameen Bank (Bangladesh) (www.grameen-info.org)

The Grameen Bank (*gram* means 'village' in Bangla) pioneered the provision of small, unsecured, loans to poor borrowers as the first microfinance organization in the world. The inspiration for the Bank came in 1974 when its founder, economist Muhammad Yunus, responded to the lack of financial services then available to the poor for their own development. Yunus lent $27 of his own money to a group of 42 families so that they could start small businesses without paying prohibitive interest rates to loan sharks. The loans were repaid and had a positive impact on the borrowers' economic development. As a consequence, in 1976 Yunus, who was at that time Head of the Rural Economics Program at the University of Chittagong in Bangladesh, started the Grameen Bank action research project that aimed to design a credit delivery system to provide banking services for the rural poor. The project tested an alternative to the status quo in which the poor were typically exploited by moneylenders if they could access debt products at all. The provision of microcredit to the poor has proved to be an innovative approach to reducing poverty that can act as a catalyst for larger-scale economic development. The Grameen Bank uses mutual trust, accountability and participation to reduce the risk of default in an innovative peer-group lending model – several borrowers come together and agree to share the responsibility for each other's repayments. The Bank also aims to address gender issues in poverty and development: 98 per cent of its borrowers are women.

After the original action research project had demonstrated the potential impact of the micro-finance model during 1976–79, the Central Bank of Bangladesh provided capital to extend the project to the Tangail district near the capital city of Dhaka. After several other successful trials the Grameen Bank Project was granted stand-alone bank status in 1983. In addition to its innovative lending model, the Grameen Bank pioneered a novel ownership structure in which borrowers owned 90 per cent of the shares, while the national government retained 10 per cent. By 2011 Grameen Bank had 8.37 million borrowers and 2,565 branches, and offered financial services in 81,379 villages covering more than 97 per cent of Bangladesh. Grameen Bank and Yunus were jointly awarded the Nobel Peace Prize in 2006.

4.6 Housing: Échale! A Tu Casa (Mexico) (www.echale.com.mx)

Mexico suffers from a severe housing shortage that particularly affects the poor. The country needs over 9 million more homes than are currently provided by the state or the private sector, and the scale of this problem is likely to increase over the next 20 years as the population of Mexicans aged 25–45 grows.

In response to this crisis, Francesco Piazzesi set up Échale! A Tu Casa to provide housing for low-income Mexican families who otherwise would struggle to afford a home. Having started as a not-for-profit, Échale has subsequently developed a business model in conjunction with support and mentoring from funders at New Ventures within the World Resources Institute that allows it to be self-sufficient and profitable.

The organization works with Mexican communities to help them self-build new homes. The Échale model works in communities to create social housing production units by offering training in both financial literacy and basic construction skills. The organization then helps set up a local credit union to facilitate savings and loans to help establish the conditions for increased home ownership and development. By building their own homes, community members are able to have a new home in roughly one month rather than waiting for years to save sufficient money to buy a pre-built house. The houses built by Échale also provide opportunities for local community members to move out of temporary, often unsafe, shelter.

Houses are designed to be environmentally sustainable and are constructed from Échale's patented building block, Adoblock, which serves as a natural insulation source and reduces reliance on heating and cooling devices. More than 90 per cent of each Adoblock is made from local soil, which reduces waste and the use of environmentally harmful materials. The blocks are produced with an Adopress, an easily operated machine that can be used directly by community members building their own homes. In addition, new homes have solar heaters, grey water bio-digestors and rainwater harvesting systems.

By 2011 more than 26,000 new homes had been built through Échale, creating 130,000 jobs and US$65 million of income for those engaging in the local micro-construction industry. Piazzesi aims to expand Échale by implementing a social franchise model in which communities that have already self-built homes will be able to assist and train other communities in the process. This model should allow 120,000 new houses to be built in Mexico by 2014.

4.7 Security and Health: Apopo (Tanzania) (www.apopo.org)

Landmines are a major problem across many post-conflict zones in Africa and are destructive both physically and economically, typically injuring many innocent people as well as severely constraining local development. APOPO (Anti-Persoonsmijnen Ontmijnende Product Ontwikkeling or Anti-Personnel Landmines Detection Product Development) is a social enterprise that uses African giant pouched rats (known as 'hero rats') as an innovative biotechnology to detect landmines in former conflict zones as well as tuberculosis in its early stages. It is a registered Belgian non-governmental organization headquartered in Tanzania.

Bart Weetjens founded APOPO in 1997 while still a student at the University of Antwerp. The existing mine-clearance methods were slow, expensive and inefficient, so Weetjens, who had a lifelong interest in rats, used his knowledge to develop the idea of training rodents for landmine detection and clearance. Weetjens knew that rats have a strong sense of smell and are intelligent and easy to train, so they could provide a cheaper, more efficient and locally available means to detect landmines. He selected the African giant pouched rat (*Cricetomys gambianus*) as the most suitable species, as it is indigenous to sub-Saharan Africa, has a long life span and is resilient to most local diseases.

In 2000 APOPO built partnerships with the Sokoine University of Agriculture and the Tanzanian People's Defence Force, and moved its headquarters to Morogoro, Tanzania. Three years later APOPO expanded its operations to Mozambique. In the same year it won the World Bank Development Marketplace Global Competition, which provided seed funding for research into another application of the rats biotechnology: tuberculosis detection. A full-scale three-year research trial of this new application began in 2010. In 2011 APOPO set up a new programme in Thailand in collaboration with the Thailand Mine Action Center and a local non-governmental organization, Peace Road Organization, that aimed to use hero rats to detect mines along the Thailand–Cambodia border.

By 2011 APOPO's rats had cleared 1.3 million square metres of suspected minefields, positively affecting more than 50,000 people, and had diagnosed over 900 tuberculosis patients in Tanzania, preventing infection from reaching an estimated 13,500 healthy people. In addition APOPO employed more than 200 staff and had over 300 rats in various stages of breeding, training or usage. The APOPO model is now being copied in Latin America and South East Asia.

These case examples are illustrative rather than exhaustive, but they aim to show the variety of socially entrepreneurial innovation that is currently evident in contexts of interest to social policy. A comparative analysis of these cases demonstrates a wide variety of approaches, models and strategic orientations with respect to the three established sectors of society. For example, while Associação Saúde Criança now works closely with formal state structures, Honey Care Africa is located firmly in private sector markets. With respect to growth, Grameen and BRAC have aimed to expand their operations aggressively, but APOPO has adopted a more measured and organic approach based not on developing a franchisable model but rather on exploring new applications of its core biotechnology. Various factors are at play in the differences between these cases, but chief among them are the entrepreneurial vision and orientation of the founder or founding managerial group and their context-specific judgements of how to maximize impact and effectiveness (see further below).

5. CHALLENGES AND LIMITATIONS

The examples above suggest that social entrepreneurship is already playing a significant role in addressing social policy voids across a range of developing countries. However, the field is still at an early stage of institutionalization and faces a number of significant critiques globally. This section outlines the main issues.

5.1 Public Legitimacy

It is a commonplace to note that societies exhibit distinct categories of organization, each of which has its own set of internal logics and rationales for action. In liberal democracies three different 'ideal-type' sectors have been identified: the public/state sector dominated by government; private/commercial markets; and civil society/informal organizations.[7] Each of these three sectors demonstrates a series of distinctive features: for example, the institutional logics and rationales for action by civil society are built upon notions of public benefit; those of the private sector focus on profit maximization; and the (functioning) state prioritizes democracy. Similarly, in terms of accountability civil society aims to incorporate stakeholder voice in its systems of planning and measurement, while the private sector demonstrates its performance through formal mechanisms of publishing audited accounts, and the state is ultimately accountable through the ballot box (see Table 10.2). These established sectors provide important normative orientations for action in most societies.[8]

Table 10.2   Institutional logics in societal sectors

	Civil society	Private sector	Public sector
Institutional logic	Public benefit	Profit maximization	Collective democracy
Ownership	Mutual	Private	Collective
Key beneficiaries	Clients	Owners	General public
Strategic focus	Social value creation	Financial value creation	Public service
Accountability	Stakeholder voice	Published accounts, stock performance	Ballot box
Resource strategy	Donations, grants, earned income, volunteers, tax breaks	Debt, equity, earned income	Taxes
Dominant organizational structure	Charity, cooperative	Private company	Departmentalized bureaucracy

However, many of the solutions developed by social entrepreneurship to address policy voids take the form of interventions that combine otherwise distinct institutional logics and models of action in innovative forms. Such action typically blurs the boundaries of the conventional institutional structures of society and challenges normative notions of the roles and responsibilities of the discrete sectors. Thus, in practice the social entrepreneurial response to policy voids has often been to develop hybrid forms of action that blend the logics and rationales of two or more of the established sectors to build new organizational structures (i.e. 'social' business), processes (i.e. work integration models), or goods and services (i.e. user-led welfare models) that correspond to complex sets of needs and demands in late modern societies better than conventional interventions do. Such hybridity often drives the innovation that provides alternative mechanisms to reframe and, thus, begins to address otherwise insoluble 'wicked problems' (Rayner 2006). Furthermore, the innovations driven by social entrepreneurship as responses to policy voids may ultimately become institutionalized in policy (see Figure 10.1). For example, the 'social business' model that simultaneously combines the logics of civil society with those of the private sector and also decouples notions of enterprise from profit maximization has been widely supported by social enterprise policy agendas in national governments, as well as at the transnational level in the United Nations Development Programme and the World Bank. Similarly, the 'shadow state' model developed in Bangladesh by BRAC and Grameen, which combines the logics of civil society and the state, is also present in other developing countries typically with the blessing of the state (e.g. India, Afghanistan and Ghana). Finally, the public–private partnership model that integrates state and private sector logics is well established in many neo-liberal democracies (and increasingly elsewhere, too), with social enterprises playing a growing role in the reformulation of state functions in several countries (e.g. the UK, the USA, parts of Latin America and East Africa).

However, crossing normative boundaries can generate public legitimacy issues, too, since the logics and rationales of action of each conventional sector are quite different and even contradictory at the normative level. As a consequence, the public legitimacy of social entrepreneurship (at both normative and cognitive levels: see Suchman 1995) can often be compromised. The new models of this sector have been variously seen as attempts to privatize the social, dismantle the state, or undermine civil society (Nicholls and Cho 2006). The reaction to the core social enterprise/social business hybrid model has been a particularly hostile since this challenges many fundamental principles of the state and civil society as not-for-profit sectors. Such loss of public

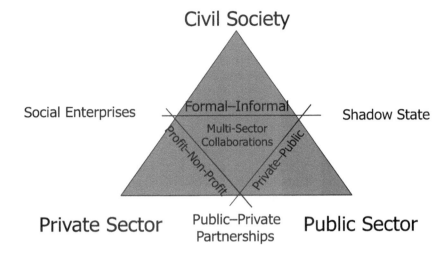

Figure 10.1   Social entrepreneurship in policy voids

legitimacy can have serious consequences in terms of access to resources, market competitiveness, policy support and staff recruitment, and is likely to persist until the hybridity of the social entrepreneurship sector is itself normatively institutionalized (but see Nicholls 2010a).

5.2 Scaling

The stated objective of many social entrepreneurs is to bring about 'systems change' or a new, more just societal 'equilibrium', rather than just ameliorate an existing situation (Bradach 2003; Martin and Osberg 2007). However, genuine systems change is a very ambitious objective and typically requires a combination of scale, geographical spread and political support. Bloom and Chatterji (2009) acknowledged these factors when they established the SCALERS model as a guide to key activities needed to achieve scale in social entrepreneurship: staffing; communicating; alliance building; lobbying; earnings generation; replicating; and stimulating market forces. Elsewhere research has focused on the institutional, rather than organizational, aspects of achieving scale, particularly in terms of building socially entrepreneurial 'eco-systems' (Dees et al. 2004; Bloom and Dees 2008).

However, despite evidence of growth in the field overall globally (see above), there are still relatively few examples of social entrepreneurship reaching a significant scale, let alone bringing about systemic change. Perhaps the only two examples thus far are micro-finance (see Grameen Bank above) and Fair Trade (see Honey Care Africa above). Both of these models have reached global scale – going beyond a single organization – and have brought about significant institutional change in terms of the societal framing of major issues that concern the poor. In the case of micro-finance, Grameen and the many subsequent organizations that adopted this model demonstrated that, contrary to accepted models of risk, the poor were extremely low-risk debtors, even when their loans were unsecured.[9] In addition, micro-finance challenged the notion that the poor lacked innovatory and entrepreneurial spirit. The consequence of these systemic changes in the perception of poor borrowers' risk was to bring them into the mainstream of financial services, so much so that today Citibank is the world's largest single holder of microcredit debt (albeit it is secondary-market, securitized debt).

In the case of Fair Trade, a combination of trade justice groups, faith-based entrepreneurs and non-governmental organizations developed an alternative model of trade that reconnected Southern producers and Northern consumers by making consumption a political and ethical choice. At the same time, Fair Trade created a more transparent and efficient supply chain that returned more of the total value chain to the producer as part of a market-driven development model. While Fair Trade products were initially sold only by dedicated alternative trade retailers and church groups, the creation of a Fair Trade certification label in 1999 built wider brand recognition and attracted mainstream retailers to list Fair Trade products so as to attract high-spending 'ethical' consumers. The result has been global sales of over $4 billion in 2010 that have directly helped 1.2 million producers in 58 countries by providing more than $100 million of additional income.[10] Perhaps even more importantly, Fair Trade has played a leading role in unlocking the 'commodity fetishism' that characterized late modern capitalism in the developed North, leading consumers to demand more information about the provenance and processes behind all the products they buy (Nicholls 2010b).

However, despite these examples there is very little evidence as yet of social entrepreneurship delivering welfare interventions – let alone systems change – on the same scale as governments. Moreover, the single issue or cause-driven nature of much social entrepreneurship, aligned with a lack of cooperation across organizations similar to that found in the not-for-profit sector, can result in a 'patchwork' or serendipitous landscape of provision compared with state-led programmes or welfare policies. This suggests that social entrepreneurship will not necessarily function well in terms of equity of access across a whole population.

5.3 Political Support

A related issue in terms of achieving scale and systemic change is the political dimension of social entrepreneurship. Perhaps surprisingly, this aspect of social change has been largely ignored in the analysis of, and commentary on, social entrepreneurship (*pace* a few exceptions such as Alvord et al. 2004). Partly this appears to be a result of the US and UK focus of the first wave of social entrepreneurship research, which positioned the field as a response to (or even opposed to) state action.[11] Nevertheless, as has already been discussed, the actual relationship between social entrepreneurship and the state is more complex, including active involvement at the policy level as well as more informal joint working. In fact, social entrepreneurship on the ground is often highly political, operating across a range of levels from direct interactions with the state to activism and lobbying in the tradition of social movements (see Zald and Davis 2005; Lounsbury and Strang 2009) and close working with both formal and informal community-level social and political structures. Indeed, social entrepreneurs are expert at identifying and mobilizing relevant sources of political support to move their mission objectives forward (Nicholls and Cho 2006).

However, recognizing the political dimension of social entre-preneurship is not merely a research opportunity; it also raises significant practical questions and challenges. First, political action often prompts a reaction and can lead social entrepreneurs into institutional confrontation or even danger. The personal attacks on Muhammad Yunus – the founder of the Grameen Bank – by the Bangladeshi government in 2010 are a response to the political influence of an individual social entrepreneur. Similarly, social enterprises operating in non-democratic contexts – such as the Non-Profit Incubator in China[12] – sometimes face repression and opposition from established political structures. Second, when social entrepreneurship addresses public welfare issues or aims to drive political change, it typically does so as private action that lacks any formal democratic legitimacy. This is particularly problematic in cases where a social enterprise acts as a shadow state (see BRAC and Grameen above). Finally, there is the more general issue of who is included in, and who is excluded from, social entrepreneurship. Much of the analysis of social entrepreneurship to date has prioritized a model of the field as driven by 'hero' entrepreneurs – extraordinary individuals with special skills and abilities, often from privileged financial and academic backgrounds. This represents an inherently elitist and disempowering vision of social entrepreneurship as an exclusive club.[13] Although this conceptualization has been increasingly challenged (e.g. Nicholls 2010a), the genuine democratization of social entrepreneurship remains a pressing challenge for the field as a whole (Nicholls and Young 2008).

5.4 Access to Finance

A second limitation to the further development of social entrepreneurship is the difficulty of accessing start-up and growth capital (Nicholls and Pharoah 2007; Nicholls 2010c). There are several reasons for this. First, as was noted above, social entrepreneurship typically occupies hybrid institutional spaces that span the logics of the state and the for-profit and not-for-profit sectors. This creates difficulties in terms of assessing risk within conventional financial modelling, particularly since social enterprises can adopt multiple (and sometimes hybrid) legal forms. It can also have the effect of reducing profitability since social entrepreneurship does not typically aim at maximizing the financial bottom line, focusing instead on creating 'blended value' (Emerson 2003) that combines social and financial performance. Linked to this is the tendency to disconnect value creation from value appropriation (Santos 2009): social enterprises rarely maximize economic returns to the owners of investment capital, *pace* cooperatives. A third challenge is investor exit. Unlike commercial firms, social enterprises rarely offer publicly listed equity (but see Hartzell 2007), preferring private debt or grant capitalization.[14] Moreover, any fully functioning secondary market for social enterprise securities has yet to emerge; and this severely limits liquidity.[15] The lack of appetite for public equity appears to be largely a function of social entrepreneurs' anxiety about ceding any organizational control to equity investors for fear that this could result in social mission drift. It is also a, sometimes visceral, reaction against the idea that social enterprises could help fuel the generation of speculative economic rents.

As a consequence of these serious barriers to conventional investment, a new 'social investment' sector is emerging that aims to provided bespoke instruments, market structures and institutions for social investors seeking a blended value return. This new market has more recently begun to coalesce around a potentially new asset class characterized as 'impact investing' (Freireich and Fulton 2009). It has been estimated that this market for social investment could amount to $1 trillion over the next few years (O'Donohoe et al. 2010). Overall, the value of global social investment – largely accounted for by cooperative assets – has been estimated at over $4 trillion (Nicholls 2010c).

5.5 Unintended Consequences

A final set of challenges for social entrepreneurship concerns its acciden-
tal or unintended consequences. While often addressing the negative
externalities resulting from private or public sector action, social entrepreneurship itself can generate problematic externalities. Thus, despite
the rhetoric that has developed around the field as always a socially
positive thing, social entrepreneurship can in fact have a 'dark side'.
There are four issues to be considered here. First, as has already been
suggested, social entrepreneurship can be elitist and exclusive and, as a
result, have negative social effects by excluding some groups from the
focus of its provision of social goods and services or its campaigns for
social change. Indeed, almost by definition, the combination of an almost
obsessive focus on a clear social mission and a market-orientated
approach to performance that is so typical of social entrepreneurs will
exclude some groups.

Second, another unintended set of consequences can arise from different framings or perceptions of the hybrid nature of social enterprises that
blend social and financial objectives. From one point of view social
enterprises are exploitative and represent the privatization of the social,
as critiques of the high interest rates offered by many micro-finance
organizations have pointed out. Such differences in perception can
undermine the societal legitimacy of social entrepreneurship and prove
disastrous in terms of access to resources and support over time (see Dart
2004; Nicholls 2009). Moreover, social entrepreneurship must face the
challenge of all innovative fields, namely to builds societal (cognitive)
legitimacy in established institutional contexts, as mentioned above (see
Suchman 1995): the so-called 'liability of newness' (Stinchcombe 1965
p. 5).

Third, social entrepreneurship could be hijacked for socially divisive or
destructive objectives and intentions, for example by secret societies or
extreme political parties. At a more normative level, the politicization
of social enterprises by successive governments in the UK and elsewhere
demonstrates how flexible social entrepreneurship can be to ideological
reinterpretation and public presentation (e.g. DTI 2002; Cabinet Office
2011).

Finally, social entrepreneurship can achieve perverse effects in cases of
operational failure (e.g. Tracey and Jarvis 2006). Since social entrepreneurship is often expressed organizationally in the form of innovative
start-ups in weak institutional spaces, it is inherently risky (as, of course,
is all entrepreneurship). As a result, it is reasonable to expect that much

social entrepreneurship will fail, though there is very limited data available on this subject.[16]

6. CONCLUSION

This chapter represents the first attempt to analyse the emergent field of social entrepreneurship within a social policy context in developing countries. To date much of the research on the subject has ignored its broad political dimensions and implications and has also failed to recognize its specific connections to, and implications for, state structures and social policy around the world. This chapter has set out to address this research lacuna. First, it established the theoretical and practical boundaries of the field and considered its scope and scale. Next, the chapter established the institutional drivers behind the evolution of social entrepreneurship and connected these to broader social policy agendas in developing countries by means of a series of short cases. The chapter also elaborated some of the challenges facing the further development of the field.

The discussion thus far leads to three final observations. First, social entrepreneurship clearly has an important role to play in helping to address social policy priorities in developing countries. Its combination of a clear mission focus with innovation and a strong, performance-driven market orientation allows social entrepreneurship to tackle seemingly insoluble 'wicked problems' (Cantor et al. 1992; Rayner 2006) in weak institutional spaces where conventional models have failed. Moreover, the sectoral and organizational hybridity that is characteristic of the field can generate solutions to institutional failures that are often sector-specific, while also building multiple relationships and connections across the conventional public, private and civil society sectors.

Second, since social entrepreneurship aims, ultimately, to achieve scale and to bring about systemic change around problems rather than just ameliorate them, it is well suited to address some of the major failures in welfare currently evident in developing countries. While it needs to be acknowledged that, in this regard, rhetoric can run ahead of reality in the discourses of social entrepreneurship, examples such as those given here illustrate the potential of the field to tackle the big social welfare issues of our time. Importantly, social entrepreneurship also typically displays a strong grounding in communities as well as a contextual sensitivity that drives bottom-up scaling approaches:[17] this maximizes effectiveness as well as demonstrating a respect for beneficiaries that rejects paternalistic, top-down development solutions.

However, while social entrepreneurship can offer solutions to welfare failures in developing countries, the third conclusion of this chapter is more challenging: social entrepreneurship can present a political problem to policymakers in developing countries. This is partly a consequence of the democratic deficit of any private organization noted above, but, more fundamentally, it concerns the role of policy development in institutionally weak contexts. Social entrepreneurship can blur the boundaries of public–private action that help define the ambit of policymaking and the responsibilities of policymakers. Thus, the institutional fluidity and innovation of social entrepreneurship may also undermine conventional notions of state action and accountability. In normatively benign scenarios, such as providing much-needed basic welfare services, this may not be of general concern, but elsewhere the effect of socially entrepreneurial action may be to dilute the responsibility of the state, on the one hand and, on the other, to open up welfare functions to commercialization and capture within a private market free-for-all. Thus, social entrepreneurship may have important limitations when compared with the tax-based state provision of welfare, particularly with respect to giving the poor and powerless voice and control over their own lives.

The investment activities of the Chinese government and other sovereign wealth funds in Africa in terms of infrastructure and other development projects may offer extreme examples of the logics of social entrepreneurship. Such projects both confront the conventional rationales of international aid and bring with them value systems and broader economic and political objectives with potentially far-reaching implications for 'investee' states.

In conclusion, while this chapter has not intended to present social entrepreneurship as a panacea for all welfare failures in developing countries, it has suggested that the field has an important, as well as potentially catalytic, role to play in resolving intractable social policy challenges. It seems clear that developing countries will shape their own economic and social welfare models independent of developed country norms, as has clearly been the case in China and India. In such complex and innovative institutional contexts the flexibility and sectoral fluidity of social entrepreneurship will be particularly well placed to continue to address social welfare failures without recourse to established models and out-dated methodologies.

NOTES

1. But see Weerawardena and Sullivan Mort (2006) and Zahra et al. (2009) for useful attempts to reconcile some key definitional issues. Bacq and Janssen (2011) also offer a valuable geographical analysis.
2. Public goods are defined here as goods that are non-rival and non-excludable. Social goods are defined here as public goods that could be delivered as private goods, but which – in developed countries, at least – are typically delivered by the state as part of its social policy agenda funded via taxation.
3. This is consistent with the non-distribution constraint typical of charities and other not-for-profits and provides an important source of legitimacy for social enterprises in welfare markets (see Clotfelter 1992). In the Continental European tradition, the distribution of profits within the social enterprise is seen as one of its defining characteristics (Nyssens 2006).
4. The image of the social entrepreneur, popularized in the United States as a heroic, independent, innovative actor working outside of established institutions, is challenged by the multiple examples of social intrapraneurship across all sectors, including the state (Nicholls 2010a). The latter also corresponds to established notions of institutional and policy entrepreneurship (Hall 1992, 1993; Lawrence and Phillips 2004).
5. See also Crouch (2011) for a discussion of the blurring between business and polity in late neo-liberal models.
6. Fair Trade is a model that provides market-driven economic development for poor producers around the world by linking them to developed-country markets and guaranteeing fair pricing and terms and conditions (see Nicholls and Opal 2005).
7. Evers (1995) suggested that the third sector is best understood as the domestic economy and, echoing the argument here concerning the boundary blurring aspects of social entrepreneurship, that civil society spans all three.
8. Although these sectors are not always configured in the same way in different contexts: see, for example, the Chinese model of 'state controlled' market capitalism.
9. However, despite its apparent success, micro-finance has also been subject to a range of criticisms both in terms of its impacts on communities (the social pressures of peer-lending structures can lead to defaulter suicides) and its financial structures (both Compartamos in Mexico and SKS in India have been subject to public condemnation over their high interest rates and potential profiteering).
10. Like micro-finance, Fair Trade has been criticized from several perspectives. For example, as a deliberate market distortion – through its minimum price setting – the model has been accused of perpetuating poor farmers' reliance on ultimately unsustainable crops, thus creating dependence. It has also been noted that the scale of Fair Trade on the ground excludes many more poor producers than it can help.
11. As has already been noted, the situation in continental Europe is very different: here, the political dimension of social entrepreneurship has long been acknowledged (see, for example, Borzaga and Defourny 2001 and Nyssens 2006).
12. Social entrepreneurship operating in welfare services in China was initially seen as a public criticism of the state since it demonstrated de facto failures in public sector provision. This position has softened more recently as part of a more general recognition by the government of the potentially useful role to be played by a more developed civil society in achieving a 'harmonious society'.
13. The main field building organizations in social entrepreneurship – Ashoka, the Schwab Foundation, and the Skoll Foundation – all focus on individuals ahead of

organizations, though Ashoka has presented its wider vision of social entrepreneurship in a more inclusive way under the general banner of 'everyone a
changemaker'.

14. This may also be a factor of sectoral life cycles. In the more mature sectors of social
    entrepreneurship, shares issues are becoming more common. Examples of successful
    initial public offerings (IPOs) include Fair Trade companies such as cafedirect (2004,
    £5 million raised, UK) and micro-finance institutions such as Compartamos (2007,
    $450 million raised, Mexico) and SKS (2010, $350 million raised, India) – though
    these IPOs have sometimes been controversial (see above).
15. Despite this, a social stock-market project has been alive in the UK for several years
    and an Impact Investing Exchange (IIX Asia) is likely to open for business in
    Singapore in 2013.
16. This lack of data reflects another fault of much of the research to date on social
    entrepreneurship, namely, a biased focus on success (Nicholls 2010a; Nicholls and
    Murdock 2011). This, in turn, reflects key field building organizations' strategic
    objectives.
17. See examples of social enterprises engaged in so-called 'frugal' innovation in
    developing countries, notably India (*Economist* 2010).

REFERENCES

Alter, K. (2006), 'Social enterprise models and their mission and money
   relationships', in A. Nicholls (ed.), *Social Entrepreneurship. New Models of
   Sustainable Social Change*, Oxford: Oxford University Press, pp. 205–32.
Alvord, S., L. Brown and C. Letts (2004), 'Social entrepreneurship and societal
   transformation: an exploratory study', *Journal of Applied Behavioral Science*,
   40(3), 260–83.
Austin, J.E. (ed.) (2004), *Social Partnering in Latin America*, Cambridge, MA:
   SEKN/Harvard Business School.
Austin, J., H. Stevenson and J. Wei-Skillern (2006), 'Social and commercial
   entrepreneurship: same, different, or both?', *Entrepreneurship: Theory and
   Practice*, **30**(1), 1–22.
Bacq, S. and F. Janssen (2011), 'The multiple faces of social entrepreneurship: a
   review of definitional issues based on geographical and thematic criteria',
   Entrepreneurship and Regional Development: An International Journal, **23**(5),
   373–403.
Bishop, M. and M. Green (2008), *Philanthrocapitalism: How the Rich Can Save
   the World and Why We Should Let Them*, London: A. and C. Black.
Bloom, P. and A. Chatterji (2009), 'Scaling social entrepreneurial impact',
   California Management Review, **51**, 114–33.
Bloom, P. and J.G. Dees (2008), 'Cultivate your ecosystem', *Stanford Social
   Innovation Review*, **6**, 46–53.
Borzaga, C. and J. Defourny (2001), *The Emergence of Social Enterprise*, New
   York: Routledge.
Bosma, N. and J. Levie (2010), 'A global comparison of social entrepreneurship',
   in *Global Entrepreneurship Monitor 2009 Executive Report*, London: GERA,
   pp. 44–51.

Bradach, J.L. (2003), 'Going to scale: the challenge of replicating social programs', *Stanford Social Innovation Review*, **1**, 19–25.

Cabinet Office (2011), *Growing the Social Investment Market: A Vision and Strategy*, London: Cabinet Office.

Cantor, R., S. Henry and S. Rayner (1992), *Making Markets: An Interdisciplinary Perspective on Economic Exchange*, London: Greenwood Press.

Chabal, P. and J. Daloz (1999), *Africa Works: Disorder as Political Instrument*, London: International African Institute.

Clotfelter, C. (1992), 'The distributional consequences of nonprofit activities', in C. Clotfelter (ed.), *Who Benefits from the Nonprofit Sector?*, Chicago, IL: University of Chicago Press, pp. 1–23.

Crouch, C. (2011), *The Strange Non-Death of Neo-Liberalism*, Cambridge: Polity Press.

Dacin, P., T. Dacin and M. Matear (2010), 'Social entrepreneurship: why we don't need a new theory and how we move forward from here', *Academy of Management Perspectives*, **24**(3), 37–57.

Dart, R. (2004), 'The legitimacy of social enterprise', *Nonprofit Management and Leadership*, **14**(4), 411–24.

Dees, J.G. (1998), *The Meaning of 'Social Entrepreneurship'*, Stanford, CA: Graduate School of Business, Stanford University.

Dees, J.G. (2010), 'Creating large-scale change: not "can" but "how"', New York: McKinsey & Co., available at http://whatmatters.mckinseydigital.com/social_entrepreneurs/creating-large-scale-change-not-can-but-how- (accessed 17 October 2011).

Dees, J.G., B. Anderson and J. Wei-Skillern (2004), 'Scaling social impact: strategies of spreading social innovations', *Stanford Social Innovation Review*, **1**, 24–32.

DTI (Department for Trade and Industry) (2002), *Social Enterprise: A Strategy for Success,* London: DTI.

Economist (2010), 'First break all the rules: the charms of frugal innovation', 15 April.

Edwards, M. (2008), *Just Another Emperor? The Myths and Realities of Philanthrocapitalism*, London: Young Foundation.

Emerson, J. (2003), 'The blended value proposition: integrating social and financial results', *California Management Review*, **45**(4), 35–51.

Evers, A. (1995), 'Part of the welfare mix: the third sector as an intermediate area', *Voluntas*, **6**(2), 159–82.

Freireich, J. and K. Fulton (2009), *Investing for Social and Environmental Impact: A Design for Catalyzing an Emerging Industry*, New York: Monitor Group.

Giddens, A. (1998), *The Third Way*, Cambridge: Polity Press.

Grenier, P. (2009), 'Social entrepreneurship in the UK: from rhetoric to reality?', in R. Zeigler (ed.), *An Introduction to Social Entrepreneurship: Voices, Preconditions, Contexts*, Cheltenham, UK and Northampton, MA, USA: Edward Elgar.

Hall, P. (1992), 'The movement from Keynesianism to Monetarism: institutional analysis and British economic policy in the 1970s', in S. Steinmo et al. (eds),

Structuring Politics: Historical Institutionalism in Comparative Perspective, Cambridge: Cambridge University Press, pp. 90–113.

Hall, P. (1993), 'Policy paradigms, social learning, and the state: the case of economic policy making in Britain', *Comparative Politics*, **25**(3), 275–96.

Hartzell, J. (2007), *Creating an Ethical Stock Exchange*, Oxford: Skoll Centre for Social Entrepreneurship, University of Oxford, available at http://www.sbs. ox.ac.uk/centres/skoll/research/Documents/Ethical%20Stock%20Exchange.pdf (accessed 4 February 2012).

IFF Research (2008), *Annual Small Business Survey 2007*, London: Department for Business, Innovation and Skills.

Karamchandani, A., M. Kubzansky and P. Frandano (2009), *Emerging Markets, Emerging Models*, New York: Monitor Group.

Kerlin, J. (ed.) (2009), *Social Enterprise: A Global Comparison*, Medford, MA: Tufts University Press.

Klein, N. (2002), *Fences and Windows*, London: Flamingo.

Lawrence, T. and N. Phillips (2004), 'From Moby Dick to Free Willy: macro-cultural discourse and institutional entrepreneurship in emerging institutional fields', *Organization*, **11**(5), 689–711.

Leadbeater, C. (1997), *The Rise of the Social Entrepreneur*, London: Demos.

Le Grand, J. (1991), 'Quasi-markets and social policy', *The Economic Journal*, **101**(408), 1256–67.

Light, P. (2008), *The Search for Social Entrepreneurship*, Washington, DC: Brookings Institution Press.

Lounsbury, M. and D. Strang (2009), 'Social entrepreneurship: success stories and logic construction', in D. Hammack and S. Heydemann (eds), *Global-ization, Philanthropy, and Civil Society*, Bloomington, IN: Indiana University Press.

Lyon, F., S. Teasdale and R. Baldock (2010), 'Approaches to measuring the scale of the social enterprise sector in the UK', Working Paper No. 43, Birmingham: Third Sector Research Centre.

Mair, J. and I. Marti (2009), 'Entrepreneurship in and around institutional voids: a case study from Bangladesh', *Journal of Business Venturing*, **24**(5), 419–35.

Martin, R. and S. Osberg (2007), 'Social entrepreneurship: the case for definition', *Stanford Social Innovation Review*, Spring, 29–39. NESST (2005), *Risky Business: The Impacts of Merging Mission and Business*, Santiago: NESST Learning Series.

Nicholls, A. (2006), 'Introduction', in A. Nicholls (ed.), *Social Entrepreneurship: New Models of Sustainable Social Change*, Oxford: Oxford University Press, pp. 1–35.

Nicholls, A. (2009), 'What gives fair trade its right to operate? Organisational legitimacy and strategic management', in K. Macdonald and S. Marshall (eds.), *Fair Trade, Corporate Accountability and Beyond: Experiments in Global Justice Governance Mechanisms*, London: Ashgate, pp. 95–121,

Nicholls, A. (2010a), 'The legitimacy of social entrepreneurship: reflexive isomorphism in a pre-paradigmatic field', *Entrepreneurship Theory and Prac-tice*, **34**(4), 611–33.

Nicholls, A. (2010b), 'Fair trade: towards an economics of virtue', *Journal of Business Ethics*, **92**, 241–55.

Nicholls, A. (2010c), 'The institutionalization of social investment: the interplay of investment logics and investor rationalities', *Journal of Social Entrepreneurship*, **1**(1), 70–100.

Nicholls, A. and A. Cho (2006), 'Social entrepreneurship: the structuration of a field', in A. Nicholls (ed.), *Social Entrepreneurship: New Models of Sustainable Change*, Oxford: Oxford University Press, pp. 99–118.

Nicholls, A. and A. Murdock (2011), *Social Innovation*, Basingstoke: Palgrave Macmillan.

Nicholls, A. and C. Opal (2005), *Fair Trade. Market-Driven Ethical Consumption*, London: Sage.

Nicholls, A. and C. Pharoah (2007), *The Landscape of Social Finance*, Oxford: Skoll Centre for Social Entrepreneurship, available at: http://www.sbs.ox.ac.uk/centres/skoll/research/Pages/socialfinance.aspx (accessed 4 February 2012).

Nicholls, A. and R. Young (2008), 'Introduction: the changing landscape of social entrepreneurship', in A. Nicholls, (ed.), *Social Entrepreneurship: New Paradigms of Sustainable Social Change* (paperback edn), Oxford: Oxford University Press, pp. vii–xxiii.

Nyssens, M. (ed.) (2006), *Social Enterprise*, London: Routledge.

O'Donohoe, N., C. Leijonhufvud and Y. Saltuk (2010), *Impact Investments: An Emerging Asset Class*, New York: JP Morgan Global Research and the Rockefeller Foundation.

Osborne, D. and T. Gaebler (1992), *Reinventing Government*, Reading, MA: Addison-Wesley.

OTS (Office of the Third Sector) (2006), *Social Enterprise Action Plan: Scaling New Heights*, London: Cabinet Office.

Prahalad, C.K. (2005), *The Fortune at the Bottom of the Pyramid: Eradicating Poverty Through Profits*, Upper Saddle River, NJ: Wharton Business School Press.

Rayner, S. (2006), 'Wicked problems: clumsy solutions – diagnoses and prescriptions for environmental ills', The Jack Beale Memorial Lecture, available at: http://www.sbs.ox.ac.uk/research/Documents/Steve%20Rayner/Steve%20Rayner,%20Jack%20Beale%20Lecture%20Wicked%20Problems.pdf (accessed 4 February 2012).

Salamon, L., H. Anheier, R. List, S. Toepler and S. Sokolowski (eds) (2003), *Global Civil Society: Dimensions of the Nonprofit Sector*, Baltimore, MD: John Hopkins University.

Santos, F. (2009), 'A positive theory of social entrepreneurship', Working Paper 2009/23/EFE/ISIC, Fontainebleu: INSEAD Social innovation Centre.

Stinchcombe, A. (1965), *Social Structure and Organizations*, Thousand Islands, CA: Sage.

Suchman, M. (1995), 'Managing legitimacy: strategic and institutional approaches', *Academy of Management Review*, **20**, 517–610.

Tracey, P. and C. Jarvis (2006), 'An enterprising failure: why a promising social franchise collapsed', *Stanford Social Innovation Review* (Spring), 66–70.

Weerawardena, J. and G. Sullivan Mort (2006), 'Investigating social entrepreneurship: a multidimensional model', *Journal of World Business*, **41**(1), 21–35.

Zahra, S., E. Gedajlovic, D. Neubaum and J. Shulman (2009), 'A typology of social entrepreneurs: motives, search processes and ethical challenges', *Journal of Business Venturing*, **24**(5), 519–32.

Zald, M. and G. Davis (2005), 'Social change, social theory, and the convergence of movements and organisations', in G. Davis et al. (eds), *Social Movements and Organization Theory*, Cambridge: Cambridge University Press, pp. 335–50.

PART IV

Scenarios and trajectories

11. Globalization and social policy in developing countries

Bob Deacon

1. INTRODUCTION AND OVERVIEW

This chapter is concerned with the ways in which world interconnectedness, which has increased rapidly since the 1980s, has affected the nature of social problems in the developing world and the nature of the social policies prescribed to address them. The chapter first defines this increased interconnectedness in terms of the concept of globalization, measured by reference to the free movement of capital and trade and to the interconnectedness engendered by technical change. The chapter then assesses the broad effects of the specific neo-liberal mode of globalization on trade-based low-wage production, on the brain drain and on trade in services. It reviews evidence of increased inequity within and between countries, and discusses the impact of globalization on global social structure, including the dis-embedding of the globalizing middle class, on the balance of power between capital and labour, on gender relations and on ethnic divisions. The focus then shifts to social policy and the several ways globalization has affected it. The chapter shows that globalization has increased economic competition and the race to the welfare bottom, enabled new global actors to intervene in the policymaking process, given rise to the emergence of a global discourse about desirable social policy and social development, encouraged a global market in services such as health and education and challenged the territorial limits of welfare obligations. The role of international non-governmental organizations (INGOs) in the development process is briefly examined. This shifting global discourse about desirable national social policy in the context of development builds on the treatment of the International Monetary Fund (IMF) and the World Bank in Chapter 3 of this volume and draws attention to the ideas about social policy emerging from the social agencies of the UN system – the International Labour Office (ILO), the World Health Organization (WHO), UNESCO and

UNICEF. The chapter next focuses on the critical juncture of the global economic crisis of 2008 in terms of whether it has given greater scope to the World Bank and the IMF on the one hand, or to the UN system on the other, to influence subsequent social policy developments. The rise of the idea of the universalizing Global Social Protection Floor is contrasted with the IMF's continued emphasis on meeting the needs of only the most vulnerable. Innovations in global social policy that are genuinely transnational are then reviewed and critically examined. These innovations include global funds for health and education, global regulations for business and labour, and the articulation and monitoring of global social rights. Finally, the chapter considers the implications of these topics for the contested terrain of global social governance. The extent to which the interests and ideas of the global South are reflected in the UN or in the G20 are briefly examined, and possible reforms to global social governance assessed. The ideas of de-globalization and world regionalism are introduced as a lead-in to Chapter 12 on South–South dialogues.

2. NEO-LIBERAL GLOBALIZATION AND ITS SOCIAL IMPACTS IN THE GLOBAL SOUTH

Here are two definitions of globalization:

> Globalisation may be thought of initially as the widening, deepening and speeding up of world-wide interconnectedness in all aspects of contemporary life. (Held et al. 1999)

> [G]lobalization (involves) tendencies to a world-wide reach, impact, or connectedness of social phenomena or to a world-encompassing awareness among social actors. (Therborn 2000)

When social scientists talk about globalization they are referring to a process within which there is a shrinking of time and space. Social phenomena in one part of the world are more closely connected to social phenomena in other parts of the world. The kind of definition that sees cross-border connections as the key to understanding globalization has to be distinguished from arguments for or against globalization. Usually such arguments and debates are about particular international policies and practices – typically economic ones – which may be associated with the wider process of globalization but are not a necessary feature of it. These disputes are usually about the form that globalization takes or the politics of globalization rather than about the fact of the shrinkage of time and space. Indeed, the debate about the neo-liberal form that globalization took within the context of the Washington Consensus from the 1980s through the 1990s and the consequential kinds of national residual and privatizing social policies promoted by global actors during that period is central to the assessment in this chapter of the impact of globalization upon social policy in a development context.

Most commentators are agreed that globalization embraces a number of dimensions, including the economic, the political, the production, the social and the cultural. The aspects of globalization which reflect this range of dimensions include:

- increased flows of foreign capital based on currency trading;
- significantly increased foreign direct investment in parts of the world;
- increased world trade with associated policies to reduce barriers to trade;
- an increased share of production associated with transnational corporations;
- global interconnectedness of production arising from changes in technology;
- increased movement – both legal and illegal – of labour;
- the global reach of forms of communication including television and the internet; and
- the globalization or 'McDonaldization' of cultural life.

These processes and other associated phenomena have in turn led to the emergence of a global civil society sharing a common political space. However, while economic activity has become more global, global political institutions tend to lag behind these developments. They are to a large extent trapped in an earlier historic epoch of intergovernmental agreements. Indeed, the reform of global political institutions and processes in order to improve global social policy is an important theme of this chapter.

The essential point is not that the world is shrinking but that during the 30 years from the mid-1970s this world was being shaped by a global political decision to end the separate state-led, often post-colonial, development projects of the 1960s which promoted import substitution in order to allow countries to build up their productive bases. This approach was replaced, in the wake of the Reagan–Thatcher anti-Keynesian economic free-market revolution of the 1970s, by the Washington Consensus, which argued that the interests of the poor were better served by opening up markets in developing countries to world trade and by allowing unconstrained international capital flows. Export-led growth replaced import substitution.

The economic and social consequences of that revolution have been profound. But the World Bank's argument that growth follows from global free trade and moreover that growth is good for the poor (Dollar and Kraay 2000) has been refuted by other, more persuasive voices (Milanovic 2003; Vandermoortele and Delamonica 2000; Mehrotra and Delamonica 2007; Voipio 2011). In general, the era of neo-liberal globalization has led to:

- minimal impacts on the comparative situation of the poor in many parts of the global South, especially Africa;
- the undermining of food security in many countries by replacing subsistence agriculture with cash crops and the consequential need to import staples at high prices;
- a huge growth in income inequalities both within and between countries;
- the undermining of the state's commitment to the welfare of all its citizens, favouring a focus on safety nets for the poor only;
- a consequential increased brain drain because of the flow of skilled doctors and nurses and other welfare professionals abroad seeking better pay and conditions; and
- low-wage job creation, especially in new export-focused tax-free zones but often of a kind which undermines global labour standards and drives down wages and working conditions elsewhere.

Thus, one consequence of the neo-liberal globalization project has been to strengthen the power of capital over that of labour. The returns of investment to capital have risen, the returns to labour have fallen. Capital is free to move across borders, labour is more restricted. Constructing cross-border trade union solidarities in defence of national welfare provision has become more difficult. Interestingly, while women as workers may have suffered some of the same effects of globalization upon their capacity to defend and improve pay and working conditions, organizations of women as women may have been strengthened by globalization's facilitating transnational networking. The growth of a global women's movement has empowered women in many developing countries in particular to confront issues of patriarchy and women-unfriendly development policies for the first time. The World Bank has celebrated the part that women's and girls' education can play in economic development, and there has been 'much to celebrate' in progress towards gender equality (UNRISD 2005). Increased cross-border movements of people, which have in part resulted from the rising inequities between countries, may have led, paradoxically, to increased identification and networking with one's country of origin. Post-war diasporas have become an important factor in some countries' policy-making. As well, new migrants' access to welfare benefits has been restricted. Globalization may have increased the importance of inter-ethnic stuggles in shaping national social policy (Chau 2004).

In sum, the state-led development strategies in Africa and Latin America of the 1960s and 1970s were challenged and largely destroyed, certainly in sub-Saharan Africa, during the structural adjustment period of the 1980s and 1990s, when the World Bank and the IMF made loans conditional on countries fulfilling the tenets of the Washington Consensus by cutting the size of the state. The collapse of the communist project in Eastern Europe gave a further twist to this. In terms of social policy in a development context, I concluded (Deacon et al. 1997) that the World Bank enthusiastically grasped the opportunity created by the collapse of the communist project. In alliance with social development NGOs, a social safety net future was being constructed both in Eastern Europe and in the developing world. This approach, I concluded, 'was challenging powerfully those defenders of universal social security based welfare states to be found in the EU and the ILO' (Deacon et al. 1997, p. 197). Thus, the World Bank played a very important role in shaping and damaging national social policy in a development and transition context in the 1980s and 1990s. Its insistence on user charges throughout this period limited access to education and health. Its beneficiary index demonstrating that public spending often benefited people other than the poor was used in effect to undermine the embryonic welfare states of Latin America, South Asia and Africa. While policy focused on the poor, the losers were often members of the urban middle class, who had depended upon state universities, hospitals and pensions for services and jobs. These losers were in danger either of being impoverished or, if they found work, of being thrown into the arms of new, global private education and health service providers, and as a consequence abandoning their historic role as state builders. This chapter returns to the issue of the abandoned middle class in Section 4, which examines the shifting global discourse about desirable social policies in a development context.

3. THE IMPACT OF GLOBALIZATION ON THE MAKING OF SOCIAL POLICY

The diverse ways in which globalization affected the way social policy is made were addressed in my *Global Social Policy and Governance* (Deacon 2007). There I made several arguments about globalization.

Globalization sets welfare states in competition with each other. This raised the prospect of a race to the welfare bottom whereby states reduced their welfare commitments for fear of losing capital investment. Evidence is now accumulating which suggests that in the global North equitable approaches to social policy may actually be sustainable whereas in conditions of neo-liberal globalization they may not be so easily replicable within the South. Indeed, Section 2 showed how the Washington Consensus has had this impact in much of the global South, in particular discouraging countries from taxing inward investment, thus undermining fiscal resources for welfare expenditure.

Globalization brings new players into the making of social policy. International organizations such as the IMF, the World Bank and the World Trade Organization (WTO), and UN agencies such as the WHO and the ILO, have, as already suggested, become more involved in prescribing country policy. This has generated a global discourse about desirable national social policy. The within-country politics of welfare has taken on a global dimension, with a struggle of ideas on national social policy being waged within and between international organizations. This point is examined in more detail in Section 4.

Globalization raises the issues with which social policy is concerned – redistribution, regulation and rights – to a supranational level that has both regional (EU, ASEAN, MERCOSUR, SADC, etc.) and global dimensions. A major question was whether the contested neo-liberal globalization described above could and should give way to a more social reformist globalization within which global or regional redistribution, regulatory and rights policies and mechanisms could be developed. The ILO, for example, produced its classic *A Fair Globalisation: Creating Opportunities for All* (2004). This issue is addressed in Section 5.

Globalization creates a global private market in social provision. Increased free trade which was the leitmotif of the new World Trade Organisation has created the possibility of mainly USA and European private health care and hospital providers, education providers, social care agencies and social insurance companies operating on a global scale and benefiting from an international middle-class market in private social provision. The International Finance Corporation agency of the World

Bank has been instrumental in advancing private investments in these sectors in developing countries. The implication of this development for sustaining cross-class solidarities within one country in the context of development is discussed in Section 4.

Globalization encourages a global movement of people that challenges territorial-based structures and assumptions of welfare obligation and entitlement. The impact of migration upon welfare provision in developing countries is profound both in terms of the loss of skilled welfare-state labour (doctors and nurses) and in terms of increased reliance on foreign remittances. International care chains have emerged within this context within which poor women from the global South care for the children of rich women in the global North. The case arises for social policy obligations to extend beyond borders with possibly a greater role for regional associations of government in making such provision. This point is revisited at the end of the chapter.

These are the broad ways in which it is argued that globalization affects social policy as a subject area and as a practice of governments and allied actors. In terms of social policy understood as sectorial policy (health, education, social protection), two points stand out. One is the role of international organizations in influencing national social policy through loans, conditional aid or technical assistance. At present the world has in effect two global ministries of health, two global ministries of education and two global ministries of social protection. During the period of the creation and influence of the UN agencies in the 1950s and 1960s and into the 1970s, global advice on sectorial policy came from the WHO, UNESCO and the ILO. Once the World Bank in the 1980s and 1990s included social sector issues in its lending policy and practice, it began in effect to operate in competition with the UN social agencies. Its policy prescriptions for developing country health, education and social protection were often at odds with the advice given by UN agencies. Furthermore, it became better endowed than the UN agencies and had more influence both in financial terms and in terms of the perceived quality of its professional staff. Related to this is the increased scope that the globalization of markets offers private providers of hospitals, pension funds and some aspects of education. In the context of neo-liberal globalization, the mix between government and private welfare provision shifted in favour of the latter in developing countries.

In social policy understood as policies and processes of redistribution, regulation and rights, a number of points stand out. The first is that, because of the perceived impact of global economic competition on a country's ability to tax in order to spend, the extent to which a country can redistribute has been brought into question. And because of fear of capital flight a country's ability to impose social regulations on business has been brought into question, too. Guaranteeing social rights becomes rather more difficult in this context. If it is true that to some extent capital has escaped national rules by virtue of its capacity to move abroad, then the political task becomes one of reinventing those rules at regional and global levels. If the global economy is to have a social purpose, global taxes and global social regulations must be geared to the realization of a set of global social rights. This issue of the global funding for global public goods is revisited in Section 5.

4.   THE SHIFTING GLOBAL DISCOURSE ON SOCIAL POLICY IN A DEVELOPMENT CONTEXT

We turn now to examine in more detail the shifting debate within and between international organizations concerning the most desirable social policy for developing countries. The dominant Washington Consensus logic summarized in Section 2 did not go unchallenged. The arguments about desirable national social policy promoted by the international organizations in the early years of the current century amounted to something approaching a 'war of position' waged between on the one hand those agencies that continued to argue for a more selective, residual role for the state (focused upon only the poor), together with a larger role for private actors in health, social protection and education provision, and on the other hand those who took the opposite view. This division of opinion often reflected a disagreement over whether the reduction of poverty was a matter of targeting specific resources (micro-credit, safety nets, workfare) on the poorest through such mechanisms and policy processes as the Poverty Reduction Strategy Papers or whether it was, on the contrary, a matter of major social and political-institutional change which would involve a shift in power relations and a significant increase in redistribution from rich to poor.

In 2006 I concluded that 'the tide has turned against the targeting and privatising view and the opportunity now exists for the UN working with sympathetic donors such as the Scandinavians and some other European countries to begin to undo the damage wrought by the Bank over the past decades' (Deacon 2007, p. 171). Around that time ideas about social policy as a desirable social investment were being reinvented, the notion that services for poor people are poor services was rediscovered, the finding that inequity might be bad for business and security was re-emerging, and the importance of middle class buy-in was being remembered. Not only were agencies such as the ILO gaining more credibility, but within the World Bank counter-tendencies for a while dominated the discourse. Below I examine one aspect of this shifting discourse in more detail, namely the emergence of the idea of a Global Social Protection Floor, and show how the global economic crisis has propelled it to centre stage; then, however, I ask whether that idea goes far enough.

Reviewing the impact of the 2008 global economic crisis on the shifting global social policy discourse, I suggested that the crisis had highlighted three strands of thinking about social policy in a development context (Deacon 2011). The first derived from the large sums granted by the historic first summit of the G20 in 2009 to the IMF. This left the IMF's parsimonious targeted approach towards protecting social expenditures only for the most vulnerable poor in a still-dominant position. The second, at the other extreme, was a few voices raising again the case for a kind of state-led development within which state capacity is central. UNCTAD's *Least Developed Countries Report 2009* argues that 'the developmentally orientated elite … should establish a social compact through which broad sections of society support the developmental project' (UNCTAD 2009, p. 51). The third was the emergence of the idea of a Global Social Protection Floor, which the global economic crisis has propelled to centre stage. Though evoking universal access to a minimum standard of welfare, the concept does not in my view go far enough in recognizing the role of the middle class in engineering improved collective well-being.

The idea of a Global Social Protection Floor had been promoted at public events bringing together UN and INGO staff. A public presentation of the campaign for a Global Social Protection Floor brought together Isabel Ortiz, then of UNDESA, now of UNICEF; Michael Cichon, Director, Social Security Department, ILO; Silvia Stefanoni, Director, HelpAgeInternational; and Gaspar Fajth, UNICEF, at a public side event at the Financing for Development Conference at Doha in December 2008. The publicity material for this event, titled 'A New Deal for People in a Global Crisis: Social Security for All', asserted that:

> The current global financial crisis is an opportunity to create a Global New Deal to deliver social protection in all countries through basic old age and disability pensions, child benefits, employment programs, and provision of social services … Social security is a human right (Articles 22 and 25 of the Universal Declaration of Human Rights) and it is affordable, a basic package is estimated to cost from 2 to 5 percent of GDP as an average. It is feasible if the international system commits to providing financial support for a Global New Deal to jump start an emergency response to the urgent social needs of our times. (Choike 2008)

Subsequently Cichon, now Director of the ILO Social Security department, argued that the concept of a Global Social Protection Floor should be mainstreamed within the ILO. This was given a boost after the G20's response to the global financial crisis focused upon giving the IMF the authority to address the social consequences of the crisis using its unreformed pro-cyclical and cost-cutting approach. The selection of the G20 and the IMF as the global agencies to address the crisis annoyed many in the UN system and, concretely, led to a meeting of the UN Chief Executives Board (UNCEB) in Paris in April 2009 which generated the UNCEB issue paper, *The Global Financial Crisis and its Impact on the Work of the UN System*. The meeting called for coordinated action across the UN system in eight key policy fields: (i) finance, (ii) trade, (ii) employment and production, (iv) environment, (v) food security, (vi) social services, empowerment and protection of people, (vii) humanitarian, security and social stability, and (viii) international cooperation for development. Most important from this chapter's point of view was the sixth policy field, in which the goal was a global 'Social Protection Floor which ensures access to basic social services, shelter, and empowerment and protection of the poor and vulnerable'. This was elaborated as a

> floor (that) could consist of two main elements: (a) public services: geographical and financial access to essential public services (water, sanitation, health, education); and (b) transfers: a basic set of essential social transfers ... to provide a minimum income security. (UNCEB 2009)

The ILO and the WHO would lead on this policy, supported by a host of other agencies such as UNICEF and UNDESA. The Global Social Protection Floor (SPF) had become UN policy. To strengthen the case for the Social Protection Floor the ILO set up an advisory committee which generated the Bachelet Report (ILO 2011a). The report also called upon the World Bank to incorporate the idea in its emerging new social protection strategy which it was finalizing in 2012. This it indeed did, suggesting a future where the World Bank and ILO contest over Social Protection Policy might not be as fundamental as in the past (World Bank 2012). At the same time the ILO conference in June 2011, focusing on the social transfers aspect of the UNCEB definition, agreed that in 2012 it would spell out a global recommendation on such a floor (ILO 2011b). However, by then the concept had been modified to refer to social protection floors as adapted to the conditions prevailing in each country – which some commentators saw as weakening it. On the other hand, the G20 meeting in Cannes in November 2011, led by the French, roundly endorsed the concept in its final communiqué. This marked a significant shift from the G20 meeting in 2008, which had focused upon the role of the IMF. At the International Labour Conference in 2012 the ILO Recommendation on Social Protection Floors was indeed agreed asserting that the SPFs should comprise at least the following basic social security guarantees:

> (a) access to a nationally defined set of goods and services, constituting *essential health care*, including maternity care that meets the criteria of availability, accessibility, acceptability and quality; (b) *basic income security for children*, at least at a nationally defined minimum level, providing access to nutrition, education, care and any other necessary goods and services; (c) *basic income security*, at least at a nationally defined minimum level, for persons *in active age* who are unable to earn sufficient income, including in particular in cases of sickness, unemployment, maternity and disability; and (d) *basic income security*, at least at a nationally defined minimum level, *for older persons*. (ILO 2012, p. 8)

Moreover these floors should be designed within a set of principles (which included universalism, non-discrimination, respect for the dignity of the recipient) and should be funded from a progressive tax base with international cooperation and support to complement national funds.

While many celebrate the advance of the idea of the Global Social Protection Floor made possible by the global economic crisis, we need to assess it in terms of whether it represents a fundamental break from the 'social-policy-as-safety-net' discourse of the 1980s and 1990s. While it is certainly an advance in global social policy to have the expression of the principles of universalism etc. clearly set out my concern, as argued above, is that since around 1990 the dominant discourse in international development has been the 'global politics of poverty alleviation', which focuses on the poor and on policies designed to lift them out of poverty, to protect them from it or to compensate them for it. Rather, what is needed is the global politics of social solidarity. Does the Global Social Protection Floor help us to make this shift? On the one hand, it has certainly contributed to persuading the ILO to shift its focus from the needs exclusively of workers to the needs of the poor, including those outside the workforce. In that sense it embraces solidarity between the poor and the workers. On the other hand, the emergence of a floor defined primarily in terms of cash or in-kind transfers and a minimum set of guarantees has not in itself shifted us far enough towards the global politics of (re)building the welfare state where the welfare needs of the state builders themselves are central. The Global Social Protection Floors or minimum social protection guarantees are still, I have argued essentially packages for the poor (Deacon 2013). The Global Social Protection Floor sidesteps the middle class and their historic role in state-led development. However in so far as the case for the social protection floor made by the ILO is always linked to extending contributory wage-related social security for the employed, it can be argued that the middle class is also considered (Cichon et al. 2011).

Why is this issue so important? Together with Shana Cohen (Deacon and Cohen 2011) I argue that, in the history of welfare states developed in the twentieth century, social policy and social development science tells us that the better way to reduce poverty is fairly consistent and involves middle-class buy-in to inclusive state welfare provision. In the context of developed countries, Goodin et al.'s (1999) comparative research of liberal, conservative and social democratic welfare states concludes that, whether the objective of policy is poverty alleviation, social inclusion or the facilitation of personal autonomy, social democratic welfare states are best at meeting it. This finding remains largely unchallenged by social policy analysts. For developing countries, Mehrotra and Jolly's (1997) comparative review of those countries with higher than expected human development indicators likewise concludes that a common feature of such human development leaders was the universal provision of social services. At the same time there is clear evidence that in both rich and poor countries more equity is good for growth, for poverty alleviation and for well-being (Wilkinson and Pickett 2009).

But, as we saw earlier, an alliance between the World Bank, the poor and development NGOs (which have an interest in meeting the needs of the poor) was constructed that challenged fundamentally the lessons of the universalism of the European social policy experience. In turn this gave rise to the OECD's Development Assistant Committee's poverty targets focused upon the poor, which in turn gave rise to the Millennium Development Goals (MDGs) that were themselves a retreat from the more universalist formulations of the UN Copenhagen Social Summit of 1995. In other words, those who constructed the global politics of poverty alleviation during the 1980s and 1990s were ignorant of the political economy of welfare-state building, which teaches us that this requires the construction of cross-class alliances and middle-class buy-in to reform.

One final twist in this global politics of poverty alleviation centres on the nature of the overseas aid business powered by the global INGO community. The neglected and impoverished middle classes of developing countries were co-opted into this project. Finnish scholar Gould (2005, pp. 148–9) has demonstrated that the aid business played a major part in seducing the professional and middle classes of developing countries from the developmental role they used to perform. Writing about Tanzania and other countries in Africa, he blamed the decline of the nationally engaged middle class on the actions of international aid agencies:

> Seduced by access to the dollar economy, they prioritise acquiring skills for ... the requirements of the aid cartel ... at the expense of contributing to the development of domestic manufacturing and processing industries that would generate actual wealth within the national economy.

There are signs of a change in thinking on this issue. Thus, Birdsall (2010, p. 159) argues:

> A focus on the middle class does not imply a lack of concern for the poor. To the contrary; in the advanced economies the poor have probably benefited from the rule of law, legal protections, and in general the greater accountability of government that a large and politically independent middle class demands, and from the universal and adequately funded education, health and social insurance programs a middle class wants and finances through the tax system.

These arguments have been reproduced by a research report of the African Development Bank (ADB 2011, p. 15):

> The middle class is also helping to improve accountability in public services through more vocal demands for better services. The middle class is better educated, better informed and has greater awareness of human rights. It is the main source of the leadership and activism that create and operate many of the nongovernmental organizations that push for greater accountability and better governance in public affairs ... policies that include the promotion of middle class growth are more cost-effective and generate more long-term poverty reducing benefits than policies that focus solely on addressing problems of the poor.

It is too soon to tell whether this report heralds a substantive shift away from the global politics of poverty alleviation to the global politics of social solidarity building.

5. ISSUES OF GLOBAL AND REGIONAL SOCIAL POLICY AND GOVERNANCE

The role of international organizations in the era of neo-liberal globalization has been not only to influence national social policies in a particular direction through the global discourse and advice associated with it but also to construct embryonic global policies and practices that also affect social policy within countries. In other words, global policies of redistribution from richer to poorer countries, global policies that regulate business activities in all countries and the global articulation of social rights that aspire to be recognized in all countries have a bearing on each country's social policies. To put it another way, the global social governance institutions which embrace global funds for health and education, global compacts between the UN and business to adhere to core labour standards, and new global conventions such as those concerning the rights of children and of persons with disabilities affect social policy in a development context. Here we consider only the case of global redistribution.

Redistribution from richer to poorer countries has traditionally taken the form of official development assistance, with all its advantages and drawbacks as discussed in various chapters throughout this volume. However, recently the related concept of global public goods has been brought into sharper focus. Global public goods are goods whose provision delivers worldwide benefits but which no one country might be inclined to finance. Among the global public goods argued for initially by Kaul et al. (1999) of the United Nations Development Programme were international equity and distributive justice (to secure a more stable world), international financial stability, health and global epidemiological surveillance, and global communications networks, peace and security. The idea that ensuring the health of the world's population might be something that is in the general interest, but that no particular national or private agency might see it as its business to undertake, has a long history. The issue has become even more apparent as globalization has increased the movement of people. If the health of each person is regarded as a public good from which we all benefit, rather than as a purely national or private matter which is the outcome of private behavioural choices and national government expenditures, then issues of equitable access to services and prevention become a matter for global health policy. Further work being undertaken by Kaul and her colleagues (Kaul et al. 2003) is now shaping a conception of global public goods within the UN system that goes beyond the mere formal economic criteria of goods which are technically non-excludable and non-rival in their consumption (e.g. world peace) to embrace goods such as basic education and health care which are (or should be) 'socially determined public goods', that is, goods which might be considered rival and excludable but which by political decision could be regarded as non-exclusive (Kaul et al. 2003, p. 83). Political decisions about this could reflect the global social rights embodied in the 1967 United Nations Covenant on Economic, Cultural and Social Rights. Another approach would be to regard as socially determined global public goods those goods listed within the internationally agreed MDGs.

In practice, global funds for several aspects of health care and health intervention have been set up in recent years, as has a global fund for primary education. There is as yet no fund for social protection. Distributive justice has yet to be recognized as a global public good, although it is under discussion by those involved in promoting the Global Social Protection Floor. These funds are financed partly through national donors, partly through philanthropic business (like the Gates Foundation) and, importantly, partly through new international taxation. The airline ticket tax has supported the Global Fund to Fight AIDS, Tuberculosis and Malaria. New ideas for other global taxes such as a financial transaction tax and a financial activities tax reached the agenda of the G20 in 2011, with some support even from the IMF.

These funds and the way they allocate monies to countries are an integral part of the relationship between globalization and social policy in a development context. The global funds might be taken as an example of how global innovative redistribution mechanisms are being established. Using the World Bank's categories of low-income and middle-income countries, the global fund first distinguishes between low-income countries that are fully eligible for monies and lower-middle-income countries that must match international funds with national funds, focus activities on the poor and vulnerable and aim to be self-sufficient over time. The procedure used for allocating funds within these constraints is based on a competition between bids from Country Co-ordinating Mechanisms within each eligible country. Where governments are non-functioning, the applications can be made by non-governmental organizations. A board of internationally appointed technical experts adjudicates between competing applications in light of the following considerations: epidemiological and socio-economic criteria, political commitment (of recipient governments), complementarities (to national effort), absorptive capacity (of governance mechanisms), soundness of project approach, feasibility, potential for sustainability, and evaluations and analysis mechanism in place. There are arguments for and against this responsive mode of resource allocation. Such an approach could miss the neediest countries, which might be unable to bid, but it does involve a partnership between national effort and global effort. At the same time there is room for debate about the implicit conditionality built into the allocation mechanism. Good national governance is likely to be rewarded (except where it is recognized that no effective government exists). On the other hand, a global fund that simply poured money into the coffers of a corrupt national government is likely to be criticized. Critics say that such funds lack democratic accountability, detract from the more systematic processes of global health funding that could be developed under the auspices of the WHO, and emphasize medical intervention at the cost of preventive public health measures. Recently there has been a move to consider how to fund and strengthen health systems. An issue here is an emerging concern to ensure governments raise their own revenues from the rich or mineral wealth rather than rely on global funds. As well, many progressive politicians in developing countries want to be free from aid dependency. A way forward would be matching funds that are offered only when national revenues are also raised.

In terms of the other two dimensions, namely global social regulation and global social rights, I concluded some years ago (Deacon 2007) that

> Global business is being asked by the UN to act in a socially responsible away. Of course there are no teeth and the idea of voluntary codes rather than enforceable rules prevails for now. There is no social clause in international trade deals but there is now a global expectation on all countries who are members of the ILO that they uphold core labour standards whether they have chosen to sign up to them or not. Despite continued international controversy about aspects of global social rights their very existence and promulgation by the UN enables others to campaign for their realisation in countries where governments have hitherto been reluctant to concede them.

Further advances in global social regulation, including especially the regulation of tax havens and the enhancement of governance mechanisms to oversee social rights adherence through the recent introduction of an individual complaints procedure, will positively affect national social policy in developing countries.

Related to these concerns about global redistribution, regulation and rights is the architecture of global social governance. An issue for developing countries has been whether they have enough say in the institutions of global social governance. Certainly they are relatively powerless in the World Bank and the IMF; campaigns to increase the number of seats on the boards have been very slow to have an impact. The WTO has been more open to developing countries' voice, which is reflected in the present impasse in the WTO Doha round of discussions. When the global South started to insist that the WTO recognized the special situation of developing countries by moderating its trade-related intellectual property rights policies which affect drug prices, or reconsidered its equal treatment policies to protect emergent nations, the debate stalled. The global South believes that the UN is much more open to its influence, leading to some countries in the North being unwilling to provide as much funds for it as needed. UNCTAD is a space within the UN system that is especially open to the influence of the global South. There have been moves to strengthen the UN with attempts to create a 'One-UN' with one lead agency in each country, under one boss with one budget and one policy, and to give more clout to the Economic and Social Committee by convening annual ministerial meetings and biennial global development forums. Some members of the South, however, have seen such moves as turning the UN into a mere development agency and further undermining its authority to manage the world's economy. Of course, crucially there is no global tax authority. Alongside the weakened UN the G20 has emerged, largely replacing the outdated G8 as a new centre of global power. An issue for the future is whether the new members of the G20 such as Brazil, China, India, South Africa and Russia speak for the middle-income countries rather than the low-income countries, and what kind of development agenda the G20 will fashion for them.

A related issue is whether advances in the supranational governance of social policy are best made at the global level or the world–regional level. I argued in 2007 that, because of the continued opposition (then) by the world superpower to any kind of strengthening of the UN system and any talk of global taxation and redistribution, an alternative route to a more systematic global governance might need to be sought in the concept of a strengthened regionalism with a social dimension. Within this scenario the European Union (EU), would be joined by the Association of South East Asian Nations (ASEAN), the African Union (AU) and similar groupings of countries in South and Latin America, in a global federation of regions linked to the L20 within which regions rather than countries had a vote. Regional social policies could then be devised that gave due recognition to diverse social and labour standards and reflected different cultural and religious approaches to social rights. Such a regional approach to a global social policy might, as we suggested, chime with the sentiments of many Southern voices that react against a Northern-driven global social democracy as strongly as they react against a Northern-driven global neo-liberalism (Bello 2004).

Since then the L20 has become the powerful G20 with EU, ASEAN and AU in attendance. Since then the AU has devised its own Social Policy Framework for Africa, and Latin American regionalism is undergoing a renaissance. Therefore we (Deacon et al. 2010, p. 224) wrote more positively that

The *argument* of this book has been that a strengthened system of world regional governance with each region adopting a social dimension to its regional integration project is the best way of securing a socially responsible globalization. The *exposition, empirical evidence and assessment* in this book suggest that developments along these lines are slowly taking place within regional associations of governments on four continents.

As I write I am engaged in discussions with the Southern African NGO community about the prospects of the Southern African Development Community establishing a regional sovereign fund financed by a tax on the regional extraction industry to finance a universal social protection grant for all southern Africans. This direction in the reform of neo-liberal globalization points also to the importance of the South–South dialogues on social policy, which are the subject of the following Chapter 12.

6. CONCLUSIONS

This chapter has described the diverse ways in which globalization has affected social policymaking, especially in developing countries, such that an understanding of national social policymaking is incomplete without reference to international actors. It has shown how the particular neo-liberal form of globalization empowered some of the external actors in the last decades of the twentieth century to drive a global politics of poverty alleviation across much of the developing world in which embryonic welfare states were destroyed. It has suggested that the global discourse about desirable national social policy has become more nuanced and contested. The concept of the Global Social Protection Floor is having an impact on building more inclusive social protection policies, but the welfare needs of the disconnected middle class are only now being addressed. The chapter has pointed to the ways in which embryonic systems of global social governance in the terrains of redistribution, regulation and rights also affect national social policy in a development context. Reviewing the debates about the responsiveness of the global architecture of social governance to the interests and voice of the global South generated the argument that such policy terrains might be better addressed at a world regional level, and invited the student to pay more attention to this level of social policy governance.

REFERENCES

ADB (African Development Bank) (2011), *The Middle of the Pyramid: Dynamics of the Middle Class in Africa*, Tunis-Belvedère: ADB.

Bello, W. (2004), *Deglobalization: Ideas for a New World Economy*, London: Zed Press.

Birdsall, N. (2010), 'The (indespensible) middle class in developing countries; or the rich and the rest, not the poor and the rest', in R. Kanbur and M. Spence (eds), *Equity in a Globalizing World*, Washington, DC: World Bank.

Chau, A. (2004), *World on Fire: How Exporting Free-Market Democracy Breeds Ethnic Hatred and Global Instability*, London: Heinemann.

Choike (2008), 'A new deal for people in a global crisis: social security for all', 27 November, available at http://www.choike.org/2009/eng/informes/7194.html (accessed 12 June 2011).

Cichon, M., C. Behrendt and V. Wodsak (2011), *The UN Social Protection Floor Initiative: Turning the Tide at the ILO Conference 2011*, Berlin: Friedrich Ebert Stiftung.

Deacon, B. (2007), *Global Social Policy and Governance*, London: Sage.

Deacon, B. (2011), 'Global social policy responses to the economic crisis', in K. Farnsworth and Z. Irving (eds), *Social Policy in Challenging Times: Economic Crisis and Welfare Systems*, Bristol: Policy Press, pp. 83–102.

Deacon, B. (2013), *Global Social Policy in the Making: The Foundations of the Social Protection Floor*, Bristol: Policy Press.

Deacon, B. and S. Cohen (2011), 'From the global politics of poverty alleviation to the global politics of social solidarity', *Global Social Policy*, **11** (2–3), 233–49.

Deacon, B., M. Hulse and P. Stubbs (1997), *Global Social Policy: International Organizations and the Future of Welfare*, London: Sage.

Deacon, B., M.C. Macovei, L. van Langenhove and N. Yeates (2010), *World Regional Social Policy and Global Governance: New Research and Policy Agendas in Africa, Latin America and Asia*, London: Routledge.

Dollar, D. and A. Kraay (2000), *Growth is Good for the Poor*, Washington, DC: Development Research Group, World Bank.

G20 (2011), G20 Heads of State Meeting in Cannes, 3–4 November 2011: Final Communiqué.

Goodin, R., B. Heady, R. Muffels and H. Dirven (1999), *The Real Worlds of Welfare*, Cambridge: Cambridge University Press.

Gould, J. (2005), *The New Conditionality: The Politics of Poverty Reduction Strategies*, London: Zed Press.

Held, D., A. McGrew, D. Goldblatt and J. Perraton (1999), *Global Transformations*, Cambridge: Polity Press.

ILO (International Labour Office) (2004), *A Fair Globalization: Creating Opportunities for All*, Report of the World Commission on the Social Dimension of Globalization, Geneva: ILO.

ILO (2011a), *Social Protection Floor for a Fair and Inclusive Globalization Report of the Advisory Group Chaired by Michelle Bachelet*, Geneva: ILO.

ILO (2011b), *Social Protection Floors for Social Justice and a Fair Globalization*, Report IV (1), International Labour Conference, 101st Session, 2012.

ILO (2012), *Recommendation Concerning National Floors of Social Protection (Social Protection Floors Recommendation), 2012 (No. 202)*, International Labour Conference, 2012, Geneva: ILO.

ILO/WHO (World Health Organization) (2009), *The Social Protection Floor: A Joint Crisis Initiative of the UN Chief Executives Board for Co-ordination on the Social Protection Floor*, Geneva: ILO/WHO.

Kaul, I., I. Grunberg and M. Stern (eds) (1999), *Global Public Goods: International Cooperation in the 21st Century*, Oxford: Oxford University Press.

Kaul, I., P. Conceicao, K. Goulven and R. Mendoza (2003), *Providing Global Public Goods*, Oxford: Oxford University Press.

Mehrotra, S. and E. Delamonica (2007), *Eliminating Human Poverty: Macro-Economic and Social Policies for Equitable Growth*, London: Zed Press.

Mehrotra, S. and R. Jolly (eds) (1997), *Development with a Human Face*, Oxford: Clarendon Press.

Milanovic, B. (2003), 'The two faces of globalization: against globalization as we know it', *World Development*, **31** (4), 667–83.

Therborn, G. (2000), 'Globalizations: dimensions, historical waves, regional effects, normative governance', *International Sociology*, **15**, 151–79.

UNCEB (UN System Chief Executives Board) (2009), *The Global Financial Crisis and Its Impact on the Work of the UN System*, New York: UNCEB.

UNCTAD (United Nations Conference on Trade and Development) (2009), *The Least Developed Countries Report 2009*, Geneva: UCTAD.

UNRISD (United Nations Research Institute for Social Development) (2005), *Gender Equality: Striving for Justice in an Unequal World*, Geneva: UNRISD.

Vandermoortele, J. and E. Delamonica (2000), *Growth is Good for the Poor: A Comment*, New York: UNICEF.

Voipio, T. (2011), *From Poverty Economics to Global Social Policy*, Kuopio: University of Eastern Finland, available at http://tinyurl.com/voipio2011book (accessed 10 June 2011).

Wilkinson, R. and K. Pickett (2009), *The Spirit Level: Why More Equal Societies Almost Always Do Better*, London: Allen Lane.

World Bank (2012), *Resilience, Equity and Opportunity: Consultations Report*, March 2012, Washington DC.

12. South–South cooperation: a new paradigm for global social policy?

Rebecca Surender and Marian Urbina-Ferretjans

INTRODUCTION: CONTEXTS AND DEFINITIONS

'South–South cooperation' is a broad term used to describe diverse types of political, economic and social cooperation among developing countries. Recently defined by the UN as 'the process, institutions and arrangements designed to promote political, economic and technical cooperation among developing countries in pursuit of common development goals' (UNCTAD 2010), the concept is rapidly gaining attention in both policy and academic forums. Although formally adopted by the UN General Assembly in 2003, the concept is much older and initially emphasized 'Technical Cooperation among Developing Countries' (TCDC). The Buenos Aires Plan of Action (BAPA) adopted by 138 states in 1978 is one of the first manifestations, providing an early conceptualization and practical guide for realizing the objectives of technical cooperation among developing countries. However, current South–South cooperation activities go well beyond technical cooperation, and address most sectors including traditional social policy areas such as health, education and social protection (UNDP 2004; Morais 2005, 2010). South–South relationships now include promotion of trade, development of regional, political and economic associations, provision of development assistance, and cooperation among developing states in multilateral negotiations with developed countries (UNCTAD 2010). This chapter focuses on those ideas and activities most relevant for the social sector and social policy.

Cooperation can take different forms – including the sharing of knowledge, experience and expertise; training; technology transfer; financial and monetary cooperation; and in-kind contributions – and is typically justified as being in both the national and the collective self-interest of developing countries. Underlying this is a rationale which posits that developing countries share common historical legacies, face many common conditions and challenges of underdevelopment, have a common interest in improving their positions in the international system, and, in many cases, have complementary resources which can be used for their mutual benefit. Most developing countries still regard the principles of equality and mutual benefit expressed in the Bandung Conference of 1955 as a central element of South–South development aid cooperation (The Reality of Aid 2010). Despite the heterogeneity of the 'global South',[1] South–South cooperation discourse emphasizes a common identity, and the proximity of experience is a key catalyst in promoting capacity development and South–South cooperation between countries.

In recent decades a growing number of Southern nations have become active in promoting South–South exchanges and responding to a range of development aid interventions. Despite its emphasis on 'mutuality' and 'partnership among equals', South–South cooperation in practice involves, in most cases, the most powerful middle-income, emerging and developing economies aiding the least-developed nations. The emerging market bloc of so-called BRICs (Brazil, Russia, India and China) is perhaps the best-known of the new group of benefactors. Another expanding lower-income group of countries also increasingly engaging in South–South exchanges, includes Colombia, Indonesia, Vietnam, Egypt, Turkey and South Africa (collectively referred as CIVETS) (Schulz 2010). While still aid recipients themselves, other emerging providers of development aid are Chile, Malaysia, Mexico, Thailand and Venezuela. Arab countries, in particular Saudi Arabia, are also an important group of development aid providers who have often used development assistance as an important tool to enhance solidarity among Arab countries (Zimmermann and Smith 2011).

Though often referred to as 'non-DAC donors',[2] 'emerging donors' or 'new donors', none of those labels really accurately define the nature or character of these new Southern benefactors. In the first instance, many of these countries have provided cooperation assistance of various kinds for decades, which makes it problematic to define them as 'emerging;' or 'new'. Likewise, defining the group by its non-membership of the Development Assistance Committee (DAC) appears inappropriate since it defines South–South cooperation by what it is not rather than from what it is. Besides, some non-DAC members such as the new European Union (EU) member states use DAC standards as a reference point, and new DAC members like South Korea are also increasingly engaged in South–South cooperation, making the DAC/non-DAC distinction less relevant. Many oppose the term 'donor' altogether, viewing it as inadequate since South–South cooperation is ideally defined in terms of partnership among countries rather than by hierarchical donor–recipient relationships (Davies 2010; The Reality of Aid 2010). (Interestingly, while there is debate about whether Arab states should be considered 'South–South development providers', they are among the few that welcome the 'donor' label: Zimmermann and Smith 2011). Finally, and perhaps most crucially, the experiences of providing development assistance are significantly diverse, and this heterogeneity makes it difficult to generalize and to refer to one single type of South–South cooperation (Davies 2010).

Regardless of this definitional complexity and heterogeneity, South–South cooperation in its various forms is undoubtedly expanding (Morais 2010). It has become an increasingly important source of funding for international development assistance, although volumes of financial support are still a relatively small proportion of DAC Official Development Assistance (ODA)[3] (Zimmermann and Smith 2011). More important, the trend has generated new ideas and models, 'complementing, challenging and providing alternatives to DAC donor practices and the multilateral institutions traditionally dominated by them' (Davies 2011). Increased South–South cooperation therefore has significant implications for traditional analytical frameworks utilized for understanding global welfare dynamics; and it raises interesting questions about its role for social policy developments in the global South.

This chapter argues that the ideas and activities of South–South cooperation in the area of welfare and social policy have implications not only for lessons about what might work (and an exceptional opportunity for reflection on the strengths and limits of North–South social development approaches) but also for important theoretical debates. The emergence of BRIC and other Southern powers as increasingly influential actors in the South appears to be changing the aid policy landscape and reopening past debates in international development, in particular regarding the optimal relationship between the economic and the social spheres of policy. Even though many of these debates are not new, we see, for the first time ever, that they are progressively driven by non-Western players.

There is growing awareness that South–South social cooperation appears to be 'mediated under a different set of normative premises, institutional actors, and policy mechanisms from traditional bilateral and intergovernmental institutions' (Urbina-Ferretjans and Surender 2012). Nonetheless, there is still a large gap in knowledge and basic descriptive information about what is unfolding. There is also interest in whether a new and distinctive South–South paradigm is emerging and, if so, what its implications are for social policy analysis concerning the conditions, processes and politics of social policy formation in developing countries. It is these two sets of concerns that the chapter explores.

SOUTH–SOUTH SOCIAL POLICY: CHARACTERISTICS, IDEAS AND PRACTICES

The volume of South–South social cooperation is difficult to estimate since most Southern providers of social assistance do not systematically collect and report detailed data disaggregated by sector. An additional challenge in assessing the volume of aid is the lack of a globally agreed definition of what exactly 'social aid' comprises. South–South development cooperation assistance is often delivered in a package that includes aid but also trade and investment. According to DAC criteria, while some of these modalities of aid would be considered Official Development Assistance (ODA), others would not (Davies 2011).

The modalities of aid also vary among South–South actors. While some countries like Turkey allocate funding through grants, the majority of countries provide aid through concessional loans (UNCTAD 2010), and a trend has been observed towards an increase in the loan component of aid among some Southern benefactors. For instance, whereas 64–70 per cent of Arab bilateral ODA during 1970–90 took the form of grants, in 2000–08 that share dropped to 36 per cent of net disbursements (World Bank 2010). This significant shift in the share of grants may reveal the increasing importance of trade and investment at the expense of aid in the package of South–South development assistance. Even so, the social sector tends to benefit more of the grant component than do other areas of cooperation, such as infrastructure, which are mainly supported through loans.

The overall estimated figures available, while limited, nevertheless provide some evidence of a steady growth in volume of assistance from non-DAC providers. In 2008 the total reported ODA from non-DAC countries amounted to US$9.5 billion in net figures. This represented an increase since 2003, when the amount was $3.4 billion and reflected both a growth in volume from individual donors and a rise in the number of countries reporting to DAC (Davies 2010). According to Zimmerman and Smith (2011), by 2009 visible gross development flows from non-DAC donors amounted to almost $11 billion and constituted approximately 8 per cent of global gross ODA. As Table 12.1 shows, this figure was made up of $7,299 million from the 20 non-DAC countries currently reporting to DAC plus estimates from BRICs based on various government sources. Among the 'BRICs' China is the main provider of development assistance with $1,947 million while Brazil provides the least, with $362 million.[4]

Table 12.1 Estimate of gross development cooperation flows from selected countries from beyond the DAC, current US$ millions

Country	Amount	Year	Source
20 countries reporting to DAC	7,299	2009	OECD/DAC statistics
Brazil	362	2009	IPEA and ABC, Brazil
China	1,947	2009	Fiscal yearbook, Ministry of Finance, China
India	488	2009/2010	Annual reports, Ministry of Foreign Affairs, India
Russia	785	2009	Russia Ministry of Finance, June 2010
South Africa	109	2009/2010	Estimates of public expenditure 2010, Foreign Affairs, National Treasury of South Africa
Estimated total	10,991		

Notes: DAC, Development Assistance Committee; OECD, Organisation for Economic Co-operation and Development; IPEA, Instituto de Pesquisa Economica Aplicada; ABC, Agencia Brasileira de Cooperacao.

Source: Zimmerman and Smith (2011).

However, the volume of aid tells only a partial story; and social policy engagement between South–South partners is perhaps better understood (and differentiated from North–South relations) in terms of its aspirations and normative underpinnings. In its broadest sense, it is articulated as an expression of solidarity and mutual respect among countries of the global South (Morais 2005; UNCTAD 2010). The strong discourse of legitimization of South–South cooperation is frequently built around the idea that the nature, aims and instruments of South–South cooperation are superior to those of North–South cooperation (Morais 2005). Accordingly, South–South cooperation is portrayed as more developmental, that is, detached from the selfish economic or strategic interests of rich countries; fair, rooted in principles of self-determination, solidarity and social justice and free of hidden governmental agendas; horizontal, in that it takes place between developing countries in a relationship of equals, without the power asymmetries and conditionality usually found in North–South cooperation; and more effective, since it utilizes more cost-effective instruments and resources, and is better adapted to the specific development needs and local contexts of recipient countries (Sanahuja 2010).

GOALS AND OBJECTIVES OF SOUTH–SOUTH SOCIAL POLICY INTERVENTIONS

Flowing from this normative underpinning, distinctive elements can be recognized in the overall objectives and goals of South–South development assistance. First, the discourse tends to emphasize, as the main focus of intervention, the development of countries and harmonization of territories and international order rather than individual social rights. The emphasis on global democratization and a more equitable international order was enshrined right from the beginning: 'Technical cooperation among developing countries ... gives expression to the developing world's determination to achieve national and collective self-reliance and to the need to bring about the new international economic order. Its emergence and rationale should therefore be viewed in this global perspective' (United Nations 1978). Typically, then, the unit of analysis and focus has been the 'nation' (or the region) rather than particular classes, groups or individuals. Social development interventions should primarily aim to promote and enhance the wellbeing of the whole population rather than specific vulnerable and disadvantaged groups.[5]

Second, mutual respect and a strong respect for national sovereignty expressed in the principle of 'non-interference in internal affairs' are also the hallmarks of this type of cooperation: 'co-operation among all countries must be based on strict observance of national sovereignty, economic independence, equal rights and non-interference in domestic affairs of nations, irrespective of their size, level of development and social and economic systems' (Buenos Aires Plan of Action 1978). The non-interference principle continues to be translated into current mechanisms of South–South cooperation, in particular in the explicit absence of macroeconomic, governance or policy conditions in the provision of development assistance. In principle, it means that grants, loans and aid are not tied to any conditions or requirements to the effect that recipient states institute specific policy responses or changes. China is probably the Southern actor that has most overtly advocated such approach. 'Each country has the right to choose, in its course of development, its own social system, development model and way of life in light of its national conditions' (FOCAC 2000, p. 7). Thus, countries providing assistance within the framework of South–South cooperation typically claim that their programmes are largely 'demand-driven', by which they mean that policies are not imposed from outside and beneficiaries articulate their needs and participate in programme/project development (UNDP 2009).

Third, and possibly most significant for the purpose of the present analysis, South–South engagement appears to be introducing a shift in the way social development is conceptualized and how social policies are justified. A re-prioritization of the economic over the social has led to greater stress on the necessity of economic growth for subsequent social development. This is perhaps most clearly articulated in Chinese assistance to Africa, where it seems not only that the notions of economic development and social development are inextricably linked but that it is strongly believed that economic growth must precede social development (Urbina-Ferretjans and Surender 2012). Social interventions must thus first and foremost be designed to support the objective of economic growth and productivity. In contrast to Western benefactors, most Southern donors thus openly justify their development assistance not only as an important mechanism to demonstrate solidarity among developing countries but also as a legitimate tool to create business opportunities and develop commercial activities. Brazil, perhaps, appears to be an exception and publically justifies its South–South cooperation in terms of purely 'altruistic' goals.

The emphasis on economic growth and productivity is not unexpected. In the context of North–South cooperation, most social development models in developing countries have been mainly supported by and based on European and North American preconceptions, values and experiences (Midgley 2004). In the same way, it is not surprising that links between economic and social policy initiatives are supported by Southern donors, since this reflects their own domestic development experiences. Most developing nations championing South–South cooperation have established their social welfare systems in the context of a 'developmental state' model. A strong and enabling role for the state and a 'productivist' social policy focused on economic growth with strong residualist elements are thus presupposed in the social sector initiatives and approaches adopted by many South–South donors.

INSTITUTIONS AND ACTORS

Countries engaged in South–South cooperation share several common institutional features. In contrast to most Western countries, most Southern donor countries do not have a designated or discrete development cooperation agency which centralizes or coordinates the provision of development aid assistance. Instead the provision of development assistance is typically divided among several institutions, though social sector assistance most often involves ministries of social development, education and health. China, for instance, despite being one of the largest participants in South–South cooperation, has not yet established a separate agency to dispense aid; and its aid and loan programme is orchestrated by a number of actors, including the Ministries of Commerce and Foreign Affairs, China Eximbank and China Development Bank (Bräutigam 2008). This difference from traditional donors in institutional arrangements is not incidental, but reflects the fact that development aid is not seen as something separate from overall economic activity but rather embedded in it.

Though South Africa and India, South–South countries championing cooperation, have recently announced the creation of new development aid agencies, in both cases the link between development aid assistance and opportunities for business is still openly recognized – and is apparent in the justification provided by the South African and Indian governments for the establishment of their agencies. In April 2012 the South African government publicly launched the South African Development Partnership Agency (SADPA) (which will replace the African Renaissance Fund), asserting that it will not only contribute to the advancement of philanthropic purposes but also serve to generate new business opportunities for the country (Tapula et al. 2011). Likewise, the Indian government has recently announced a proposal to set up the so-called Indian Agency for Partnership and Development. In response to questions about whether India should be a provider of aid to other developing nations, given its own aid recipient status and high levels of poverty and poor development, supporters of India's foreign aid programme have referred precisely to the role of the aid agency in opening business opportunities and expanding India's domestic agenda by stimulating the economy and ensuring regional peace (*Guardian* 2011). Thus, South–South development aid cooperation appears to have established much stronger and more overt links between development aid and economic issues than do most Western donors (Woods 2008).

Since South–South cooperation is primarily state-led, particular importance is attributed to national governments as key actors, and most cooperation agreements are driven by dialogue between 'lending' and 'borrower' governments. Consequently, civil society organizations have frequently raised concerns that South–South development cooperation has provided few opportunities for civil society participations. The importance of involving actors other than governments was recognized more than a decade ago in the San Jose meeting (1997): 'it would be desirable to develop and strengthen a partnership among the public and private sectors, entrepreneurs, non-governmental organizations, community- based organizations and civil society', most South–South social policy initiatives nevertheless continue to be largely taken by governments. Many consequently argue that the limited transparency and inclusiveness in the decision-making process and provision of South–South cooperation precludes real democratic ownership of South–South development cooperation (The Reality of Aid 2010).

Equally, mobilization of expertise from the private sector is also largely absent from South–South social cooperation. Although, in their assistance to African countries, Chinese companies have in some cases contributed to the provision of basic social services such as health care and education in the communities surrounding the mines the companies operate, on the whole few countries articulate the promotion of partnership with the private sector (UNDP 2009). Instead, the public sector constitutes the major source of expertise for South–South social cooperation, with many public organizations using technical capacity strengthened with past assistance from donor and international organizations.

Despite a comparative lack of engagement with sub-national constituencies, such as NGOs, civil society or the private sector, South–South cooperation does involve relationships at the supranational level, beyond nation states. Although in most cases countries establish South–South cooperation without a formal dialogue or platform of cooperation (and instead engage in piecemeal and ad hoc relationships), joint efforts have been promoted at the subregional, regional and inter-regional levels forming multilateral mechanisms and pluri-lateral alliances (Deacon et al. 2010; Morais 2010). These developments increasingly blur the traditional neat divisions between national, regional and global social policy. In fact, while in the industrialized world the European Union appears the most prominent example of regional integration, there are several examples of how social policy in the South is gradually evolving from an essentially state-led affair to including many actors with complex interlinkages between different geographical levels of policymaking (Van Langenhove and Macovei 2010). Examples include Social Mercado Común del Sur (MERCOSUR) in Latin America, ASEAN Socio-Cultural Community (ASCC) in Asia and the Pacific, the Organisation of African Unity–New Partnership for Africa's Development (OAU–NEPAD), the Forum on China–Africa Cooperation (FOCAC), and the India–Brazil–South Africa (IBSA) Partnerships.

Important differences exist, however, between these subregional and regional forums. In Africa, there have been significant achievements in the development of South–South social policies at regional and subregional levels through the African Union (AU), the Economic Community of West African States (ECOWAS) or the Southern African Development Community (SADC). Cross-border cooperation and processes for lesson learning have been instituted in the area of education and health, for both disease control and service delivery, and dialogue has been established at different levels, from political declarations to concrete initiatives on the ground (Deacon et al. 2010). In contrast, in Latin America social policy has not been regarded as a major component of South–South subregional and regional cooperation. While dialogues are taking place throughout MERCOSUR about regional labour and social security regulations and mutually recognized educational qualifications, there has been a very soft regulation and articulation of social rights on the continent (Deacon et al. 2010). Equally, in South and East Asia the general absence of supranationalist elements to ASEAN and SAAR has resulted in minimal progress in regional social policy (Deacon et al. 2010).

INSTRUMENTS AND MECHANISMS

South–South social development cooperation includes a wide range of instruments and mechanisms, including training and capacity building programmes, scholarships, technical cooperation, knowledge-sharing and exchange of experiences in the social sector, humanitarian assistance, building of social infrastructure, provision of equipment and material goods, volunteer programmes, or teams of doctors, generally given through projects which could be financed in the form of grants or zero-interest or concessional loans.[6] Interestingly, as indicated earlier, the strong principle that one sovereign state cannot instruct or advise on the macro policy environment of another sovereign state (UNCTAD 2010) also means that budgetary support is mainly targeted to particular project-level interventions rather than to the implementation of national social policies and programmes. Despite this broad diversity of activities,

South–South cooperation tends to focus mainly on instruments and mechanisms supporting infrastructure and production sectors (UNCTAD 2010).

However, as other chapters in this volume show, many Southern donor countries are increasingly moving towards providing social protection throughout the life cycle of their populations through a combination of social insurance, social assistance and access to social services. Such commitment is exemplified by large-scale programmes for non-contributory social pensions, grants, and benefits for children, the elderly and the disabled such as the Child Support, Old Age Pension and Disability Grants in South Africa; the Programa de Benefício de Prestação Continuada (BPC) and Bolsa Família in Brazil; and the National Old Age Pension Scheme (NOAPs) and the Integrated Child Development Services Scheme in India. However, while comprehensive social protection is recognized as a key element for a more inclusive society within its own borders, at present on the whole there is little generalization of this model in the aid programmes for other Southern countries. Most South–South development aid does not target 'pro-poor' instruments – whether social insurance, social assistance, cash transfers or services – as currently prompted by Western aid institutions (Urbina-Ferretjans and Surender 2012).

Though the Buenos Aires Action Plan identified a number of areas requiring targeted and redistributive interventions, including employment, development of human resources, health, and the integration of women in development, these recommendations did not imply prioritization. Instead, South–South cooperation still largely appears to provide more support to infrastructure and economic or productive sectors than to social sectors (UNCTAD 2010; The Reality of Aid 2010), and Southern donors tend to concentrate their assistance on fairly defined areas. In particular, new emerging economies such as China and some Arab countries have focused most of their development assistance on infrastructure projects (UNCTAD 2010). For instance, during 2002–07, an estimated 54 per cent of China's total support to Africa was devoted to infrastructure and public works (Lum et al. 2009). By the end of 2007, Arab financial institutions allocated 51 per cent of their financial support to infrastructure projects and 9 per cent to social sectors.[7]

Though it is true that substantial assistance from Southern donors encompasses health and education initiatives, the specific instruments and mechanisms utilized reveal a focus on a 'productivist' approach to development, even within these social sectors. For instance, in the area of education Sino–African assistance focuses on the tertiary level: on building universities and providing scholarships to African students to complete vocation and technical education and higher-education degrees in Chinese universities. While Western donors' focus on universal access to primary education appears to be guided by a pro-poor approach which emphasizes redistribution, gender and socioeconomic equality, and social rights, China's education strategy reflects a productivist approach to development in which vocational and higher education are drivers of economic development.

Likewise, in the area of health traditional donors are increasingly focusing on the provision of technical assistance, capacity building and sector-wide policy dialogue rather than investing in public health infrastructure or providing health services at the grass-roots level. While some Western aid continues to be channelled to NGOs to provide clinical services and public health interventions, there has been a distinct turn to more macro or systems-wide solutions for delivering health, most recently through market-based social insurance initiatives (WHO 2010). In contrast, China directly provides services through building hospitals and health centres, and sending medical teams to African countries to provide health services at the community level.

There are, however, exceptions. A recent South–South cooperation project worth more than US$520,000 between Brazil and Timor-Leste (with the assistance of the International Labour Organization, ILO) contributed towards the establishment of a social security system in Timor-Leste. The initiative included the creation of training instruments to strengthen capacity in the field of social security protection, and the development of a strategy for framing the relevant public policies (ILO 2010). Similarly, the Africa–Brazil Cooperation Programme on Social Development, in partnership with the United Kingdom's Department for International Development and the International Poverty Centre, sought to promote international technical cooperation between developing countries to foster social protection policies. Likewise, Cuban health assistance to Timor-Leste has been characterized by a strong emphasis on capacity development at the grass-roots level, contributing through large-scale training programmes to the empowerment of poor and vulnerable populations. Cuban's aid has also focused on developing a public service ethos among Timor-Leste's health workers (Anderson 2010). Nevertheless, while these two countries promote assistance instruments and mechanisms that clearly reflect their own domestic social development approaches and experiences, most South–South interventions are typically directed at infrastructure and economic productivity, and those interventions which are more explicitly 'social' such as health and education are largely justified in terms of their functions in accumulating human resource and capacity building.

IMPLICATIONS OF SOUTH–SOUTH COOPERATION FOR SOCIAL POLICY PRACTICES AND DEBATES

The increasing involvement of Southern partners in South–South social cooperation has many practical and substantive implications for global social welfare. It raises important questions about whether a new and coherent 'model' of social development is emerging, how it differs from traditional North–South policy prescriptions, whether it will influence and guide the social policies of developing counties, and, most crucially, whether it will achieve more effective results in terms of poverty reduction and economic and social development in the global South. Important questions are also raised about how this new dynamic might potentially influence the views and practices of 'Western' development and international governance institutions and global social policy debates about the politics and determinants of social policy in developing countries more generally.

As demonstrated throughout this chapter, Southern development aid partners are a diverse and heterogeneous group, and it is not clear that a unique and distinctive model for social development can be unequivocally identified. However, it is possible to detect a sufficient number of common features and characteristics to justify referring to an emerging 'South–South approach'. Along the various dimensions of policy goals, institutions and instruments we see key similarities. South–South development assistance is provided not only in the form of aid (frequently disparaged as 'charity' by both donors and recipients) but also trade and investment activities. This approach emphasizes support through 'productivist' rather than 'welfarist' interventions on the assumption that this will generate structural changes and eventual welfare gains for all. This developmental approach contrasts with the practices of traditional donors more reluctant to mix investment activities with official flows channelled through development agencies (UNCTAD 2010). Lessons, experiences and knowledge-sharing between Southern partners appear to be inspired by an approach which advocates general economic development rather than poverty eradication as the primary objective of South–South cooperation. This strategy is significantly different from the targeted, pro-poor interventions currently supported by Western donors, although the overall objectives might be the same. Furthermore, the approach is distinguished by a renewed emphasis on the role of the state and state-led development, less reliance on the NGO sector and civil society, and a rejection of the use of conditionality-based lending.

What any of this means at the level of outcomes for the poorest countries remains to be seen. At a minimum, South–South cooperation has contributed to a redistribution of resources from those developing countries that have more to those that have less. Cooperation in the social sector has opened up new and alternative sources of funding and has become increasingly important in providing more financial resources for welfare and social policy in the South. There are indications that joint South–South coordination is also increasing the bargaining power of 'the South' in obtaining additional funding and support. It has been suggested that regional formations (South–South cooperation beyond the national bilateral level) provide increased access and influence over policy development for small and developing countries (Yeates 2005; Deacon et al. 2010) and have contributed to a better redistribution of resources among those countries with less voice (Deacon et al. 2010; UNCTAD 2010).

Arguably, though, the importance of development assistance from providers beyond the DAC lies primarily not in its volume but rather in the way in which this assistance potentially transforms international and multilateral development cooperation by contributing new ideas and modalities, as well as by increasing the policy options available to partner countries. No longer captive to a single model (be it a Washington Consensus or a post-Washington Consensus), aid recipient countries now have greater choice and more alternatives. Growing evidence shows that this is welcomed by recipient countries, which find the lack of standardized policy formulas very attractive; Chinese engagement in the African continent has been widely welcomed by African governments, almost without exception (Alden et al. 2008; Bräutigam 2008, 2009).

Some observers are beginning to forecast, however, that this 'aid diversity' brings not only opportunities but also challenges, that South–South relationships will inevitably face the same problems and pitfalls as North–South engagement, and that new patterns of inequality, hierarchy and 'layering' will simply replace the old ones. Research indicates that differences within the global South have widened in recent years; and it remains to be seen whether this will have any impact on the discourse of solidarity that has developed and whether in time there will be a trends towards a 'South within the South' (Ladd 2010). In this context, there is a risk of the least-developed countries (LDCs) losing their opportunity to raise their voice (even within the global South) and to safeguard their prospects for further economic and social development (Ladd 2010; Malhotra 2010). In the context of China–Africa cooperation, it has been suggested that China's relations with African states, rather than redistributing resources, have accentuated the existing inequalities. According to this view, Sino–African cooperation has reproduced traditional North–South trade patterns in which poor countries export cheap raw materials to richer ones which manufacture the imported inexpensive materials and obtain most of the profits (UNCTAD 2010). Equally, in the arena of social development studies suggest that South–South cooperation presents the same problems and challenges of North–South engagement concerning inequality, ownership and sustainability (Morais 2005); and it has been suggested that 'South–South cooperation may be more efficient and less wasteful than the west's grand gestures, but it is no less self-interested' (Melville and Owen 2005).

A crucial question remains regarding the extent to which South–South cooperation is indeed developmental and improves the social welfare of the population, especially the most vulnerable in the 'Global South'. Certainly, the overall results achieved by South–South cooperation appear still grossly insufficient: as recently asserted by the UNDP (2004), 'A quarter century after the Buenos Aires Conference, cooperation among developing countries has a proven track record and acknowledged value. But the Plan of Action has not been fully implemented, and collective self-reliance and increased capacity to integrate into the world economy remain distant goals for most developing countries'.

While the impact on the ground may remain negligible, there are early signs that these new developments are nevertheless influencing global social policy agendas and discourse. One key question is to what extent and in which direction South–South approaches may be shaping Western ideas about welfare and social policy in developing countries. As Chapter 3 indicates, international development institutions now constitute an influential and dominant global dimension to the social policy agendas of developing countries; and it is vital to assess the extent to which South–South cooperation will affect North–South ideas and practices of social development assistance. Debates about this issue are commonly heated and polarized. Some believe that the practices and standards of Southern partners, in particular China on issues such as good governance, respect for human rights, transparency, accountability and fight against corruption, are different from those of the West and undermine the position of the traditional donor community (Naim 2007). Others argue that emerging donors have no interest in or intention of challenging or replacing the current internationally agreed 'rules' of development aid, and so the West has little to fear (Woods 2008).

Whatever the viewpoint, subtle changes do seem to be under way. Emerging research suggests that policy exchanges, learning and transfer have begun to take place between Southern donors and several Western traditional donors regarding the instruments, institutions and objectives of social development. While any influence of a South–South 'model' on

Western ideas and practice is still at a very early stage, and we are not suggesting that a radical paradigm shift is imminent, nevertheless, this research shows that some receptiveness to changes in social policy thinking among some OECD–DAC members (Urbina-Ferretjans and Surender forthcoming). It is certainly the case that the Western donor community, in particular OECD–DAC members, have been actively attempting to engage China and other emerging nations in a policy dialogue (Paulo and Reisen 2010). Attempts at more inclusive dialogues and mutual learning have been evident at so-called High Level Forums on Aid Effectiveness held in Accra (Ghana) and Busan (South Korea) in 2008 and 2011 respectively. In Ghana, 'the role of middle-income countries as both providers and recipients of aid' was acknowledged and 'the importance and particularities of South–South cooperation' was actively embraced. In Busan, the eagerness of cooperation with Southern players was openly recognized, and they were welcomed without being required to accept the established and agreed norms and rules: 'The principles, commitments and actions agreed in the outcome document in Busan shall be the reference for South–South partners on a voluntary basis.' There are strong indications then that 'the aid architecture of the future might turn out to be a synthesis of established and new approaches' (Paulo and Reisen 2010).

CONCLUSIONS

The new position of emerging and developing economies as global actors in development cooperation, through so called South–South cooperation, and its growing impact on the 'architecture' and discourses of global governance are generating mounting debate. They raise the all-important issue of whether these new international development practices among developing countries will promote a more inclusive, democratic and developmental social policy than traditional North–South approaches have. The implications of these processes may ultimately affect the objectives of social policy and the types of instruments and institutions required to achieve them in developing countries. South–South relations appear to support poverty reduction and social development by securing productive activities which contribute in turn to economic development and employment opportunities. South–South cooperation resurrects past social policy debates on the interdependence of economic and social rights and the mutually reinforcing role of pro-growth and pro-poor approaches. While not mutually exclusive, these different frames do ultimately affect the choice of policy instruments on the ground. Certainly, South–South cooperation has reignited core development debates about protection, production and the role of social policy.

It is interesting to note that South–South cooperation has gained further impetus in recent years despite a difficult global context affected by economic downturn and financial crisis. While it was anticipated that, as a result of the current global economic downturn, Southern donor nations might come under pressure to focus more on domestic issues (UNCTAD), several scholars now suggest that the crisis may in fact contribute to increased Southern solidarity (UNCTAD) and strengthen South–South social initiatives. Hence we observe that the volume of South–South aid flows appears to progressively increase, as does the political will to maintain this type of cooperation. China, Brazil, India and Korea have all recently stated their intention to provide or even increase support to the African region in the coming years (UNCTAD 2010). Meanwhile, as a result of the global recession, aid from traditional Western donors, in particular OECD–DAC members, has dropped and pressure on the aid budgets of OECD countries may mount in coming years.

South–South cooperation in the field of social development has been relatively successful, and knowledge sharing and transfer are clearly taking place among and between developing countries throughout the global South. Though many observers forecast that South–South cooperation will suffer from the same challenges as North–South cooperation concerning ownership, sustainability and power relations, the dominant rhetoric is that South–South relations bring a new 'altruistic' approach, free from political interests and historic exploitation. Although the empirical reality does not always correspond with the normative aspirations and polemical language (on both sides of the debate) regardless, South–South cooperation seems to be here to stay (Morais 2010) and Southern actors appear to be increasingly involved and influential in welfare and social policy at national, regional and global levels. These new developments will undoubtedly have significant consequences not only for social and welfare strategies in developing countries but also for existing international development institutions and global social policy debates.

NOTES

1. 'The use of the term "South" to refer to developing countries collectively has been part of the shorthand of international relations since the 1970s. It rests on the fact that

all the world's industrially developed countries (with the exception of Australia and
New Zealand) lie to the north of its developing countries. The term does not imply that
all developing countries are similar and can be lumped together in one category. What
it does highlight is that although developing countries range across the spectrum in
every economic, social and political attribute, they all share a set of vulnerabilities and
challenges' (UNDP 2004, p. i)

2. The Organisation for Economic Co-operation and Development (OECD)'s Develop-
    ment Assistance Committee (DAC) is a forum for selected OECD member states to
    discuss issues surrounding aid, development and poverty reduction in developing
    countries.

3. OECD definition of Official Development Assistance (ODA): 'Grants or Loans to
    countries and territories on Part I of the Development Assistance Committee (DAC)
    List of Aid Recipients (developing countries) which are: (a) undertaken by the official
    sector; (b) with promotion of economic development and welfare as the main
    objective; (c) at concessional financial terms [if a loan, having a Grant Element (q.v.)
    of at least 25 per cent]. In addition to financial flows, Technical Co-operation (q.v.) is
    included in aid. Grants, Loans and credits for military purposes are excluded. For the
    treatment of the forgiveness of Loans originally extended for military purposes, see
    Notes on Definitions and Measurement below. Transfer payments to private indi-
    viduals (e.g. pensions, reparations or insurance payouts) are in general not counted'
    (DAC Glossary of Key Terms and Concepts, http://www.oecd.org/document/32/
    0,3746,en_2649_33721_42632800_1_1_1_1,00.html#ODA).

4. This figure does not represent the total amount of development assistance provided by
    Southern partners since many of them, including significant providers, do not report to
    DAC (Zimmermann and Smith 2011).

5. Nonetheless, the India–Brazil–South Africa (IBSA) Dialogue Forum has emphasized
    the focus on the poor; and more recent South–South statements suggest more attention
    to targeting the needs of vulnerable and disadvantaged groups: 'We call upon the
    international community to make all the necessary efforts to fight poverty, social
    exclusion and inequality bearing in mind the special needs of developing countries,
    especially LDCs, small islands and African Countries. We support technical and
    financial cooperation as means to contribute to the achievement of sustainable social
    development, with social protection, full employment, and decent work policies and
    programmes, giving special attention to the most vulnerable groups, such as the poor,
    women, youth, migrants and persons with disabilities' (BRICS Information Centre,
    2nd BRIC Summit of Heads of State and Government: Joint Statement, Brasilia, 15
    April 2010; http://www.brics.utoronto.ca/docs/100415-leaders.html).

6. Concessional loans are loans that are extended on substantially more generous terms
    than market loans. The concessionality is achieved either through interest rates below
    those available on the market or by grace periods, or a combination of these.
    Concessional loans typically have long grace periods (IMF 2003). A grant-like flow is
    a transaction in which the donor country retains formal title to repayment but has
    expressed its intention in the commitment to hold the proceeds of repayment in the
    borrowing country. (DAC Glossary of Key Terms and Concepts, http://www.oecd.org/
    document/32/0,3746,en_2649_33721_42632800_1_1_1_1,00.html#ODA.)

7. The Arab financial institutions include ADFD, KFAED, SFD, AFESD, AMF, BADEA,
    OFID and IsDB. The percentage of funds in the social sector might be underestimated
    since some of the institutions include social sectors under the category 'other' (World
    Bank 2010).

REFERENCES

Alden, C., D. Large and R. Soares de Oliveira (eds) (2008), *China Returns to Africa: A Rising Power and a Continent Embrace*, London: Hurst & Company.

Anderson, T. (2010), 'Cuban health cooperation in Timor Leste and the South West Pacific', available at http://www.realityofaid.org/userfiles/roareports/roareport_eca617f3d4.pdf# (accessed 20 April 2012).

Bräutigam, D. (2008), *China's African Aid: Transatlantic Challenges*, Washington, DC: The German Marshall Fund of the United States.

Bräutigam, D. (2009), *The Dragon's Gift: The Real Story of China in Africa*, Oxford: Oxford University Press.

Davies, P. (2010), 'South–South cooperation: moving towards a new aid dynamic', in International Policy Centre for Inclusive Growth – UNDP, *Poverty in Focus: South–South Cooperation: The Same Old Game or a New Paradigm?*, Number 20, Brasilia: Bureau for Development Policy, UNDP.

Davies, P. (2011), 'Toward a new development cooperation dynamic', in *Transnational Issues, Multilateral Solutions? The Future of Development Cooperation*, The Canadian Development Report 2011, Ottawa: The North–South Institute.

Deacon B., C. Macovei Maria, L. Van Langenhove and N. Yeates (eds) (2010), *World-regional Social Policy and Global Governance: New Research and Policy Agendas in Africa, Asia, Europe and Latin America*, London: Routledge.

Forum of China and Africa Cooperation (FOCAC) (2000), *Beijing Declaration 2000*, Beijing: FOCAC.

Guardian (2011), 'India to create central foreign aid agency', 26 July, available at http://www.guardian.co.uk/global-development/2011/jul/26/india-foreign-aid-agency (accessed 20 April 2012).

ILO (International Labour Organization) (2010), 'Timor-Leste to receive funding for social security development from Brazil: South–South cooperation project worth more than $500,000', 16 June, Geneva: ILO.

IMF (International Monetary Fund) (2003), *External Debt Statistics: Guide for Compilers and Users – Appendix III, Glossary*, Washington, DC: IMF.

Ladd, P. (2010), 'Between a rock and a hard place: LDCs in a G-20 world', in International Policy Centre for Inclusive Growth – UNDP, *Poverty in Focus: South–South Cooperation: The Same Old Game or a New Paradigm?*, Number 20, Brasilia: Bureau for Development Policy, UNDP.

Lum, T., H. Fisher, J. Gomez-Granger and A. Leland (2009), *China's Foreign Aid Activities in Africa, Latin America, and Southeast Asia*, CRS Report for Congress, Washington, DC: Congressional Research Service.

Malhotra, K. (2010), 'South–South cooperation: Potential benefits for the Least Developed Countries', in International Policy Centre for Inclusive Growth – UNDP, *Poverty in Focus: South–South Cooperation: The Same Old Game or a New Paradigm?*, Number 20, Brasilia: Bureau for Development Policy, UNDP.

Melville, C. and O. Owen (2005), 'China and Africa: a new era of "South–South cooperation"', Open Democracy, available at http://www.opendemocracy.net/globalization-G8/south_2658.jsp (accessed 29 March 2010).

Midgley, J. (2004), 'Social development and social welfare: implications for social policy', in P. Kennett (ed.), *A Handbook on Comparative Social Policy*, Cheltenham, UK and Northampton, MA, USA: Edward Elgar, pp. 217–38.

Morais de Sá e Silva, M. (2005), 'South–South cooperation, policy transfer and best-practice reasoning: the transfer of the Solidarity in Literacy Program from Brazil to Mozambique', Working Paper no. 406, The Hague: Institute of Social Studies.

Morais de Sá e Silva, M. (2010), 'How did we get there? The pathways of South–South cooperation', in International Policy Centre for Inclusive Growth – UNDP, *Poverty in Focus: South–South Cooperation: The Same Old Game or a New Paradigm?*, Number 20, Brasilia: Bureau for Development Policy, UNDP.

Naim, M. (2007), 'Rogue aid', *Foreign Policy*, **159** (March/April), 95–6.

Paulo, S. and H. Reisen (2010), 'Eastern donors and Western soft law: towards a DAC donor peer review of China and India?', *Development Policy Review*, **28** (5), 535–52.

The Reality of Aid (2010), 'South–South Cooperation: A Challenge to the Aid System?', available at http://www.realityofaid.org/userfiles/roareports/roa report_08b0595377.pdf# (accessed 20 April 2012).

Sanahuja, J.A. (2010), 'Post-liberal regionalism: S–S cooperation in Latin America and the Caribbean', in International Policy Centre for Inclusive Growth – UNDP, *Poverty in Focus: South–South Cooperation: The Same Old Game or a New Paradigm?*, Number 20, Brasilia: Bureau for Development Policy, UNDP.

Schulz, N.-S. (2010), *The Third Wave of Development Players*, Policy Brief no. 60, Madrid: FRIDE, available at http://www.fride.org/publication/818/the-third- (accessed 20 April 2012).

Tapula, T., P. De Kock and K. Sturman (2011), 'South Africa's development partnership agency: a burden or blessing?', South African Institute of International Affairs, available at http://www.saiia.org.za/diplomatic-pouch/south-africa-s-development-partnership-agency-a-burden-or-blessing.html (accessed 20 April 2010).

United Nations (UN) (1978), *Buenos Aires Plan of Action for Promoting and Implementing Technical Co-operationamong Developing Countries 1978*, New York: United Nations.

UNCTAD (United Nations Conference on Trade and Development) (2010), *Economic Development in Africa, Report 2010: South–South Cooperation: Africa and the New Forms of Development Partnerships*, Geneva: UNCTAD.

UNDP (United Nations Development Programme) (2004), *Forging a Global South: United Nations Day for South–South Cooperation*, New York: UNDP.

UNDP (2009), *Enhancing South–South and Triangular Cooperation. Study of the Current Situation and Existing Good Practices in Policy, Institutions, and Operation of South–South and Triangular Cooperation*, New York: Special Unit for South–South Cooperation, UNDP.

Urbina-Ferretjans, M. and R. Surender (2012), 'China's developmental model in Africa: a new era for global social policy?', in M. Kilkey et al. (eds), *Social Policy Review*, **24**, Bristol: Policy Press, pp. 183–202.

Urbina-Ferretjans, M. and R. Surender (forthcoming 2013), 'Social policy in the context of new global actors: how far is China's developmental model in Africa impacting traditional donors?', *Global Social Policy*.

Van Langenhove, L. and M.C. Macovei (2010), 'Regional formation and global governance', in B. Deacon et al. (eds), *World-Regional Social Policy and Global Governance: New Research and Policy Agendas in Africa, Asia, Europe and Latin America*, London: Routledge.

WHO (World Health Organization) (2010), *The World Health Report – Health Systems Financing: The Path to Universal Coverage*, Geneva: WHO.

Woods, N. (2008), 'Whose aid? Whose influence? China, emerging donors and the silent revolution in development assistance', *International Affairs*, **84** (6), 1205–21.

World Bank (2010), *Arab Development Assistance: Four Decades of Cooperation*, Washington, DC: World Bank.

Yeates, N. (2005), 'Globalization and social policy in a development context', Social Policy and Development, Paper no. 18, Geneva: United Nations Research Institute for Social Development.

Zimmermann, F. and K. Smith (2011), 'More actors, more money, more ideas for international development co-operation', *Journal of International Development*, **23**, 722–38.

13. Conclusion: towards the analysis of social policy in a developing world

Robert Walker

Social policy is increasingly a reality in the developing world. It typically comprises a rather complex web of legislation, institutions and provision that seeks to meet the kind of individual and social needs that are not adequately met by markets, be it for reasons of effectiveness or ideology. But social policy also exists as a language of enquiry and this too is becoming increasingly evident in developing countries alongside development studies. Social policy analysis takes the first form of social policy as its subject matter and applies a set of concepts and methods to understand its nature, origins and effectiveness.

This volume is about both kinds of social policy. Authors have sought to elucidate much better than hitherto the social policies and institutions that exist in developing countries, to explain their form, evolution and trajectories and to consider their effectiveness and sustainability. In so doing they have used, but also questioned, concepts, theories, typologies and approaches to analysis that form the core of academic social policy as it has developed in the global North. From its origins with the social reformers of the later nineteenth century, social policy taught in higher education has gradually been released from a reform driven agenda focussed on the role of the state within a nation state. It now adopts a more neutral position apprised of the myriad of institutions that interact in the design, delivery and challenge of social policy at local, national and multinational level. It lies at the confluence of disciplines drawing on, combining and shaping theories better to understand a phenomenon that consumes some 10 per cent of global wealth, has helped to extend life and enhance its quality for billions of people and yet seemingly proves powerless to prevent 22 per cent of the world's population from surviving on $1.25 per day, at risk from malnutrition, the natural elements and preventable disease (World Bank, 2012).

Nevertheless, while social policy is increasingly taught globally, alongside adjunct disciplines such as public policy, public management, public administration and public economics with which it shares some subject matter, it has remained a moot point how far its conceptual repertoire has expanded fully to embrace the circumstances of the developing world. This volume has demonstrated that social policy, the discipline, can engage productively with the subject matter of social policy in developing countries; providing explanations, problematising the taken for granted, offering alternative accounts and trajectories, and facilitating cross-national theory building and learning. But equally the social policy discipline is not comprehensive, all-explaining or static. Like any discipline, the concepts, theories and methods that define social policy analysis develop and are refreshed through their engagement with empirical worlds that are themselves different and changing. Hence, the volume points to assertions, concepts and perspectives that are not in alignment with experiences in developing countries. It offers, too, insights from the South that deserve to shift approaches to social policy, both the subject matter and the discipline, in the global North.

This final chapter first considers history and the ways that it has shaped social policy institutions in the developing world, noting limitations of explanatory theories developed in the North. It then focuses on the different set of institutions that interact with states in the South – NGOs, donors and business – often in the context of informal labour markets and social relationships. The goals of social policy are considered next again drawing attention to broad differences between South and North. Four illustrative policy instruments are then discussed, viewed through the universal lens of pluralistic evaluation and thereby considering their different objectives, operative constraints, funding models, delivery mechanisms, effectiveness and unintended consequences. Finally, attention shifts to the sustainability of social policy in the developing world and to the potential of social policy analysis to better understand it.

HISTORY'S LEGACY

Social policy analysis contends that context and history is important not only accounting for the kinds of policy in place or absent but also their effectiveness (Klein and Marmor, 2006). Hence, history frames both the volume as a whole and individual chapters, as authors seek to explain and evaluate the diverse range of social policies and policy models found in developing countries.

Rebecca Surender, in Chapter 1, takes a broad historical and geographical perspective on the development of social policy in the developing world, referencing as a vantage point the experience in the industrial North. The taken for granted view is that the welfare state is a product of democracy, capable states, formal labour markets with division of labour, robust financial institutions and established legal systems. Many developing countries cannot be characterised as such for states are sometimes fragile, governments are often weak, laws may be difficult to enforce and taxes hard to collect from those immersed in multiple activities in an informal economy. However, as Surender points out, many Northern welfare states were established under authoritarian, pre-democratic systems in transition from agrarian to industrialised economies.

A greater difference, therefore, between the social policy regimes in the North and those in developing countries is that many of the latter are products of colonialism and arguably inherited 'foreign' traditions or had them externally imposed. For a short while after independence, many countries sought to build and celebrate their new nationhood by investing in social policy, echoing what had happened in Europe almost a century before. However, they were soon to be influenced by a new form of colonialism as US conceptions of residualist welfare took hold in international organisations such as the World Bank that were legitimated with reference to neoliberal economics. This was the period of the Washington Consensus and structural adjustment. Developing countries were urged – and indeed, through conditionality imposed by international donors, coerced – first, to prioritise economic growth over social development, and then to stem the growth of social expenditure even before the rhetoric of rolling back the state could have had any real meaning. Health, education and pensions were increasingly commodified and provided by the private sector while the state's social role was limited to residual safety nets. This had the effect of limiting the responsibilities of the state and dissociating it from the interests of the emergent or potential middle class. Bob Deacon argues, in Chapter 11, that a middle class disconnected from the benefits of state welfare is a distinguishing feature of developing countries that has only recently been addressed. Indeed he agrees with David Lewis who argues in Chapter 4 that the energies of the middle classes have been diverted away from engagement in economic production to service professionally the needs of international aid agencies.

To the extent that the state is weak, democracy fragile and the middle class is neither driving economic growth nor benefiting from collective public welfare, many of the traditional theories of the origins of Western welfare states do not hold. These include:

- the *power resources model* and *conflict theories* that prioritise working class influence being exerted through trade unions and social democratic parties (Korpi, 1983; O'Connor and Olsen, 1998);
- *functionalist theories* that view welfare polices as a more or less mediated, developmental, rationalist response to the manifestation or recognition of social needs arising often from industrialisation;
- *teleological models* such as T.H. Marshall's (1950) assumed progression through the state conferring and supporting civil and then political rights to the full expression of social ones; and
- various *convergence theories* that postulate an increasing similarity of policy resulting from shared historical and developmental experiences (Flora and Heidenheimer, 1977; Visser and Hemerijck, 2000).

Of course, the state is not weak in all developing countries and productivist models can be applied to explain the exceptionally rapid development of countries such as Singapore, Korea and latterly China, Rwanda and Ghana where strong and sometimes authoritarian governments have used state power to promote economic growth, sometimes through selective support for increasingly large industrial conglomerates. However, more generally applicable are historical institutional models that point to the importance of path dependency in which perceived policy options are shaped by the interests and potential of existing institutions and the experience of the past (Klein and Marmor, 2006).

Abu Sharkh and Gough (2010) have sought to categorise welfare regimes in the developing world, noting the importance of international actors and informal provision: proto-welfare states; successful and failing informal security regimes; and insecurity regimes. The first regime category, mostly comprising countries of industrialised southern South America and the ex-Soviet Union, once had established systems of provision that were partially dismantled in response to neoliberal pressures during the era of the Washington Consensus and, in the latter case, an ideological backlash against the state. The second regime grouping is fairly heterogeneous, mainly low-income countries with high growth rates that seem to deliver moderately good welfare outcomes with limited spending; unfortunately the existence of successful informal welfare is not empirically determined by Abu Sharkh and Gough but rather presumed by way of an explanation for positive welfare outcomes. The group includes many of the developmental states of China and South East Asia, which grew economically through state-led macroeconomic planning, and also the remaining countries in South and Central America.

Abu Sharkh and Gough divide 'failing' informal regimes into two. The first, signalled by high illiteracy rates, has countries of the Indian sub-continent as its core, generally democratic with a plethora of policies but without effective health, schooling or security, and with highly gendered outcomes. The second group of countries with 'failing' welfare systems includes South Africa, Namibia, Botswana, Zimbabwe and Kenya; all exhibit high mortality despite increased welfare spending which is largely a consequence of the spread of HIV/Aids. Finally, countries characterised as insecurity regimes are, with the exception of Papua New Guinea, all located in sub-Saharan Africa and are characterised by low and falling life expectancy; over half have been designated by the UK Department of International Development (DFID, 2012) as countries where 'the government cannot or will not deliver its basic functions to the majority of its people, including the poor'.

While the categorisation developed by Abu Sharkh and Gough can be criticised on technical grounds (confounding of the results by measurement error), it hints at the diversity of welfare provision in the developing world and connects it to the historical and cultural legacy that Surender reviews in Chapter 2.

INSTITUTIONS AND NETWORK GOVERNANCE

The tight tripartite structure of corporatist welfare states engaging government employers and trade unions, typified by Germany, is generally replaced in the South by a much looser association between NGOs, donor and international development organisations and government. Social policy, in this context, becomes the product of networks of relationships seldom bounded by the borders of a single country such that accountability to a national populace can be tenuous even when strong democratic structures are present. In some respects, this is a model that is coming to be replicated in the European Union as the Commission is accorded more authority in matters of social policy and nation states necessarily lose sovereignty to supra-national European institutions.

As explained in Chapter 2, the weak capacity and limited legitimacy of states in the developing world are often central to understanding the varieties of welfare arrangements. Frequently the role of the state – conceived in most Northern welfare states not only as legislator and regulator but also as provider – is complemented, and arguably sometimes usurped, by international donors and NGOs operating in developing countries. Quite often there is a shared interest in promoting increased activity by NGOs and the private sector in policy arenas that have typically been the preserve of governments in the global North. The justification often given is that the state in the South frequently lacks the administrative capacity to deliver complex services, is more likely to be hijacked by sectional interests than the private sector or NGOs, and lacks the drive towards greater efficiency that is imposed by the discipline of the profit motive. Whatever the justification, the private sector and, perhaps, especially NGOs are much more important in the South than are their counterpart in the North.

NGOs

As David Lewis explains in Chapter 4, a key consideration in the policy dynamic is the nature of the working relationships between institutions. Network governance theorists, attracted by alliteration, identify five forms of relationship: cooperative; coordinative; collaborative; collegial; and conflictual (Brown and Keast, 2003; Danley, 2012). To these, Lewis might want to add catalytic, contractual and competitive based on his analysis of the relationship between state and NGOs, noting that the nature of such relationships vary between particular settings and over time.

For much of the period of the Washington Consensus, NGOs were represented by many donors as a desirable alternative to government. They had competitive advantages in terms of cost effectiveness, willingness to innovate, and ability to work on a local scale to service and represent local communities while not being captured by special interest groups. Governments and NGOs were thereby placed in a competitive relationship but with donor funding favouring NGOs at the expense of states. Lewis demonstrates that the advantages of NGOs are in fact less clear-cut due to issues of unclear accountability, elite capture, duplication, patchwork coverage and a failure to bring innovation to scale. Consequently, competition readily becomes conflict between NGOs and the state.

Nevertheless, NGOs have successfully established a major and frequently dominant role in the implementation and delivery of social policy services in many developing countries that has been sustained over long periods. Sometimes NGOs substitute for government provision; sometimes they supplement it in relationships that can be cooperative and collaborative. They also fulfil similar functions to those that they often perform in Northern welfare states, those of advocacy and catalyst, identifying and giving voice to new issues and pioneering suitable interventions. The roles that NGOs play are very context specific, and differ between local and international NGOs, with culture and history shaping relationships such that generalisations need heavy qualification. Lewis, though, juxtaposes the contribution and the challenges associated with the expanded role of NGOs. They are flexible and offer effective delivery but may be lacking in accountability and quality control. They are powerful advocates but sometimes fall short on legitimacy. They can successfully identify and promote issues but generally lack the ability to deliver sustained and universal provision which results in 'patchwork' coverage. Finally, they can offer complementarity but there remains the risk of them sidelining the state. Lewis further concludes that NGOs are not inherently neutral providers of services but, as non-state actors, represent values that condition their behaviour *vis-à-vis* government and other welfare institutions.

Such is true of all social policy institutions. The values are in part structural, determined by competition for influence, roles and resources; they are partly shaped from within through the necessity of reconciling goals with constraints; and they are partly influenced from without by the presumptions, interests and behaviour of other institutions. NGOs are dependent on the state for legitimacy and for resources (though generally less so in developing countries than in advanced welfare systems because their funding is often external, coming from abroad). However, their continued existence is conditional on the state not expanding to take over their role which generates values in favour of curbing state influence. Moreover, potentially they are also threatened by the emergence of the kind of social entrepreneurial organisations discussed by Alex Nicholls in Chapter 10 that prioritise social outcomes above profit but nevertheless operate under market principles and compete on innovation, effectiveness and efficiency.

Donors

Donor countries constitute another set of welfare institutions that play a crucial role in shaping social policy in developing countries. They are comprised primarily of OECD countries (represented on the Development Assistance Committee, DAC) but are increasingly being joined by others (engaged in South–South cooperation as described in Chapter 12). In addition there are the international development institutions. These constitute the focus of Chapter 3 in which Antje Vetterlein demonstrates that they bring distinct and decisive interests and values to the welfare governance of developing countries. Some, such as the United Nations Development Programme, exert influence by shaping the analytic discourse, promoting explanatory and variously prescriptive models of development. Others – the World Bank and the International Monetary

Fund in particular – exert a direct influence by recommending and often funding particular courses of action. In both cases the analysis and prescription are presented as objective and rationalistic but are underpinned by values that are profoundly ideological as Vetterlein's comparison of the Washington and post-Washington Consensuses demonstrates. The first period was premised on the assumption that economic growth is the optimal means of achieving poverty reduction and was itself a reaction to Keynsian policies of stimulating demand through large scale infrastructure projects. Growth was purported to be possible only by keeping savings high and inflation low and by allowing a free market to flourish unfettered by extensive regulation or government expenditure and productive activity. Such was the power and influence of the Bretton Woods organisations that they were placed in collaborative relationships with governments of the political right and conflictual and coercive ones with those of the left. As alternatives to the state, relationships with NGOs and the private sector were cooperative and, in terms of provision, contractual. However, NGOs and private firms frequently found themselves in competition to win lucrative contracts funded via the World Bank and IMF.

The post-Washington Consensus is underpinned by a different analysis as Vetterlein explains. It is one that views development more holistically and not just in economic terms. It acknowledges the need for growth to be sustained, equitable and democratic and understands that poverty reduction may be a precondition for growth rather than vice-versa. This new policy discourse is changing the nature of relationships between institutions because it implies different roles and ways of working. The language of country ownership and participation prioritises the role of the state and, with weak democracies and limited informational infrastructures, establishes NGOs as the voice of the people. Nevertheless, the powerful actors promoted during the era of the Washington Consensus remain in situ with expertise and experience in the delivery of services that continue to shape provision and constrain the role of the state.

While the post-Washington Consensus is more participative than its predecessor in striving to be consensual between international development organisations and nation states, it remains ideological beneath the rationalistic and factual presentation. It prioritises growth and poverty reduction above other policy goals and is based on the model of capitalist democracies that characterises OECD countries. This ideology is not inert but expressed in terms of the conditions that must be met in return for financial support, in the channelling of support, and in the uses to which it is allowed to be put. The holistic approach could actually increase the control of development institutions, limiting the ability of national states to play off donors against each other or to spread funding across different projects or policy areas. Moreover, Vetterlein argues that the very nature of international institutions prioritises one form of knowledge, quantitative, over all others and promotes oversimplification of analysis and policy prescriptive underpinned by standardisation and measurable performance indicators. As a consequence, relationships with nation states are, if not coercive, generally more contractual than collegial, more coordinative and directive than cooperative.

South–South cooperation, development assistance between developing countries, is ostensibly premised on very different principles than North–South aid but, as Rebecca Surender and Marian Urbina-Ferretjans demonstrate in Chapter 12, all is not as it seems. South–South assistance is presented as being cooperative and horizontal without power asymmetries and conditionality. It is ostensibly developmental and detached from the economic interests of donors, fair in terms of prioritising self-determination, solidarity and social justice, and more effective in that it is better adapted to the needs and resources of recipient countries (Morais, 2005).

The principle of self-determination, non-interference, permits state-to-state transactions irrespective of judgements about the capacity or morality of recipient governments. In time, therefore, South–South aid may strengthen state institutions but without necessarily fostering the democracy thought to have supported the development of welfare provisions in the global North. The aid has also tended to focus on the nation as the beneficiary rather than disadvantaged sub-regions or groups. This inherently risks reinforcing latent inequalities. Notions of solidarity and justice may also find expression at the level of nation states rather than that of individual citizens, reflected in the fact that NGOs, and civil society more generally, report being sidelined in this process. While not coercive, donor countries in the South do seem to be seeking to export strategies of development, including the model of the developmental state, that worked for them on the presumption that it will work for others. Somewhat ironically, therefore, South–South assistance has tended to follow the direction of the Washington Consensus, prioritising economic growth before social development, funding infrastructure projects and those aspects of social services with a direct productivist rationale. Resources have been directed towards funding higher rather than primary education and to acute medicine rather than public health or grass roots primary provision.

The presence of alternative sources of aid has inevitably changed the network dynamics, increasing the bargaining power of recipient countries. Their governments can now place donor countries in the position of competing for influence. Moreover, they can choose between assistance premised on diverse models of development or decide to package them together. NGOs are possibly weakened relative to recipient governments, while private sector organisations may stand to benefit from infrastructure investment.

Business

With important exceptions, including health services in the US and occupational pensions and social care in the UK, the private sector is conspicuously absent from social policy provision in OECD countries. It has had to confront monopoly state provision able to exploit economies of scale through compulsory membership. The state is also able to subsidise coverage of low-income and vulnerable groups by risk pooling, intergenerational transfers and pay-as-you-go funding systems. Moreover, state systems were often instigated due to palpable evidence of market failure or to avoid this occurring.

The situation is potentially very different in the developing world where weak and weakened states have not the authority or competence to instigate universal provision and where citizens with money use it to buy their own 'social' protection. Moreover, the private sector was a favoured agent of provision during the era of the Washington Consensus and in some sectors and countries it has retained monopoly expertise (although in education and health care faith-based provision is often strong). Therefore, the private sector looks set to remain a powerful player in welfare provision in the developing world although Jane Doherty and Diane McIntyre argue, in Chapter 6, that the governance relationships need to change. Focusing on health, they show how difficult it is to ensure wide access and avoid increased inequalities and demonstrate that in developing countries provision is often uncoordinated, of poor quality and provided by inadequately trained single proprietors.

The example of deregulation in South Africa is used to illustrate that an unfettered market in health insurance does not inevitably lower costs or make it affordable to more than a minority of the population. Instead, they argue for greater regulation and for national health insurance, as proposed in India and recently in South Africa itself. Under such a system, which would be funded by a mix of taxation on insurance, the state would become the single active purchaser of health services from private, public and civil society suppliers. The goal, then, is to shift the power balance from private provider to consumer by making the state a monopoly purchaser. The obvious challenge for many developing countries is the limited legitimacy and capacity of state institutions to take on this role. In part, this is a legacy of attempts by international development institutions to promote the private sector at the expense of the state, but reflects, too, a failure of national political institutions compounded by the difficulties of establishing a productive tax base in the absence of a substantial formal economy.

Whereas social policy making in the global North is still largely conducted within the confines of the nation state, variously the outcome of seeking to reconcile the competing interests of employers, labour and government, social policy in the developing world is the product of a greater number of actors. Moreover, many of the policy actors in the developing world reside outside the nation state and have responsibilities that extend beyond it. Clearly, therefore, the dimensionality of the analytic models evolved in the North has to be expanded and the models developed to cope with this added complexity. A possible by-product of such refinement might be models that could be adapted to analyse responses of the industrially developed world to the aftermath of the Great Recession of 2008 that have entailed a complex network of national and international actors. Arguably globalisation itself calls for the increasing cross-national coalescence of economic and social policy as illustrated by the Open Method of Coordination pioneered by the European Union.

INFORMALITY

As already emphasised, advanced welfare states are premised on a structural symbiosis between a strong and competent state and a formal taxable economy with enforceable employment contracts and typically sustained employment; the competent state is dependent on the market for its income while the market requires the state for regulation and the enforcement of law. In developing countries this symbiosis is often missing with informality characterising state citizen relations as well as labour market activity. Access to politics, public services and employment often depends explicitly on who one knows, the group to which one belongs, what one will do in return for favours given, and what favours need to be returned. Viewed from the North such dynamics smack of illegality, corruption and nepotism; experienced in some societies in the South, they are normal, necessary and appropriate.

Estimates suggest that about 60 per cent of employment in developing regions is comprised of own account workers and family members (Bacchetta et al., 2009). In South Asia, the proportion rises to almost 76 per cent and averages 71 per cent in Sub-Saharan Africa and 69 per cent in Oceania. Rates are much lower in Western Asia (29 per cent) and in Latin America and the Caribbean (33 per cent) but still three times higher than in the developed world. This informality is often twinned with poverty in a symbiotic relationship that perpetuates the demand and supply of low-income labour (Pellissery and Walker, 2007). It also generally impedes governments in their attempt to build generous welfare systems funded by contributions and/or taxes levied directly on employers and employees. This is because the potential tax base is largely inaccessible to state authorities since it is unrecorded. Nevertheless the informal economy provides the livelihood for billions of people and creates its own characteristic web of welfare.

As Sony Pellissery explains in Chapter 5, policy responses to the informal economy and labour market have ranged from ignoring it, through expecting it to decline in response to increased formality, to seeking to eradicate it. The first strategy denies the possibility of good policy design, the second has proved to be incorrect, while the last seems largely to have been ineffectual. Pellissery therefore proposes seeking a better understanding of informality and developing social policies that work with it. He reports strategies: to support informal workers to organise themselves as trade unions and slum dwellers as residents' organisations to gain influence through collective voice; to accord natural and acquired rights to livelihoods and housing equal or possibly greater status than legal titles; and extending social security to informal workers, a strategy also discussed by Robert Walker in Chapter 7.

Pellissery's strategy of accommodation is unlikely to be without critics. Capitalism can only thrive through the accumulation of capital that can be protected and accessed through legal title and therefore supporting systems that undermine the concept of defensible individual ownership might be considered to constrain economic development. Likewise, perpetuating a culture of 'corruption' is likely to be thought to inhibit inward overseas investment. For citizens, corruption such as the bribery necessary to access public services is proven to be individually and collectively inefficient and to penalise most those who are poorest and hence unable to pay bribes (Gupta et al., 2002). Furthermore, the informal labour market helps to sustain poverty level wages by inhibiting investment in both human and technological capital and preventing the accumulation of profits necessary to reward innovation and risk taking. Moreover, the expansion of social protection into the informal sector can only be achieved by those states with adequate capacity to identify, regulate and police employment, and informality conspires against the state acquiring such capacity.

In defence of Pellissery's position is the scale and persistence of informality in developing countries, a double-edged sword that serves to perpetuate poverty but provides incomes necessary for survival. Indeed Walker argues, in Chapter 7, that traditional social security systems that protect only persons who are unable to work are unsuitable in societies in which full-time employment is insufficient to lift people out of poverty. One might hope that measures that strengthen the bargaining position of workers in the informal economy will ultimately shift the balance of power, increase wages and trigger the positive investment cycle enjoyed by the advanced economies. It should be recognised, though, as Pellissery notes, that informality has increased markedly in many OECD countries with governments having become increasingly less willing to ensure employment protection for fear of losing out to global competition. Informality is a matter of degree and, insofar as the labour market is concerned, may be spreading northwards.

Informality in the labour market is echoed in many developing countries by the supply of welfare. The family, nuclear and extended, is often the locus of subsistence and sustenance and the distinction between cash income, domestic work and care work is much less clear than in developed market economies. Such resources as exist, material and social, are generally shared among family members and between members of clan and tribe. Often such exchanges are obligated by culture and custom, codified in philosophical traditions and religion, and manifest in more or less explicit requirements for reciprocity. State welfare provision, in such settings, frequently becomes an extension of established informal welfare exchanges. Individualised payments become a shared resource and access to them is quite likely to be mediated through established systems of obligation and reciprocity that looks like nepotism and corruption through the lens of a formal welfare state. In the absence of formal welfare provision, it is these kinds of systems of exchange that Abu Sharkh and Gough (2010) presume (without direct evidence) explain the positive outcomes of successful informal welfare regimes. Fractured by HIV/Aids they might function less effectively to meet increased needs but it is less clear why (and if) they would work less well on the Indian sub continent or in the insecurity states that Abu Sharkh and Gough identify in sub-Saharan Africa.

POLICY GOALS

The diversity of experience of developing countries is a recurring theme throughout the book and generalisation is as dangerous as it is useful.

These dangers acknowledged, the strategic welfare goals of developing countries do often differ from those evident in the North. In part this stems from the differing historical legacies discussed above. Welfare provision in the North was initiated and developed as part of the currency of political exchange that variously reconciled the interests of competing classes, assuaged social unrest and dissent, forged national consciousness and allegiances and/or allowed for the realisation of shared communal values. In the South, provisions have more often been a response to extreme poverty or to economic, humanitarian or political crisis and have more frequently been encouraged, imposed and/or delivered from outside. Alternatively social policies have been the instrumental components of a developmental strategy to support or drive forward economic growth, rather than responses to the expressed wants of citizens. Social policy in the South has therefore more often than in the North been imposed top down on people by governments, or been imposed on governments by international institutions rather than being fought for and won by the local populace.

These broad differences in the dynamics of policy making are reflected in subtle but important differentiation in the goals of welfare and translate into different modes of delivery. To the extent that policy has focussed on poverty alleviation, welfare provision has more often reflected the liberal or residualist regimes of the North than either corporatist or social democratic ones (Titmuss, 1974; Esping-Andersen, 1990). This has resulted in the neglect of collectivist goals to do with social solidarity or social cohesion and tended to produce parallel systems of provision. One system typically comprises basic or crises provision accessed by the demonstration of need, often required to be chronic or extreme. The other form of provision is frequently supplied through the market. Often, as a consequence, state of the art provision for the wealthy exists alongside very basic services emulating Tizard's (1975; Penn, 2004) much quoted assertion (repeated in Chapter 11) that 'services for the poor are poor services'. Moreover, this pattern of provision leaves a variable proportion of the population without access to formal services, reliant on informal support and without a vested interest in state provision that might translate into demands for improvement. Rather than social welfare provision being a glue holding society together it can be divisive, reinforcing the negative stereotypes attaching to people in poverty based on individualistic rather than structural explanations. In such scenarios stigma attaches to welfare provision, legitimating derogatory, self-reinforcing urban myths such as the one prevalent in South Africa in the mid 2000s that the introduction of

Disability Grant had generated a market for TB infected saliva that was injected in order to access the benefit.

Productivist goals are frequent drivers of welfare state provision in the global North. They are manifest, for example, in the investment in research and higher education and signalled by the political interest aroused by country rankings of OECD PISA (Programme for International Student Assessment) scores. However, they are considerably more prominent in many developing countries and, as Surender and Urbina-Ferretjans report in Chapter 12, much promoted in South–South exchange. Sometimes, especially where economic success is demonstrable and widely shared, productivist policies can be integrative. The Singapore Central Provident Fund is a much cited example (CPFB, 2012). A colonial legacy to provide old age pensions, the compulsory saving scheme was embraced by the post-colonial People's Action Party, being consistent with the leadership's development goals. The self-funding scheme was (and remains) based on 'save-as-you-earn' principles and permitted the government to use the assets of the fund to support economic and social development. The fund has diversified as Singapore has developed economically to embrace house purchase, health care, family protection and support for tertiary education and also to provide investment opportunities especially for the more affluent. The scheme promotes individualistic values such as self-reliance, the work ethic (participation is based on employment) and family support while encouraging intergenerational solidarity, pooling risk and giving members a stake in society.

However, productivist goals perhaps more often lead to the neglect of social policy and to increasing inequality as the more affluent and accomplished gain most from developmentalist social policy and as the result of growth that is not determinedly pro-poor. Furthermore, if the economy lags behind social investment leading to an over-educated workforce, emigration may be an unavoidable consequence bringing very mixed consequences as remittances substitute for loss of human and social capital.

More so than in the North, social policy goals are remedial. That is they are designed primarily to address factors that at a structural level are holding back development and to ameliorate, at a social and personal level, the consequences of crises that have already occurred. Implicit is the idea that things could have been different and that the problems to be addressed are the result of political or personal failings. Social policy is therefore inherently judgmental, a medicine or even a punishment rather than a stimulus or an aspiration. Early childhood development schemes promoted by the World Bank are but one good example (Penn, 2004).

The claim, based largely on experience in the US is that such schemes, which teach improved parenting skills, can reduce poverty and are most beneficial for children growing up in the poorest households. The implication is that parents in poverty are poor parents and that poor countries have many poor parents. (Leaving aside confounding factors in the US evidence in which 'low income' is conflated with 'multi problem', there is little accommodation in the policy guidelines for cultural and environmental differences between the USA and developing countries, a feature that Viruru [2001] terms cultural colonialism.)

Policies in the South and North have also been shaped by rather different emphases given to the notion of rights. While the aforementioned progression from civil rights to political rights and social rights aptly captures the development of many welfare states in the North, it is much less true of the countries in the South. The latter have had to contend with colonialism, military and authoritarian regimes, tribal and ethnic conflict, civil wars and criminal exploitation from within and without. In the absence of legal and political rights, reformers have more often turned to the concept of human rights, sometimes, as in the case of South Africa, embedded in national constitutions, and on other occasions made available in universal declarations epitomized by the UN Declaration on Human Rights. However, it has often proved a daunting challenge to translate global principles and rhetoric into the reality of practical policies.

So, while many goals of social policy are shared across North and South, they tend in the latter to be remedial, individualistic rather than collective, targeted more often than universal, and frequently imposed top down or from outside.

INSTRUMENTS: CONSTRAINTS AND EFFECTIVENESS

Turning to policy instruments, the volume covers four that seek to provide cash or services to people who cannot readily acquire it through the labour market, a generic goal of social policy. It is important to recognise that two of the instruments – micro-finance and conditional cash transfers – could justifiably be said to have been invented or re-invented in the global South. One, public works, is now largely confined to developing countries, while the fourth, social security, is a defining feature of Northern welfare states but has proved difficult to establish in the developing world. Such coverage is not of course comprehensive since there are many more policies than there are developing countries. Moreover, because the instruments covered are either designed to reflect, or are adapted to, circumstances that are characteristic or common in developing countries, taken in isolation they serve to exaggerate differences between North and South. These differences can be illuminating when incorporated into a social policy analysis.

Constraints

Robert Walker, in Chapter 7, focuses on social security, broadly defined as both a social goal and as a suite of mechanisms including insurance systems and tax-funded schemes. Historically, this has been a policy sector developed for the comparatively affluent in developing countries rather than the universal provision associated with welfare states in the North. More recently, in the post-Washington Consensus era, it has benefited from the growing recognition of social protection. The chapter focuses on instruments designed to fit alongside constraints imposed by limited finance, lack of administrative capacity and the prevalence of informality in the labour market and society that sometimes shades into corruption: universal pensions; micro-insurance; and various ways of servicing the social security needs of informal workers.

Similar constraints shape the diverse initiatives that Alex Nicholls groups under the term social entrepreneurship in Chapter 10: micro-credit; Fair Trade; self-build housing; social medicine and rat-based biotechnology that each marks an innovative low resource solution to a generic problem. They are pertinent, too, in explaining why the conditional cash transfer schemes, discussed by Paul Dornan and Catherine Porter in Chapter 8, first appeared on a large scale in developing countries and why public works programmes, covered by Anna McCord and Charles Meth in Chapter 9, retain an important role in developing countries whereas they have declined in importance in the North or else morphed into active labour market programmes. In each case, flexibility, simplicity, economy, robustness and scalability are required to respond to the informal dynamics, limited infrastructures and cultural specificity that characterises many low-income countries.

Objectives

Clearly, the diverse range of policy instruments represents a response to a large set of different social needs and so is characterised by discrete, if often multiple, objectives. However, they are for the most part targeted on the unmet needs of low-income groups, be it for health care, education or employment, and are therefore special rather than universal schemes. In some cases, for example micro-credit and outreach social insurance targeted on informal workers, there is the implicit expectation that the service will provide the mechanism through which users will eventually enter the mainstream, to become normal and self-sufficient, but not without the help of special measures.

In terms of the World Bank's (2010, 2012) three-fold characterisation of policy objectives as preventive, promotional and protective, referred to by Dornan and Porter in Chapter 8, more are protective, limiting the negative impact of events that have already occurred rather than preventive (expanding social security) or promotional (micro-credit and education). Of course, this cannot be read to reflect the balance of provision in the developing world but certainly the current aspiration of the World Bank (2012) is to encourage a shift towards promotion and prevention, whereas the local political and humanitarian imperative is often to respond to current suffering.

The conditional cash transfers discussed by Dornan and Porter seek to ameliorate current poverty through cash payments, while preventing intergenerational transmission by ensuring, as a condition of receipt, that parents invest in the human capital of their children through education and preventative healthcare. These objectives evidence the paternalism frequently associated with remedial policies. The policy rationale is that parents in poverty, when forced to make hard choices, may sacrifice expenditure on health or education to meet more pressing short term needs for cash. Conditional cash transfers are designed to shift the balance of the decision in favour of the human capital investment upon which the transfer payment is conditioned. However, the implicit underlying assumption is that low-income parents, left to their own devices, will deliberately choose to deprive their children of good health and education by spending cash on other things. To the extent that there is any evidence at all for such an assumption it derives from studies of 'multi-problem' families in high-income countries rather than low-income ones. Generally, research points to low-income parents making great personal sacrifices to do the best by their children in both the North and the South (Streuli et al., 2011; Walker et al., 2013).

Funding

Financing, both its level and the method, is of course fundamental to the design and effectiveness of social policies and the crux of political and ideological argument. It has often been argued that some developing countries are simply too poor to afford social policy although, following detailed analyses by the ILO, Walker concludes in Chapter 7 that such a proposition is largely untrue since the cost of providing a basic infra-structure is typically between just 2 and 5 per cent of GDP. Nevertheless, this still leaves open how such funds would be raised in countries with fragile governments, unsophisticated administrative infrastructures and limited public trust. Much of the tax base is hidden from view in the informal economy and some of it is lost to other countries when significant numbers of citizens work abroad. Nevertheless customs duties, sales taxes, associational taxation (bargains struck between tax-payers and the tax authorities) and 'forfeit' systems (taxes paid by small businesses on directly observable characteristics) have all proved viable mechanisms in difficult situations.

There is likewise much debate and variation in the balance struck between public and private funding, between tax-funded schemes and insurance systems and between the flexibility of pay-as-you-go funding, when expenditure is met from current revenues, and the supposed discipline of funded schemes where saving has to take place before spending is permitted. There is the suggestion that government provident schemes (entailing compulsory personal saving) and micro-insurance and micro-credit schemes (in which funders and spenders voluntarily partici-pate together) are more prevalent in developing countries than in the North. Perhaps, too, there is more consideration of the viability of basic or minimum income guarantee schemes that mean all individuals are unconditionally granted a tax-funded income without recourse to a means test or work requirement (Parijs, 2000; Standing and Samson, 2004).

Financing social policy is always a challenge but the decision is a political one to do with priorities rather than an absolute one about what can be afforded.

Delivery

Much of the innovation discussed in the chapters on instruments reflects modes of delivery that enable the informal sector to be reached in seemingly chaotic urban areas and in distant small rural communities where trust in government and other agencies is limited. The Grameen Bank (Chapter 10) is based on peer-group lending, exploiting the notion that people trust people like themselves, and is similar to the long established credit unions in the global North that are also important in Latin America and, in the Échale scheme in Mexico, help to finance self-build housing. Micro credit, directed to low-income women, was the initial core of BRAC in Bangladesh which has now expanded into health provision, manufacturing and retailing. Indeed, creating livelihoods based on mutual trust, rather than passive protection, is an important element in proactive social provision. Honey Care Africa links micro finance, skills training and extension services to support 9,000 small-scale beekeepers. Similarly, the Kiara District Co-operative in Gujurat (trading as Amul) collects and processes 1.5 million litres of milk daily from 669,546 producer members, turning micro-production into large-scale processing and marketing.

While the above examples replace the state, empowering individuals to come together to support themselves, there are important examples in Chapter 7 of the state adapting better to engage with the needs and lives of citizens. One instance is Ghana's Informal Sector Fund (SIS) which primarily seeks to provide for retirement, but also enables members to access micro credit to support livelihoods and to withdraw part of their contributions to cope with financial shocks and urgent expenses. Similarly, public works schemes (Chapters 8 and 9) can provide a flexible, direct and targeted response to need with the potential benefit that enrolment can be through self-selection. Self enrolment means people in need offer their labour in return for payment, thereby allowing participants autonomy while minimising the bureaucracy needed to undertake assessment and to manage abuse. Nevertheless, public works implemented on a large scale impose significant financial and organisational demands on the state to devise and manage meaningful work opportunities, ideally building lasting public assets while relying on a rotating, largely unskilled labour force (Chapter 9). Moreover, while, as McCall notes, such schemes are very similar to employment, people are recruited on the basis of need rather than ability to do a job, which radically changes the work relationship making it akin to conditional cash transfers as Dornan and Porter suggest.

Simplified administration is one attraction of universal non-contributory pensions, such as those in Mauritius (Chapter 7), which avoid the need for complex means tests and more readily provide protection to persons outside the formal labour market. Where means testing is applied there are examples of creative accommodation to limited administrative capacity and outreach. For example, area-based targeting in Brazil and Mexico means that schemes can be delivered without individualised means tests, in effect being universal and non-discriminatory within the target areas.

Effectiveness

There have been demonstrable falls in poverty, improvements in health status, and increases in life expectancies and rises in literacy rates in many developing countries over the last two decades, probably driven by both economic growth and increasing provision (UNDP, 2012). However, there remains an enormous gap in material wellbeing between the global North and South, and increasing differentials within the developing world as income inequalities increase and variations in the competence of domestic institutions become more apparent (OECD, 2011). Moreover, there is a dearth of information about what policies work and even more so with respect to what policies are working well in situ.

Information available on policy effectiveness is largely of three kinds. First, there is evidence of policies that have been sustained and widely adopted (Chapter 7); this is valuable in determining the nature of the existing policy mix but such policies may be largely symbolic, supported by vested interests, simply fashionable within the policy community or politically expedient rather than being effective. Secondly, there are policies about which proponents are enthusiastic and active in promoting (Chapter 10); this evidence is suspect – the heart or the quest for market opportunities risk overwhelming rationality – but is nevertheless important as a source of potentially worthwhile policy ideas. Thirdly, an increasing number of projects have been carefully evaluated as proto-types and, especially when funded by the World Bank and other agencies influenced by US-style policy evaluation, have exploited random assignment methodology (Chapter 8; Walker, 2010). This last kind of evidence focuses on impact, necessarily assessed against a small number of outcomes, rather than on processes of implementation and environmental influences. The challenges in using this evidence lie in determining: which elements, or combinations of elements, in the policy mix actually drive the outcomes; how transportable the policy is to different socio-economic and cultural contexts; and whether a small-scale project can successfully be run at a large scale with sustainable levels of resources and staff and management that are average rather than exceptional (as those involved in pilot innovations often are).

There is as yet a shortage of systematic analysis that distinguishes between the concept of effectiveness and the various forms of efficiency. Effectiveness addresses the issue of whether policy objectives are met while efficiency asks about the costs of attaining the objectives. Perhaps to too great an extent, policy attention has tended to focus on economic efficiency rather than on targeting and administrative efficiency. There has, for example, been much international concern – expressed most loudly during the Washington Consensus but still evident in policy papers – about work disincentives potentially created by provision of social assistance even at very low levels of benefit (Chapters 3, 7, 8 and 9); about state provision and state borrowing crowding out the private sector and increasing the cost of private investment (Chapters 2 and 6); and about the loss of international competitiveness resulting from increased welfare expenditure (Chapters 2 and 3). Less attention has been given to targeting efficiency concerning the proportion of eligible populations being reached, the adequacy of the support received and leakage of considerable sums to ineligible populations (Chapters 7 and 8; Robles, 2012; Pellissery, 2009). Discussion of administrative efficiency has perhaps understandably concerned limited state capacity and modes of delivery that circumvent this limitation but at the cost of neglecting issues to do with service quality and promotion of the dignity of service users (ILO, 2012).

Unintended Consequences

An important aspect of policy effectiveness relates to effects of implementation that are unanticipated, particularly those with detrimental consequences. In Chapter 8, Dornan and Porter identify a number of such effects that have accompanied some conditional cash transfer schemes. They include: stimulating gaming on the part of beneficiaries in an attempt to meet the sometimes unrealistic outcomes required by the conditionality; diverting attention from inadequate benefits and poor service delivery; and perpetuating belief in individualistic causes of poverty in situations where it is structural in origin. In the context of specific conditional policies, Dornan and Porter report unexpected negative effects on children including being ostracised because their parents receive benefits and being forced to take on additional domestic chores in order to facilitate their parents' participation in public works programmes.

The negative framing of poverty in the public mind is not one limited to conditional cash transfers. There is evidence that because of the way that poverty is widely perceived as being caused by individual inadequacy, policies that address the problem are themselves often viewed as being inherently stigmatising (Walker et al., 2013). There are pragmatic policy reasons for not challenging such an assertion that can be traced back to the principle of less eligibility under the British Poor Law; stigma stems demand, arguably separating the 'deserving' from the 'undeserving'. Equally, stigma lowers targeting efficiency and policy effectiveness by deterring the eligible and can also erode social cohesion. Where policies are allocated on a geographic basis, entire localities can become stigmatised and neighbourhoods set against neighbourhoods, while individual targeting, especially when accompanied by lack of clarity about eligibility criteria, can result in resentment and anger (Chapter 8).

Setting policy expectations too high can exacerbate issues of stigma and undermine the sustainability of policies. McCord and Meth (Chapter 9) stress that small-scale public works provision (PWP) may benefit individual participants but is unlikely to be more than a short-term palliative in the context of ongoing mass unemployment and adverse incorporation. To expect PWP to trigger large-scale labour market engagement and job progression is unrealistic, and in the event that this does not occur, participants may serve as scapegoats and/or the public may lose faith in the particular policy or, indeed, in the ability of governments successfully to effect beneficial change.

The advance of social entrepreneurship, discussed in Chapter 10, is partly a response to the perceived deficiencies or limits of government and to market failure. To the extent that entrepreneurialism is successful, it may trigger mistrust and opposition among institutions, further weaken the ability of other institutions to play a role in social provision, and possibly undermine the legitimacy of government. Where social enterprises fail to meet the needs of individuals this can precipitate additional hardship – micro-enterprises are very vulnerable and resultant over-indebtedness has been reported to cause family breakdown and social stress (Dichter and Harper, 2007). Where they fail as institutions, there may well be demands for them to be bailed out by already hard-pressed governments. If excessive claims for the sector are made that cannot be achieved, this may further lessen people's belief in innovation and in governance generally, already low in many developing countries.

SUSTAINABILITY IN A GLOBAL CONTEXT

Designing and delivering social policy is inherently complex. Multiple stakeholders bring competing interests, and different expectations for effectiveness and efficiency, that are held in tension against demands for voice, justice and dignity, while being constrained by resources and technical limitations. In many countries in the developing world, the need for social policy still exceeds political demand for it. This is partially because social policy in the South has been strongly influenced by international development organisations and donors that, in helping to deliver welfare, have sometimes unintentionally usurped the role of national governments or, during the period of structural adjustment, done so deliberately for ideological reasons.

Deacon, in Chapter 11, opines that the tide has turned against the neoliberal orthodoxy that insisted on private provision at the expense of the state and on narrowly targeted residual assistance restricted to those in subsistence poverty. He also recognises the inter-connectedness of international markets, the power of private providers of social services operating globally, and the scale of international migrations which all limit the freedom of states to build and fund adequate welfare systems. In response, he envisages a global architecture of social governance concerned with global redistribution, regulation and rights. Although he acknowledges the recent coalescence of global international organisations around the UN's commitment to establishing a global social protection floor (ILO, 2011), his instinct is that such policy architecture could develop most readily from regional associations of governments that would need to reconcile a narrower range of interests than the intractable number confronted by global bodies.

The UN commitment to a global social protection floor is nevertheless likely to have more than solely symbolic significance. The ILO's version of the floor was unanimously[1] approved as a Recommendation to its 185 member countries in June 2012 and, although it is not legally binding on governments as an ILO Convention would be, it establishes a framework of principles and guidelines within which social policies can be developed and assessed (ILO, 2012). It determines that all countries should provide: essential health care; basic income security for children providing access to nutrition, education and care; and basic income security at a nationally defined minimum level for older persons and for those of active age who are unable to earn sufficient income. Deacon might critique the emphasis on minimum provisions as perpetuating an exclusionary discourse on poverty that fails to embrace the middle class, but nations are encouraged to 'seek to provide higher levels of protection to as many people as possible, reflecting economic and fiscal capacities of Members, and as soon as possible' (ILO, 2012, p. 12). There is also no global fund to support implementation of the Recommendation akin to that for Aids, tuberculosis and malaria about which Deacon writes in Chapter 12. Nevertheless, the Recommendation empowers national governments by stipulating that the social protection floors should be financed from national resources, while encouraging countries 'whose economic and fiscal capacities are insufficient to implement the guarantees' to 'seek international cooperation and support that complement their own efforts' (ibid., p. 12).

The ILO Recommendation arguably re-establishes the expectation that all countries should proactively engage in establishing a coherent social policy as a fundamental component of national governance; this after decades when social policy was viewed as being peripheral, redundant or counterproductive. The Recommendation is eclectic with regard to the instruments used to establish the floors and, while the drafting reflects the tripartite composition of the ILO, the only UN body to bring together governments, trade unions and employers, it requires 'consultation with other relevant and representative organisations of persons concerned' (ibid., p. 6). As illustrative of a new global orthodoxy, the movement toward establishing social protection floors runs the risk of becoming too dominant, being too inflexible, prioritising established institutions and accommodating the interests of donors more readily than the needs and aspirations of developing countries. Though it is still early days, it looks as if social policy is back at the heart of governance.

The same movement could also provide a major stimulus to social policy analysis, both in its disciplinary-based and more applied forms. The Recommendation establishes a set of internationally agreed principles against which the welfare systems of all countries, North and South, can be assessed. There is work to be done to operationalise these principles and to develop means by which they might be assessed, and scope to design performance and outcome indicators against which progress could be established. There will be endless possibilities for theory building to understand which policies, if any, countries adopt, and for policy learning in determining which policies prove to be most effective and in which particular settings. There will be opportunities, too, to establish whether reaching the protection floors become goals in themselves or waypoints en route to more generous provision, and whether governments in the North choose to allow their systems to slip in the direction of the basic floors.

On the applied side, the demand is to use the Recommendation to shape reality. This will entail building political support and momentum on the one hand, and developing guidance on funding, design, implementation, monitoring and evaluation on the other. The ILO and other UN organisations are mobilised to lead in these processes but it is likely that the World Bank and IMF will become involved. Already NGOs are gearing up to influence the process and one would expect other providers and actors to enter the network of governance. Social policy analysis provides a core set of concepts and understandings available to enhance the policy making of all these groups of actors, concepts that stand to be revised and further improved in the context of the developing world.

NOTE

1.   There was one abstention, Panama.

REFERENCES

Abu Sharkh, M. and I. Gough (2010) 'Global welfare regimes: a cluster analysis', *Global Social Policy*, 10(1), 27–58.

Bacchetta, M., E. Ernst and J. Bustamante (2009) *Globalization and Informal Jobs in Developing Countries*, Geneva: International Labour Office and the Secretariat of the World Trade Organization.

Brown, K. and R. Keast (2003) 'Citizen–government engagement: community connection through networked arrangements', *Asian Journal of Public Administration*, 25(1), 107–131.

CPFB (2012) *Central Provident Fund: General information*, available at http://mycpf.cpf.gov.sg/Members/Gen-Info/mbr-Gen-info.htm (accessed July 2012).

Danley, S. (2012) *Neighbourhood Negotiation: Network Governance in Post-Katrina New Orleans*, Oxford: University of Oxford DPhil thesis.

DFID (2012) *Fragile States*, London: Department for International Development, available at http://webarchive.nationalarchives.gov.uk/+/http://www.dfid.gov.uk/fightingpoverty/fragile_states.asp.

Dichter, T. and M. Harper (2007) *What's Wrong with Microfinance?* Rugby: Practical Action Publishing.

Esping-Andersen, G. (1990) *The Three Worlds of Welfare Capitalism*, Princeton: Princeton University Press.

Flora, P. and A. Heidenheimer (1977) *The Development of Welfare States in Europe and America*, New Brunswick, NJ and London: Transaction Books.

Gupta, S., H. Davoodi and R. Alonso-Terme (2002) 'Does corruption affect income inequality and poverty?', *Economics of Governance*, 3, 23–45.

ILO (2011) *Social Protection Floor for a Fair and Inclusive Globalization*, Geneva: Report of the Advisory Group chaired by Michelle Bachelet, Convened by the ILO with the collaboration of the WHO.

ILO (2012) *Text of the Recommendation Concerning National Floors of Social Protection*, Geneva: Provisional Record, One hundred and first Session.

Klein, R. and T. Marmor (2006) 'Reflections on policy analysis: putting it together again', in M. Moran, M. Rein and R. Goodin (eds), *The Oxford Handbook on Public Policy*, Oxford: Oxford University Press, pp. 892–912.

Korpi, W. (1983) *The Democratic Class Struggle*, London: Routledge.

Marshall, T.H. (1950) *Citizenship and Social Class and Other Essays*, Cambridge: Cambridge University Press.

Morais, M. (2005) 'South–South cooperation, policy transfer and best-practice reasoning: the transfer of the Solidarity in Literacy Program from Brazil to Mozambique', ISS Working Paper Series, n. 406, The Hague: ISS.

O'Connor, J. and G. Olsen (1998) *Power Resources Theory and the Welfare State: A Critical Approach: Essays Collected in Honour of Walter Korpi*, Toronto: University of Toronto Press.

OECD (2011) 'Growing income inequality in OECD countries: what drives it and how can policy tackle it?', Paper prepared for Forum, Paris, 2 May, available at www.oecd.org/dataoecd/32/20/47723414.pdf

Parijs, Van, P. (2000) 'A basic income for all: if you really care about freedom, give people an unconditional income', *Boston Review*, October/November, available at http://bostonreview.net/BR25.5/vanparijs.html.

Pellissery, S. (2009) *The Politics of Social Protection in Rural India: A Network Approach to Study Policy Processes*, Saarbrücken: VDM Verlag

Pellissery, S. and R. Walker (2007) 'Social security options for informal sector workers: emergent economies and the Asia and Pacific region', *Social Policy and Administration*, 41(4), 401–409.

Penn, H. (2004) 'Childcare and early childhood development programmes and policies: their relationship to eradicating child poverty', CHIP Report 8, London: Childhood Poverty Research and Policy Centre.

Robles, G. (2012) 'Targeting efficiency and the costs of Oportunidades in urban Mexico', Paper presented in the Human Development and Capability Association Conference 2012, Jakarta, Indonesia, 5–7 September.

Standing, G. and M. Samson (2004) *A Basic Income Grant for South Africa*, Johannesburg: Juta Academic

Streuli, N., U. Vennam and M. Woodhead (2011) 'Increasing choice or inequality? Pathways through early education in Andhra Pradesh, India', Working Paper 58, Studies in Early Childhood Transitions, The Hague, The Netherlands: Bernard van Leer Foundation.

Titmuss, R. (1974) *Social Policy: An Introduction*, London: Allen and Unwin

Tizard, J. (1975) 'Low Cost Daycare', Speech at a UK Department of Health Conference at Sunningdale convened by the Minister of Health, David Owen.

UNDP (2012) *Sustainability and Equity: A Better Future for All*, Human Development Report 2011, New York: United Nations Development Program.

Viruru, R. (2001) *Early Childhood Education: Postcolonial Perspectives from India*, London: Sage.

Visser, J. and A. Hemerijck (2000) 'Learning and mimicking: how European states adjust', Paper read at COST A 15 Conference 'European Welfare States: Domestic and International Challenges', 6–8 October, Cologne.

Walker, R. (2010) 'Evaluation research', in *ISSA Social Security Research and Policy Manual: Supporting Research in Social Security Institutions in Low- and Middle-Income Countries*, Geneva: International Social Security Association, pp. 94–139.

Walker, R. et al. (2013) 'Poverty in global perspective: is shame a common denominator?' *Journal of Social Policy*, in press.

World Bank (2010) *Building Resilience and Opportunity: The World Bank's Social Protection and Labour Strategy 2012–2022. Concept Note*, Washington, DC: World Bank.

World Bank (2012) *An Update to the World Bank's Estimates of Consumption Poverty in the Developing World*, Washington, DC: World Bank.

Index